JEAN-LUC NANCY
AND PLURAL THINKING

SUNY series in Contemporary French Thought

David Pettigrew and François Raffoul, editors

JEAN-LUC NANCY AND PLURAL THINKING

Expositions of World, Ontology, Politics, and Sense

EDITED BY

PETER GRATTON
MARIE-EVE MORIN

STATE UNIVERSITY OF NEW YORK PRESS

Published by
STATE UNIVERSITY OF NEW YORK PRESS, ALBANY

Printed in the United States of America

For information, contact
State University of New York Press, Albany, NY
www.sunypress.edu

Production, Eileen Meehan
Marketing, Anne M. Valentine

Library of Congress Cataloging-in-Publication Data

Jean-Luc Nancy and plural thinking : expositions of world, ontology, politics, and sense / edited by Peter Gratton and Marie-Eve Morin.
p. cm. — (SUNY series in contemporary French thought)
Includes bibliographical references and index.
ISBN 978-1-4384-4226-6 (pbk. : alk. paper)
ISBN 978-1-4384-4227-3 (hardcover : alk. paper)
1. Nancy, Jean-Luc. I. Gratton, Peter. II. Morin, Marie-Eve.

B2430.N364J43 2012
194—dc23 2011025882

10 9 8 7 6 5 4 3 2 1

CONTENTS

ACKNOWLEDGMENTS

We would like to thank François Raffoul and David Pettigrew, the series editors, for their support of this project from its earliest stages. We would also like to thank Andrew Kenyon, assistant acquisitions editor at SUNY Press, for his assistance in bringing this project to completion. We want to acknowledge the support from the University of Alberta and the help of Octavian Ion and Mike Lockhart with the editing of the volume and the compiling of the bibliography. Finally, our deepest gratitude goes to Jean-Luc Nancy, who always responded, even through hardship and illness, thoughtfully to the interview questions we sent his way.

ABBREVIATIONS

WORKS BY JEAN-LUC NANCY

ARE “Les arts se font les uns contre les autres,” in *Art, regard, écoute: La perception à l'œuvre* (St-Denis: Les Presses Universitaires de Vincennes, 2000).

BP *The Birth to Presence*, trans. Brian Holmes et al. (Stanford: Stanford University Press, 1993).

BSP *Being Singular Plural*, trans. Robert Richardson and Anne O'Byrne (Stanford: Stanford University Press, 2000).

C *Corpus*, trans. Richard A. Rand (New York: Fordham University Press, 2008).

CW *The Creation of the World* or *Globalization*, trans. François Raffoul and David Pettigrew (Albany, NY: The State University of New York Press, 2007).

D *Dis-Enclosure: The Deconstruction of Christianity*, trans. Bettina Bergo, Gabriel Malenfant and Michael B. Smith (New York: Fordham University Press, 2008).

EF *The Experience of Freedom*, trans. Bridget McDonald (Stanford: Stanford University Press, 1993).

FT *A Finite Thinking*, trans. Simon Sparks (Stanford: Stanford University Press, 2003).

GI *The Ground of the Image*, trans. Jeff Fort (New York: Fordham University Press, 2005).

GT *The Gravity of Thought*, trans. François Raffoul and Gregory Recco (New York: Humanities Press, 1997).

IC *The Inoperative Community*, ed. Peter Connor (Minneapolis: University of Minnesota Press, 1991).

IRS *L'« il y a » du rapport sexuel* (Paris: Galilée, 2001).

M *The Muses*, trans. Peggy Kamuf (Stanford: Stanford University Press, 1997).

MA *Multiple Arts: The Muses II*, ed. Simon Sparks (Stanford: Stanford University Press, 2006).

NM Jean-Luc Nancy and Philippe Lacoue-Labarthe, "The Nazi Myth," trans. Brian Holmes, *Critical Inquiry* 16:2 (Winter 1990), pp. 291–312.

OC *On the Commerce of Thinking: Of Books and Bookstores*, trans. David Wills (New York: Fordham University Press, 2009).

RP Philippe Lacoue-Labarthe and Jean-Luc Nancy, *Retreating the Political*, ed. Simon Sparks (New York: Routledge, 1997).

SW *The Sense of the World*, trans. Jeffery Librett (Minneapolis: University of Minnesota, 1997).

TS "Within my breast, alas, two souls . . . ," *Topoi* 25:1–2 (2006), pp. 69–71.

TD *The Truth of Democracy*, trans. Pascale-Anne Brault and Michael Naas (New York: Fordham University Press, 2010).

WM "War of Monotheism," trans. Amanda McDonald, *Postcolonial Studies* 6:1 (2003), pp. 51–53.

OTHER FREQUENTLY CITED WORKS

BT Martin Heidegger, *Being and Time*, trans. J. Macquarrie & E. Robinson (New York: Harper and Row, 1962).

CP Carl Schmitt, *The Concept of the Political*, expanded edition, trans. George Schwab (Chicago: The University of Chicago Press, 2007)

FCM Martin Heidegger, *The Fundamental Concept of Metaphysics: World, Finitude, Solitude*, trans. William McNeill and Nicholas Walker (Bloomington: Indiana University Press, 1996).

OT Jacques Derrida, *On Touching—Jean-Luc Nancy*, trans. Christine Irizarry (Stanford: Stanford University Press, 2005).

QT Martin Heidegger, *The Question Concerning Technology and Other Essays*, trans. William Lovitt (New York: Harper and Row, 1977).

INTRODUCTION

Peter Gratton and Marie-Eve Morin

In *On the Commerce of Thinking: Of Books and Bookstores*, Nancy provides an apt meditation on what it means to read in a world in which books have become status symbols and often sit without disturbing us (in the strong sense) on coffee tables and library shelves. Beyond the commodity fetishism of the object, long gone are the days in which the world itself was thought to be a "great book" (OC, 23). This loss of the importance of books, Nancy argues, has meant that we risk missing the "new stakes, new sense or lost sense," unique to each work of writing, senses that would bind and unbind us in our reading. In order to do so, what is required is a "play of opening and closing" in reading by which a book becomes the "subject of a reading" (OC, 35–36). The "closing" of the book refers to the new, literally the unedited (*inédit*), that remains forever illegible to the eyes that scan and remain open onto each page, that is, to what can never be captured synoptically in each reading (OC, 27).

No doubt, all introductions to books like this one are metonymic of the appeal by books in general: calling on the reader to proceed further, to move on to the essays in order to take in what has been left all-too-unedited or what is new (*inédit*) in this very book. Nancy notes,

> A book is an address or an appeal. Beneath the melodic line of its singing there intones, without interruption, the continuous bass of its invitation, of its request, injunction, or prayer: "Read me! Read me!" (And that prayer murmurs still, even when the author declares "Don't read me!" or "Throw my book away!"). (OC, 12)

We will begin with no such grand declarations. Offered here nevertheless, between the opening and closing of the binding of this book, is a singular-plural exposition of Nancy's plural thinking, divided and linked among four sections on the world, ontology, politics, and sense.

One of the most read and prominent of contemporary French philosophers, Nancy has published more than twenty-five books, along with numerous contributions to journals, art catalogues, and other volumes. He has written on major thinkers in the history of European philosophy, such as Descartes, Kant, Schelling, Hegel, Nietzsche, Marx, and Heidegger, and has engaged contemporary French thinkers such as Lacan, Bataille, Blanchot, and Derrida. Nancy's work touches on issues as diverse as psychoanalysis, hermeneutics, globalization, community, Nazism, resurrection, Christian painting, German Romanticism, modern dance, and film and has been influential in reconfiguring numerous debates in Continental philosophy. In *Being Singular Plural*, Nancy addresses the question of the "with" at the heart of Heidegger's fundamental ontology. Reinitializing Heidegger's analytic of Dasein, Nancy sets out to do no less than reorient our thinking of being to its spacing and plurality, and thus to the plurality of thought and genres of thinking (e.g., artistic, political, theological) necessary for taking on this very plurality. In *The Sense of the World* and *The Creation of the World* or *Globalization*, Nancy provides an important intervention into the question of globalization and what it means to "create" a world beyond the senselessness provided by modern techno-capitalism. In his *Dis-Enclosure: The Deconstruction of Christianity*, he argues that if the world no longer has a meaning or sense provided by a transcendent God, this also means that the world is sense itself. That is to say, we must respond to the world as it is without recourse to transcendental discourses, including the still-theological discourses of modernity operating within the logic of Christianity and its messianism. While charting this rethinking of what "sense" and "world" means, especially in his encounters with the texts of Blanchot and Derrida, Nancy also argues that far from a separation from the world, art presents and brings to the fore, as he argues in *The Evidence of Film*, the world itself. Art is nothing other than a plurality of art forms that takes in and gives back another sense of the world in its infinite variety.

Nancy thus continues to address the most pertinent questions remaining after Nietzsche's proclamation of the death of God. What makes Nancy's work particularly provocative is his care always to write in such a way as to respond to the contemporary situation; his texts are rarely just abstract discussions of age-old philosophical problems. For example, Nancy addresses questions of the sense of the world in light of a certain view of the world as resource that is part of economic globalization. His writings on Christianity not only come at a time of supposed secularism in western Europe, but also at a time of rising fundamentalisms, from the Christian and other religious traditions. It should also be said that Nancy's work on the deconstruction of Christianity, long awaited, comes after the so-called "theological turn" in phenomenology and post-phenomenology, marked out and discussed by such thinkers as John Caputo, Jacques Derrida, Dominique Janicaud, and Gianni Vattimo. And Nancy's work on the subject of the political continues to reverberate in contemporary discussions of communities and communitarianism. All of this is led by Nancy's claim that we must reposition and reintialize—that is, "expose" in its double sense—our thinking of the world, ontology, politics, and sense in the wake of the world's immanence.

EXPOSITIONS OF THE WORLD: CREATION, GLOBALIZATION, AND THE LEGACIES OF CHRISTIANITY

The first section of this book delimits Nancy's "sense of the world" in terms of its mundane, immanent character. Nancy's work circles around what he said some time ago in an essay "The End of the World": "There is no longer any world: no longer a *mundus*, a *cosmos*, a composed and complete order (from) within which one might find a place, a dwelling, and the elements of an orientation" (*SW*, 4). For Nancy, this lack of order to the world is our common lot after the death of God and the senselessness of any ideological alternative. In such works as *The Sense of the World*, *The Creation of the World* or *Globalization*, and *Dis-Enclosure*, Nancy centers his thought in this principle (one that is not itself a transcendent principle): "the meaning of the world does not occur as a reference to something external to the world" (*CW*, 43). The only site of praxis is therefore this disordered world, the unsightly, unworldly space (*immonde*) of modernity wrought by globalization and the cataclysmic devastation it brings about. But this praxis is also a task for thinking, which, as Heidegger argued before him, requires deconstructing the history of ontology in order to expose another sense to the world, one which does not come from another "world" behind or beyond this one. The world is *all there is*, but this does not mean we can simply leave behind ontotheology and the Christian heritage of the West. Nancy, for his part, argues that thinking the "world-forming" (*mondialisation*), still possible in the wake of globalization, means thinking again the Christian *creatio ex nihilo*, thus showing the resources still left in a theological tradition whose legacy, for better or worse, includes deconstruction and all manner of thinking through the meaning of the "end of the world."

François Raffoul begins this section with an account of Nancy's globalization in light of the Christian notion of creation. Raffoul's chapter, "The Creation of the World," first reviews Nancy's considerations on the threats of certain forms of globalization. By emphasizing the theme of "creation," Raffoul argues that Nancy offers a powerful rethinking of the sense of the world, one that furthers the Heideggerian concept of being-in-the-world to take on the current political stakes of globalization. In this way, Nancy denotes a post-onto-theological conception of creation *ex nihilo*, of political praxis, that necessitates a sense of the world unallied to its representability in the mind of God.

But, as Christina Smerick argues in her chapter, "No Other Place to Be: Globalization, Monotheism, and *Salut* in Nancy," this conception of the world is one still beholden to the Christian tradition. In this way, Smerick notes, for Nancy there is no thinking the future of thought without deconstructing Christianity. This necessitates, in Smerick's chapter, a review of Nancy's deconstructive reading of Christianity as it is linked to his accounts of globalization and the "demonstration" of the sense of the world. She notes that Nancy offers a version of Christianity that is quite removed from its lived, existing versions, but nevertheless his claims for rethinking Christianity should be championed if we are to put at bay the ultimate nihilism of a death drive at the heart of globalization, which makes Nancy's contributions in this area all too timely.

Alfonso Cariolato's chapter, "Christianity's Other Resource: Jean-Luc Nancy and the Deconstruction of Faith," traces further Nancy's "deconstruction" of Christianity, summarizing its implications for thinking the "closure" of Western metaphysics and onto-theology. Cariolato notes the repercussions for thinking the inseparability of deconstruction and Christianity, and in the end offers an example of the resources left within the Christian tradition for unworking the notions of community, a concern in Nancy's writings as well. Reading the Epistle of James, Cariolato argues for a *poiēsis* (making) and a notion of glory that testify to the singularity of each one as unique, thus unworking from within any presuppositions of immanent communities. In this way, Cariolato lays bare a faith in nothing but the fragile existence of each one along the tattered edges of what is thinkable.

This is not to suggest, however, that Nancy's "deconstruction of Christianity" may not simply return to the very theologies it supposedly puts in question. Jacques Derrida, in *Le Toucher*, argued that Nancy took up resources within the philosophical tradition, including the notions of fraternity and community, whose Christian, indeed Catholic, provenance (no small matter, given Nancy's early attachment to Catholic political organizations) threatened to overpower whatever displacement he was attempting. One risks taking on the tradition in such a way, Derrida argued, that one is merely repeating the tradition in full. This is a point that also concerns Martin McQuillan, whose chapter, "Deconstruction and Globalization: The World according to Jean-Luc Nancy," provides a critical overview of Nancy's work on globalization and *déclosion*. McQuillan argues that Nancy wrongly looks to Christianity for a sense of the world beyond global capitalism. Strategically, this can be done by looking for common Christian and atheistic resources in "nihilism," he argues, with the upshot of countering the moves of various forms of fundamentalism all-too-evident in today's geopolitics. In this way, McQuillan notes, Nancy's deconstruction of Christianity should be rethought in order to stand on the side of a certain form of reason under attack by fundamentalists. This requires, he argues, rethinking Nancy's use of such concepts as "creation *ex nihilo*," given their theological provenance and their link to the worldviews of those all-too-busy finding a way to return this world to nothingness in the name of their revelation.

EXPOSITIONS OF ONTOLOGY, OR A POST-DECONSTRUCTIVE REALISM

Reading *The Sense of the World*, *Being Singular Plural*, *Corpus*, and other key texts in Nancy's explicit writings on ontology, one is opened onto "exscriptive" writing, which often begins and ends with catalogued lists (rocks, lizards, skin, grass, etc.) that seems to offer barely an ontology. Nancy's prose is often elusive, but at the heart of his texts is an attempt to rethink the very act of "writing" as "exscription," a movement of sense always in excess of the inscribed meaning that allows writing to touch the thing. This requires a particular bare writing because in order to testify to the "spacing of an indefinite plurality of singularities," Nancy must refuse the gesture through which his writing would offer a system, a *logos*, by which to grasp and hold being, *ontos* (*BSP*, 35). In this way, Nancy sets out to describe what he calls the "*différance* of the real" by rethinking the disseminative deferral/difference of Derridean *différance* in terms of the writing of the real, or rather the real as a form of "writing," as a form of communication of sense between, with, and among things (*FT*, 136). For Nancy, this originary "exscription" of sense provides the basis for what Derrida dubs "an absolute, irredentist, and post-deconstructive realism," that is, "an absolute realism, but irreducible to any of the tradition's realisms" (*OT*, 46). In turn, this sends Nancy searching for means of writing the contact or inscribing the touch of existing bodies, providing in this way a thorough "haptological" realism.

This haptological realism is explained in the first chapter of this section in Anne O'Byrne's "Nancy's Materialist Ontology." Describing what she calls Nancy's "ontology in motion," O'Byrne sketches out the stakes of Nancy's materialist ontology, which she says contests the main lines of traditional materialisms. In particular, Nancy locates the sense of the world in the displacements of meaning, the changing elements of material bodies, which she contends shows an attunement for corporeal being rather than matter as such. In doing so, she argues that he upends the Cartesian *res extensa* while offering a conception of singularity in line with what she suggestively dubs "natal finitude."

Graham Harman, for his part, is skeptical that such a thinking of bodies offers much more than a tip of the hat to the being of objects. Harman begins his chapter, "On Interface: Nancy's Weights and Masses," by arguing that, of those aligned with post-structuralism, it is the work of Nancy that offers most to "object-oriented philosophy." He is critical of Nancy's thicket of self-references and parenthetical phrases—an often heard critique about Nancy's writing style—but he contends that in fact Nancy's cataloguing and listing of things has much in common with the "carnal phenomenology" of Alphonso Lingis, among those thinkers Harman champions. In his other works, Harman has argued, in line with Quentin Meillassoux's "speculative realism," that by giving up on all manner of realism, Continental philosophy has thus handed over the real to mystics and theologians. Yet, he sees little to be found in Nancy's notion of "touch" to overcome this situation. For Harman, although promising, this "touch" of the real has less to do with thinking objects as such than with turning them into something indeterminate that doesn't necessarily touch or weigh on other things.

On the other hand, Peter Gratton, in his chapter, "The Speculative Challenge and Nancy's Post-Deconstructive Realism," argues that Nancy's thinking of contact is well suited to confront Quentin Meillassoux's so-called "speculative challenge" to contemporary philosophy. By repeatedly marking the relation between things in terms of the same "*à même*" ("right at" or "at the heart of") that Nancy has long used to describe the relation within and among things, Meillassoux offers an entrée back to the heart of Nancy's work. In turn, Nancy provides an avenue for unworking what Meillassoux's "speculative" method must affirm, namely the "dualism" between things as they appear (the phenomenal) and things as they are (the noumenal). The point, Gratton argues, is to rethink the real as exscriptions of sense passing along *à même* the things themselves without answering the speculative challenge with a redoubled opposition between thinker and things.

EXPOSITIONS OF THE POLITICAL: JUSTICE, FREEDOM, EQUALITY

Nancy first came to wide prominence in the English-speaking world after the translation and publication of *The Inoperative Community*. The words that infuse this work (*désœuvrement* or unworking, communication, Heideggerian *Mitsein*, or Being-with, etc.) are found in all of his writings, making it impossible to tease out Nancy's political from nonpolitical works. What Nancy thus offers is a thoroughgoing political ontology. Following up on Heidegger's argument in *Being and Time* that being-in-the-world is always already *being-with*, Nancy contends that any notion of community must be thought in terms of "being-ecstatic of Being itself" (*IC*, 6). Weighing the legacy of all manner of communisms, Nancy argues that this originary being-with or the "being-ecstatic," explored at length in *Being Singular Plural*, requires a thinking of politics that charts its way between the rough waters of liberal atomism and religious and authoritarian "worked" or "essentialized" communities. We know well, he notes, the *telos* of the logics of fully immanent communities, and the praxis before us, as ever, is to avoid the "thanatology" and suicidal logic that would make any given community live up to "the criteria of pure immanence" (*IC*, 12). No doubt, Nancy's call for a politics that "opens onto a community . . . that does not weave a superior, immortal, or transmortal life between subjects" will be found wanting by readers looking to Nancy for a world-historical program. "Willing the world, but not willing a subject of the world (neither substance nor author nor master)," Nancy writes, nevertheless, "is the only way to escape the *immonde*," and is thus not without its consequences (*CW*, 49). It is for this reason that Nancy argues for a displacing of the regime of thought, including the traditional thinking of political subjectivity, that has heretofore "permitted" but a limited set of "options" for the political (*TD*, 9): atomistic globalization or essentialized authoritarianisms, market freedoms or deadened corporatist socialisms, etc. This requires a rethinking of justice, freedom, and equality that measures up to the "division of the sharing-out of the incalculable, and therefore, strictly speaking, the unsharable" that always "exceeds the political" (*TD*, 17).

The task of this section is thus to take the measure of the political, there where it meets its limit in that which always exceeds it. In his chapter, "Archi-ethics, Justice and the Suspension of History in the Writing of Jean-Luc Nancy," B. C. Hutchens begins by arguing that Nancy contests traditional conceptions of equality premised on subjectivity and the sovereign individual. By doing so, Nancy calls for understanding a "sharing of relations" among singularities that gives rise to but is not derived from political states, classes, or social structures. Nancy hence offers a thinking of the "suspension of history" to the march of the progress of the further immancence of fully worked communities. Justice, if there is any, must answer, Hutchens argues, to freedom's groundlessness, not the supposed substance of communities always already put in question by the free being-with of each singular existent sharing the world.

Andrew Norris situates this thinking of the sharing of the world in his chapter, "Jean-Luc Nancy on the Political after Heidegger and Schmitt," by showing the relation between Nancy's account of the inoperative community and his rethinking of Heidegger and Schmitt's concepts of the political. Norris argues that Nancy furthers Heidegger's conceptions of Being-with to rethink notions of justice and all manner of political institutions and norms, which in turn contests Schmittian biological conceptions of community. Nevertheless, Norris contends that in the end Nancy does not avoid Heidegger's dictum from the "Letter on Humanism" that thinking is the highest praxis. In this way, he argues, while Nancy offers much to reconceptualizing the political, his work remains curiously abstracted from politics as it is practiced in the everyday.

In his chapter, David Pettigrew attempts to fill this lacuna by linking Nancy to his own work on the genocidal regimes of post-Cold War Yugoslavia. His "The Task of Justice" provides a masterful overview of Nancy's work connecting finitude and justice. For Nancy, Pettigrew argues, each being is "singular" in the finitude of their existence, one that is theirs alone—a singularity to be thought in relation to Heidegger's conception of being-towards-death. What the finite singular that is each of us testifies to is what Pettigrew calls the task of justice. Laying out this task against a Levinasian version of ethics, Pettigrew grounds his analysis in what is still left to be thought in the wake of the horrors of the 1990s-era massacres in the former Yugoslavia.

EXPOSITIONS OF SENSE: ART AND THE LIMITS OF REPRESENTATION

Readers should hear the multiple meanings of the French *sens* in the title of this section: meaning, sensation, and also direction. Nancy's influential writings on the multiple arts touch (to use his favored term) on all these meanings, and one should not miss the fact that his work on poetry, film, dance, painting, techno-music, and all manner of artworks also indelibly concern bodily sensations such as seeing, hearing, and touching, as well as the question of meaning and the sense of the world for us today. Nancy's writings on the arts include the two volumes of *The Muses*, *Multiple Arts*, *The Sense of the World*, *The Evidence of Film*, *Noli me tangere*, *The Ground of the Image*, and *Listening*. In many of these works, Nancy critiques both the Hegelian view of the death of art, which sublates all art in the name of its idea, and the Heideggerian reduction of the work of art to an originary poetic thinking. For Nancy, what is missed in these accounts is the sensuous aspect of art, one that disorients any sense that we would want to give to the arts from the side of philosophy. The point, he argues, is to testify to the inadequacy of any signification or representation of artworks or the arts as such.

In the first chapter of this section, "De-monstration and the *Sens* of Art," Stephen Barker reads Nancy's *The Muses* as extending his meditations on the "sense of the world." For Barker, artworks break themselves into ever increasing categories from the inside due to their excess of sense. They thus "de-monstrate," or show from out of themselves, the fragmentary sense of the world. Disorienting, this sense of the world, however, is not only non-sense, but rather an excess of sense that disrupts any figuring of the art, and indeed any figuring of art in its relationship to the world. Such a figuring, he suggests, would simply be "monstrous."

William Watkin's chapter, "Poetry and Plurality: On a Part of Jean-Luc Nancy's *The Muses*," develops Nancy's thinking of this "excess of sense" described by Barker in order to conceive the arts in the wake of his work. Calling for what he dubs a "promiscuous" poetics, Watkin first reviews Nancy's thinking of the multiple arts in the two volumes of *The Muses*. Traditionally, Watkin notes, poetic practice had been reduced by philosophers such as Plato, Hegel, and Heidegger to concepts and thoughts said to underlay the arts' material exterior. Although Nancy calls into question such a dualism between material exterior and conceptual interior, Watkin counters that Nancy does so by reinscribing the dualism between the "whole" and the "parts" of arts. In this way, poetry, as but one of the "whole" of arts, would be similar in essence to all other arts, and any investigation of the whole (the "multiple arts") is thus *a fortiori* extendable to the part of the arts known as poetry. Rethinking poetry promiscuously, however, means accepting a conception of the arts as too slippery to be subsumed under this rigid, traditional schema.

It is the end of such rigid representation and schema that is the focus of the last chapter in this section. Beginning with Dan Pagis's remarkable poem, "Written in Pencil in the Sealed Freight Car," Andrew Benjamin's "Forbidding, Knowing, Continuing. On Representing the Shoah," reads Nancy's own contribution to thinking about writing and representation after the Shoah. For Benjamin, Nancy's meditations on the logic of representation throughout his work come to fruition in his reflections on the Shoah, particularly in *The Ground of the Image*, where Nancy shows the fragility of each and every image. Ultimately, the question Benjamin evokes is what Nancy's considerations mean for the "act of continuity" after the Shoah and what such continuing on would mean for philosophy, poetry, thinking about Judaism, and our common being-together.

The last chapter of this book returns us explicitly to the "commerce of thinking" in the form of an interview with Nancy vis-à-vis the questions raised in the critical engagements in this volume. The dialogues that make up this book do not end with this interview. Each book, Nancy writes, "is a dialogue," one that opens itself beyond its own avowed significance to the sense of the world to which it is exscribed. As such, we hope in this book to provide no less than, as Nancy writes, a "world" that "comes to mingle with the plurality of worlds" that already "inhabit" the reader (OC, 23).

These "mêlée of worlds" on offer in the excellent contributions here are meant to take the measure of the weight of Nancy's thought. This will take the form of an ever-interrupted dialogue with his plural thinking, one that should not be reduced, by definition, merely to that thought subsumed under the proper name Jean-Luc Nancy because it communicates in this volume and elsewhere beyond this name. We end with an exscription from Nancy:

> May there be, each time, in the scrolling of a volume, in the binding of a book, a burst of sense that shines and is eclipsed, and so on further and further, from book to book, . . . always echoing from one to another, indefinitely and each time unique. . . . Whoever really reads it, enters into nothing less than commerce with it. (OC, 14)

PART ONE

EXPOSITIONS OF THE WORLD

Creation, Globalization, and the Legacies of Christianity

ONE

THE CREATION OF THE WORLD

François Raffoul

In *The Creation of the World* or *Globalization*,[1] Nancy seeks to reappropriate the term *mondialisation* for his rethinking of the world through the motif of creation, which itself is a term borrowed, he recognizes, from the tradition of monotheism. It is a matter, he explains, of grasping the world "according to one of its constant motifs in the Western tradition—to the extent that it is also the tradition of monotheism—namely the motif of creation" (CW, 50). This recourse to a Christian theme is all the more surprising in light of Nancy's work on the deconstruction of Christianity.[2] However, Nancy argues that he seeks to understand creation in a radically nontheological way. " 'Creation,' " he writes, "is a motif, or a concept that we must grasp outside of its theological context" (CW, 50). Furthermore, he clarifies that the motif of creation plays a key role in the self-deconstruction of Christianity and monotheism that Nancy follows, as it points to a self-deconstruction of the creator in its creation. This thinking of an a-theological creation is intimately connected to the deconstruction of Christianity that Nancy pursues, if it is the case, as Nancy claims, that "it is theology itself that has stripped itself of a God distinct from the world" (CW, 50). Finally, the motif of creation might give us access to the world as Nancy rethinks it: "the world is not given," he writes, "the world is its own creation . . . this is what 'creation' means" (CW, 109). It is the main purpose of this chapter to elucidate the difficulties of these claims and explore the senses of such a non- or a-theological creation. Ultimately, we want to ask how these claims give us access to the world as Nancy thematizes it. Indeed, at stake in this reappropriation of the motif of creation is the access to the worldhood of the world, its being as world. The goal of the following pages is to enter further into Nancy's thinking of the world, once it is referred to an a-theological creation *ex nihilo*, from nothing, an *ex nihilo* that breaks any reliance on a divine author as the world opens in it.

THE GLOBAL AND THE WORLDLY

In *The Creation of the World* or *Globalization*, Nancy's reflection on the being-world of the world unfolds through a contrast drawn between two terms often used interchangeably, namely globalization and *mondialisation* (world-forming, world-creating). Nancy analyses and exploits the fact that this term possesses two meanings for designating the phenomenon known in English simply as "globalization": world-forming or world-creating and globalization. The two words seem, at first glance, to be indistinguishable, converging in the designation of the same phenomenon, that is, the unification of all parts of the world. In fact, for Nancy, they reveal two quite distinct, if not opposite, senses. The term "globalization," Nancy notes, has established itself in the areas of the world "that use English for the contemporary information exchange," whereas *mondialisation* does not allow itself to be translated as easily and would even be of the order of the "untranslatable" (CW, 27). In contrast to *mondialisation*, globalization is a process that indicates an "enclosure in the undifferentiated sphere of a unitotality" that is perfectly accessible and transparent for a mastery without remainder (CW, 28). Therefore, it is not insignificant that *mondialisation* maintains a certain untranslatability and nonmasterability in the face of a globalization that stands for the integral translatability of all meanings and all phenomena. Nancy refers to globality as a "totality grasped as a whole," an "indistinct totality," whereas the world, the worldly, and world-forming call to mind a "process in expansion," in reference to the world of humans, of culture, and of nations in a differentiated set. In the final analysis, what interests Nancy in this distinction is world-forming's crucial reference to the world's horizon as a space of human relations, as a space of meaning held in common, and as a space of significance. The global is not the worldly, and in fact for Nancy the global marks the disintegration of the sense of the world: In the extension of the global, the world no longer makes sense as world.

For this reason, in *Dis-Enclosure*, Nancy writes that the world "no longer acknowledges itself as holding a world-view, or a sense of the world that might accompany this globalization." The world is taken as a world-market, and the sense of the world is reduced to a mere "accumulation and circulation of capitals" (*D*, 30). This disintegration of sense—of the sense of the world—takes place in the phenomenon of globalization, a phenomenon by which the West has both established dominance and exceeded itself (to the point where the "West can no longer be called the West" [*D*, 29]) to take the form of the global. Nancy's reflection is rooted in an analysis of our present time as well as the historical trajectory of the West that has led to the point where sense itself has become questionable. It becomes urgent at such a time, Nancy argues, to reengage the history of the West through which this process of disintegration or decomposition of sense has occurred. "Our time is thus one in which it is urgent that the West—or what remains of it—analyze its own becoming, turn back [*se retourne sur*] to examine its provenance and its trajectory, and question itself concerning the process of decomposition of sense to which it has given rise" (*D*, 30). It is thus in this context of a disintegration—indeed (self)deconstruction—of sense that Nancy seeks to engage that history. Sense itself has been reduced to a general equivalence of values amid the accumulation and circulation of capital in which an indefinite technological growth without end increases the gap between the haves and the have-nots. The accumulation of globalization accentuates the concentration of wealth that leads to the exclusion of those on the margins thrown into poverty.

Globalization, far from being a becoming-world or a world-forming, leads to what Nancy calls the un-world (*l'im-monde*). "The world has lost its capacity to 'form a world' [*faire monde*]: it seems only to have gained that capacity of proliferating, to the extent of its means, the 'un-world' [*im-monde*]" (*CW*, 34). The uniformity of globalization, produced by an economical and technological logic, leads to "a global injustice against the background of general equivalence" (*CW*, 54). It leads to the opposite of an inhabitable world, an inhuman un-world. At stake is nothing less than two possible destinies of our humanity, of our time. On the one hand, Nancy describes globalization as "the suppression of all world-forming of the world" and as "an unprecedented geopolitical, economic, and ecological catastrophe" (*CW*, 50). On the other hand, there remains the possibility of an authentic world-forming, that is, of a making of the world and of a making sense that Nancy will call a "creation" of the world. This creation of the world means, as he makes clear, "immediately, without delay, reopening each possible struggle for a world, that is, for what must form the contrary" of globality (*CW*, 54).[3] The question, henceforth, becomes the following: "How are we to conceive of, precisely, a world where we only find a globe, an astral universe, or earth without sky . . .?" (*CW*, 47). Globality does not open a path, a way, or a direction; rather, it furiously turns on itself and on its absence of perspective and orientation, thereby exacerbating itself as blind technological and economical exploitation. The profound nihilism of the logic of globalization is here revealed: "everything takes place as if the world affected and permeated itself with a death drive that soon would have nothing else to destroy than the world itself" (*CW*, 34).[4]

Nancy's thinking of the world hence begins with the following fact: The world destroys itself in the logic of globalization. This is not hyperbole, but is indeed the fact from which any reflection on the sense of the world must originate (*CW*, 35). The thought of the world, of the being-world of the world, is thus rendered possible, paradoxically, when the world is in the process of destroying itself. Nancy notes the relation between the process of technologic and economic planetary domination and the disintegration of the world as a "convergence of knowledge, ethics, and social well-being" (*CW*, 34). Everything happens as if the access to totality, in the sense of the global and of the planetary, marks the end of orientation and sense. Nevertheless, it is paradoxically by virtue of the event of globalization—for Nancy, the suppression of the world—that the world is in the position to appear as such. This is why Nancy begins his thought of the world with an analysis of globalization, that is, of the destruction of the world.

THE ABSOLUTE EVENT OF THE WORLD

Nancy argues that the absoluteness of the event of the world is its disconnection from any transcendence, from any relation to or dependence on a world beyond this world. The world is no longer referred to a transcendence, to a beyond, to a god outside and distinct from the world. God, for Nancy, amounts to this: another world placed next to this world, other than this world. "[F]or a God distinct from the world would be another world" (*CW*, 44–45). Thus, he argues, "at the end of monotheism, there is the world without God, that is to say, *without another world*" (*CW*, 50; my emphasis). God is what is outside the world. However, "Whoever speaks of 'the world' renounces any appeal to 'another world' or a 'beyond-the-world' [*outre-monde*]" (*CW*, 37). This is why, in this rethinking of the world, it is a matter of showing how the world occurs or happens outside the theological scenario and how the sense of the world cannot be referred to an external and transcendent model. There is no model for the world, as the world is no longer reduced to or adjusted to a representation of another world (or to a principle subtending this world:The world is an-archic). What used to stand in the way of or obstruct, this thinking of the world as anarchic event was the division of the totality of being according to the tripartite structure of nature–man–God. Now, however, an authentic thinking of the world, Nancy states, "never crosses over these edges to occupy a place overlooking itself" (*CW*, 43). The world does not get crossed over (it does not have an outside). Rather, it is traversed from beginning to end, from one edge to another, but never in order to access an outside or a beyond that would be the site of the divine. And, if one "leaves this world," it is not to attain another world; it is simply no longer being-in-the-world and no longer having a world. To that extent, "this world" is the only world. Thus, to die is to leave the world, as world, and no longer to leave this world for another world. To no longer be is to no longer be in the world.

Devoid of an external principle, happening outside representation, the world therefore can only refer to itself, and its meaning only arises from itself. When Nancy speaks of "sense" (*sens*), he does not intend by this term *signification*, that is, as an accomplished or given meaning, but rather intends the opening of the possibility of a production of significance. Sense is not given, but to be invented, to be created, *ex nihilo*. Because the sense of the world does not refer to another world, it is first and foremost a making-sense, which is the world as such: The world makes sense of itself and by itself. Sense is never a reference to an outside world, but a self-reference, the very structure of selfhood for Nancy. This is why the expression, "the sense of the world [*le sens du monde*]," cannot signify the sense of the world as an objective genitive, an encompassing view of the world as totality on the basis of an external standpoint that would follow Wittgenstein's dictum that "the meaning of the world must be situated outside the world." Understood in the subjective genitive, produced from the internal references of the world, "one could say that worldhood (*mondialité*) is the symbolization of the world, the way in which the world symbolizes in itself with itself, in which it articulates itself by making a circulation of meaning possible without reference to another world" (CW, 53). The world only refers to itself and it "circulates," Nancy tells us, "between all those who stand in it [*s'y tiennent*], each time singular and singularly sharing a same possibility that none of them, anyplace or any God outside of this world, accomplishes" (CW, 43). It is in this sense that the world is not of the order of substance, support, or foundation: the world does not presuppose itself. It exists as an extension of itself, as a gap from itself, without ground or against the background of nothing.[5]

The world is an absolute event, an event that is absolutely freed from any reference to an exterior: The world is ab-solute, detached, without connection. Nancy thus speaks of "the" world and speaks of its absolutization as one of the senses of "world-forming." The world is absolute but nonetheless finite, because, as we will see, it comes from nothing in order to return to nothing, and it is only itself a growth of/from nothing. The conjunction of a finitude and of an absolute, the world is an absolute finitude. No longer adjusted to a representation or a vision, a worldview, the world manifests its mode of being as an excess with regard to this vision. The world exceeds its representation; it leaves it, and it appears outside this model, excessive, eccentric, and singular. As the excess of a pure event, founded on nothing, outside representation, the world escapes from all horizons of calculability (in opposition to the logic of economic and technological globalization). A world in excess has the mode of being an unpredictable event, not as a matter of a choice between given possibilities. It is, rather, "a violent decision without appeal, for it decides [*tranche*] between all and nothing—or more exactly it makes some thing be in place of nothing [*elle fait être quelque chose au lieu de rien*]" (CW, 59; my emphasis). It is a question of a decision about "what is in no way given in advance, but which constitutes the eruption of the new, that is unpredictable because it is without face, and thus the 'beginning of a series of appearances' by which Kant defines freedom in its relation to the world" (CW, 59).

According to the very structure of the event, the world then happens *as* incalculable, in the mode of what Jacques Derrida refers to as the possibility of the impossible. For Derrida, the impossible, which he writes as im-possible to mark its excess with prior conditions of possibility, is possible and takes place as im-possible. In fact, according to Derrida, which Nancy follows, the im-possible is the very structure of the event.[6] The possibility of the world "must not be the object of a programmatic and certain calculation. . . . It must be the possibility of the impossible (according to a logic used often by Derrida), it must know itself as such, that is to say, know that it happens also in the incalculable and the unassignable" (CW, 49). The impossible, in this context, does not mean that which is not simply possible, and therefore without effects. The impossible, or the im-possible, means that which happens outside the conditions of possibility offered in advance by a subject of representation, outside the transcendental conditions of possibility, which, for Nancy, render impossible the subject of this experience of the world.

We need to hold together the following two statements: The transcendental makes experience impossible; the im-possible is the possibility of the experience. The world happens as such as im-possible. Derrida often writes that an event or an invention is only possible as im-possible. This is why Nancy will specify, "Our question thus becomes clearly question of the impossible experience or the experience of the impossible: an experience removed from the conditions of possibility of a finite experience, and which is nevertheless an experience" (CW, 65). This experience is the experience of the world as excess with respect to the conditions of anticipating possibilities. Experience takes place in the excess of the im-possible as the structure of the event.

The world is thus excessive, exceeding the transcendental conditions of possibility of representation, but it nevertheless establishes a proper stance. The world is without foundation (without representation), but it holds a stance in this nothing: The world, "essentially, is not the representation of a universe (cosmos) nor that of a here below (a humiliated world, if not condemned by Christianity)," but the excess of an *ethos* or of a *habitus*, excess of a stance "by which the world stands by itself, configures itself, and exposes itself in itself, relates to itself without referring to any given principle or to any determined end" (CW, 47). Not a substance, but a stance: "The stance of the world is the experience it makes of itself" (CW, 43).

Nancy explains that the world, if it does not want to be a land of exile or simply the un-world that it is becoming today, must be the place of a possible inhabiting. Above all, the world is a place. More precisely, it is the place of a possible taking-place, where there is "a genuine place, one in which things can genuinely take place in it (in this world)" (CW, 42). The world is the place of any taking-place, of any possible taking-place, the place where "there is room for everyone [*tout le monde*]" (CW, 42). The world is the place and the dimension of a possibility to inhabit, to coexist. The world "is only for those who inhabit it" (CW, 42). Such a place is the opening of a dimension, which is properly the opening of the world, from a void. It is from this void, this nothing, that the world opens, *ex nihilo*. The world itself, as it is always "without given," takes on the meaning of a creation if it is the case that the "withdrawal of any given . . . forms the heart of a thinking of creation" (CW, 69).

To think the world as nonrepresentable, that is, outside of onto-theology,[7] necessitates, according to Nancy, an appeal to the motif of creation, but importantly, as nontheological creation *ex nihilo*. Creation is thus, on Nancy's reading, in its content and its logic, a nontheological notion, if it is the case that creating can only be *ex nihilo*, emergence from nothing, and not from a transcendent creator. For Nancy, creation is a motif that must be grasped "outside of its theological context" (CW, 50). Creation is even characterized as "a nodal point in a 'deconstruction of monotheism,'" precisely to the extent that creation resides in the *ex nihilo*. "The idea of creation . . . is above all the idea of the *ex nihilo*" (CW, 51).

This event without given opens the space of creation, a creation of the world without given but properly *ex nihilo*, by which the creator annihilates itself—deconstructs itself—in its creation. What is peculiar to the very notion of a creation for Nancy is precisely that it is not a production from a given by a transcendent producer. In *Dis-Enclosure*, he explains that the "idea of creatio *ex nihilo*, inasmuch as it is clearly distinguished from any form of production or fabrication, essentially covers the dual motif of an absence of necessity and the existence of a given without reason, having neither foundation nor principle for its gift" (*D*, 24). The creation of the world is *ex nihilo*, letting the world appear as a nothing-given, and is "neither reason nor ground sustains the world" (CW, 120, n. 20). The world as such forms a "resonance without reason," Nancy writes suggestively (CW, 47).[8] Nothing is given, all is to be invented, to be created, and the world is created from nothing. This does not mean, Nancy is quick to point out, that it is "fabricated with nothing by a particularly ingenious producer. It means instead that it is not fabricated, produced by no producer" (*CW*, 51). Thus, if "creation means anything, it is the exact opposite of any form of production," which presupposes a given, a project, and a producer (*CW*, 51).

Understood nontheologically, creation deconstructs the reference to an author or creator, which explains why Nancy claims that creation is a motif that participates in the deconstruction of monotheism. A thought of creation, *ex nihilo*, deconstructs onto-theology, deconstructs the reference to a creator. In *Being Singular Plural*, Nancy explains that the concept of creation of the world "represents the origin as originarily shared, spaced between us and between all beings. This, in turn, contributes to rendering the concept of the 'author' of the world untenable."[9] What creation shows is that the so-called "creator" becomes indistinguishable from its "creation." If creation is *ex nihilo* (and it must be because it is not a production from a given), that means not that the creator starts from nothing, but that the creator *is* the *nihil*, and that this *nihil* is not prior to creation, such that "only the *ex* remains" (*BSP*, 16). That "ex" is distributive: The origin is not a preexisting supreme being but the dis-position of the appearing, and creation is nothing but the ex-position of being as singular plural.

ABSENTHEISM, NOT ATHEISM

In *The Creation of the World* or *Globalization*, Nancy shows how the world as problem and as the proper site of human existence was obscured by the classical figures of onto-theology and representational thinking, all the while, paradoxically and silently, onto-theology was undermined from within. The question of the world, writes Nancy in a striking passage, has formed "the self-deconstruction that undermines from within onto-theology" (*CW*, 41). The world emerged as a proper philosophical problem against the background of a self-deconstruction of onto-theology, and it is precisely onto-theology that, having put into play as absolute existence, is correlative to a disappearance of God in the world. In the classical representation of the world, one finds the supposition of a subject, a position that is outside of the world, a vantage point from where the world may be able to be seen and represented. The world thus supposed an observer of the world, a *cosmotheoros*, that is to say, a subject-of-the-world representing the world in front of itself as an object, a subject that keeps the world in its gaze, in its sight, in such a way that the world is thus represented as "a world dependent on the gaze of a subject-of-the-world [*sujet-du-monde*]" (*CW*, 40). As for this subject, it is, of course, not of this world, not "in" the world in the sense of being-in-the-world: It is not worldly. Positioning itself outside the world, such a subject gains, so to speak, a theological status. Onto-theology reveals itself in the positioning of such a subject: "Even without a religious representation, such a subject, implicit or explicit, perpetuates the position of the creating, organizing, and addressing God, (if not the addressee) of the world" (*CW*, 40). The becoming-world of the world is characterized as a "detheologization." As we have noted, for Nancy God names the position of another world placed next to this world. Nancy's thought of the world, however, is the thought of an absolute immanence in opposition to the tradition of transcendence. Nevertheless, Nancy claims that the world, the question of the being-world of the world, undermines from within onto-theology, which self-deconstructs and confirms the world in its radical immanence. He states it very clearly: in classical onto-theology, in the end it was a matter of nothing else than the world (the only world there is): "there is no need of a prolonged study to notice that, already in the most classical metaphysical representations of that God, nothing else was at stake, in the end, than the world itself, in itself, and for itself" (*CW*, 41). The metaphysical thought of God questioned the being-world of the world, for what, in effect, did the classical transcendences of onto-theology provide an account, if not the world? They outlined its immanent structure, supplied "a reason internal to the general order of things," and in the end "elaborated nothing else than the immanent relation of the world to itself (*CW*, 41). God is effectively the God *of the world*, the subject of the world, of its fabrication, of its maintenance and of its destination. Of the world, God was the creator, the organizer. Therefore, Nancy identifies a "becoming-world of the world" in the classical figures of onto-theology: Descartes' "continual creation" (maintenance of the world), Spinoza's *Deus sive natura* (God as the world), Malebranche's "vision in God," and Leibniz's "monad of monads." In each instance, it is a question of the world, of its truth and of its sense. It is to this extent that the question of the world will have formed the self-deconstruction of onto-theology, and that the God of metaphysics has merged with the world, indeed has become the world. In this sense, onto-theology self-deconstructs in atheism, or rather, into what Nancy calls an "absentheism."

There is a tendency to contrast the Christian age with the modern atheistic period, a schema that Nancy rejects. Instead, one needs to understand how monotheism and Christianity in particular have structured the West through and through, including modern atheism. In this sense, the "only atheism that can be actual is the one that contemplates the reality of its Christian provenance" (*D*, 140; trans. modified). One finds, for example in the Kantian corpus, both the denial of the Christian reference (modernity itself is built, according to Nancy, on the denial of the Christian sources that are present within it) and at the same time the maintaining of Christian motifs, such as the universal, law, human rights, freedom, conscience, the individual, reason itself, and so on. Regarding the persistence of Christian motifs in the modern age, Nancy also includes the relation to nature and the reference to the intimate certainty at the heart of Rousseau, the dimension of eschatology and the salvation of man in Marx, the call of conscience and original *Schuldigsein* in Heidegger, and so on. Relying on what he calls a "deconstructive" knowledge, Nancy stresses that the most salient features of the modern understanding of the world "and sometimes its most visibly atheist, atheistic, or atheological traits" must be approached "in their strictly and fundamentally monotheist provenance" (*D*, 32). This is why Nancy insists, "Let us therefore, very simply but very firmly, posit that any analysis that claims to find a *deviation* of the modern world from Christian reference forgets or denies that the modern world is itself the unfolding of Christianity" (*D*, 143–144; trans. slightly modified).

Nancy thus stresses that the opposition between atheism and theism, which is undeniable given that a-theism is the negation of theism, nevertheless conceals the profound connection between atheism to theism. A-theism is the negation of theism, but "we should not overlook to what degree this negation retains the essence of what it negates" (*D*, 16). This statement needs to be reversed: If atheism harbors a deep dependency with respect to theism, it will be a matter for Nancy of showing how "monotheism is in truth atheism," that is, deconstructs itself as atheism, a still enigmatic formulation which Nancy will understand in terms of a self-annihilating of God in its creation (*D*, 35). Atheism is not the simple refutation of theism, and theism somehow would lead to atheism in an essential way. Christianity "shelters within itself—better: more intimately within itself than itself, within or without itself—the principle of a world without God" (*D*, 35).

We saw how for Nancy the God of onto-theology, in a peculiar kenosis or self-emptying, was "progressively stripped of the divine attributes of an independent existence and only retained those of the existence of the world considered in its immanence" (*CW*, 44), which amounts to saying that the subject of the world (God) disappears in order for the world to appear as subject of itself. This is what the self-deconstruction of Christianity gives us to think: the self-deconstruction of God in its creation, the absenting of God in the world. The becoming-world of the world indicates that the world loses its status as object (of vision) in order to reach the status of subject (previously occupied by God as independent existence). Henceforth, there is nothing but the world as subject of itself. Not a subject in the sense of a prior substantial ground, not proceeding from a ground or a basis, but in the sense that the world appears as the ex- of its extension, as a relation to itself. "The world does not presuppose itself: it is only coextensive to its extension as world, to the spacing of its places between which its resonances reverberate" (CW, 43). The God of religious representation, as subject of the world, as self-subsisting and sustaining, as substance of the world, is henceforth thought as emptying itself in the opening of the world. Following this understanding of kenosis in divine creation,[10] Nancy explains that the God of onto-theology "has produced itself (or deconstructed itself) as subject of the world, that is, as world-subject. In so doing, it suppressed itself as God-Supreme-Being and transformed itself, losing itself therein, in the existence for-itself of the world without an outside (neither outside of the world nor a world from the outside)" (CW, 44). God thus disappears, but in the world, which immediately means that we can no longer speak meaningfully in terms of being within the world (*dans-le-monde*) in the sense of something that is contained within something else, but in terms of being-in-the-world (*au-monde*). The preposition "*au*," "in," explains Nancy, represents in French what encapsulates the entire problem of the world.

From the theological understanding of creation as the "result of an accomplished divine action," one moves to the notion of an "unceasing activity and actuality of this world in its singularity (singularity of singularities)" (CW, 65). Creation is a *mise-en-monde* or *mise-au-monde*, as Nancy writes it, a bringing or coming into the world. In French, *mettre au monde* has the colloquial sense of giving birth. However, Nancy clarifies: " 'Coming to the world' means birth and death, emerging from nothing and going to nothing" (CW, 74). One sense of the world, the creation as a state of affairs of the given world, "yields to another (creation as bringing forth [*mise au monde*] a world—an active sense that is nothing else than the first sense of *creatio*)" (CW, 65). Not held by an author or subject, the world is surrendered without origin to itself, an abandonment by and to itself: The world is poor. This poverty, which is not misery but the being-abandoned as such, is the nothing that the world manifests: Emerging from nothing, resting on nothing, going to nothing, the world is, writes Nancy in an striking passage, "the nothing itself, if one can speak in this way, or rather nothing growing [*croissant*] as something" (CW, 51). Commenting on the etymological links between growing (*croissant*), being born (*naître*), to grow (*croître*), *cresco* and *creo*, Nancy connects creation with growth as movement of the world. "In creation, a growth grows from nothing and this nothing takes care of itself, cultivates its growth" (CW, 51). To that extent, the nothing grows. "If the world is the growth of/from nothing [*croissance de rien*]—an expression of a redoubtable ambiguity—it is because it only depends on itself, while this 'self' is given from nowhere but from itself" (CW, 51). The world is created from nothing, that is to say, as nothing, not in the sense of nothingness, but in the sense of nothing given and nothing of reason. Coming from nothing signifies: the presentation of nothing, not in the sense of a phenomenology of the unapparent or of negative theology, but in the sense where "that nothing gives itself and that nothing shows itself—and that is what is" (*CW*, 123, n. 24).

Creation lies entirely in the *ex nihilo* and not in the position of a theism, against which Nancy proclaims, not simply an a-theism, but an absentheism: a world without God, a world without another world: "At the end of monotheism, there is world without God, that is to say, without another world, but we still need to reflect on what this means, for we know nothing of it, no truth, neither 'theistic' nor 'atheistic'—let us say, provisionally, as an initial attempt, that it is absentheistic" (*CW*, 50–51). God is absent in the creation of the world and disappears in the world, and Nancy clarifies that this "absentheism" designates "an absent God and an absence in place of God" (*CW*, 120, n. 23). A creation no longer referred to theology, but to the ex nihilo, without a transcendent creator (in which the creator disappears and self–deconstructs in its creation), a creation *à même* itself, a creation of itself, and from itself.

This creation of the world deprived of a subject becomes an unpredictable appearance, an irruption of the new, an absolute beginning, a dis-posing openness (the *ex* of *ex nihilo* as *différance*), ultimately the opening of the world, its eclosure (*éclosion*). The nothing of creation *ex nihilo* is the one "that opens in God when God withdraws in it (and in sum *from* it) in the act of creating. God annihilates itself [*s'anéantit*] as a 'self' or as a distinct being in order to 'withdraw' in his act—which makes the opening of the world" (*CW*, 70). The creator necessarily disappears in its act, "and with this disappearance a decisive episode of the entire movement that I have sometimes named the 'deconstruction of Christianity' occurs, a movement that is nothing but the most intrinsic and proper movement of monotheism as the integral absenting of God in the unity that reduces it in and where it dissolves" (*CW*, 68). The self-deconstruction of God is the opening of the world ("the opening of the world in the world is the result of a destitution or a deconstruction of Christianity" [*D*, 78]) such that the creation of the world occurs as the self-emptying of God, an opening from a void, that is, an ex-appropriative opening: "The unique God, whose unicity is the correlate of the creating act, cannot precede its creation, any more that it can subsist above it or apart from it in some way. It merges with it: Merging with it, it withdraws in it and withdrawing there it empties itself there, emptying itself it is nothing other than the opening of this void. Only the opening is divine, but the divine is nothing more than the opening" (*CW*, 70). We are now able to understand better in what sense Nancy appropriates the term *mondialisation* in his rethinking of the world, and how a nontheological creation figures in his thought. The creation of the world is a subjective genitive, the advent of the world from nothing, from itself, *ex nihilo*.

NOTES

1. Jean-Luc Nancy, *The Creation of the World* or *Globalization*, trans. François Raffoul and David Pettigrew (Albany, NY: SUNY Press, 2007). Henceforth cited as *CW*.

2. Jean-Luc Nancy, *Dis-Enclosure: The Deconstruction of Christianity*, trans. Bettina Bergo, Gabriel Malenfant, and Michael B. Smith (New York: Fordham University Press, 2008). Henceforth cited as *D*. I have occasionally modified the translation and I indicate it as appropriate.

3. Another formulation by Nancy of this alternative reads: "can what is called 'globalization' give rise to a world, or to its contrary?" (*CW*, 29).

4. Let us note here with respect to this nihilism the crucial place and role of the nothing, apparent in the antinomy between the global and the worldly, the role that the nothing plays in the world, in its event as in its destruction or in its destruction as event. In *Dis-Enclosure*, Nancy warns us not to "confuse" this nothing or this void with nihilism (*D*, 8), as he had explained, in *The Creation of The World* or *Globalization*, that the nothing in the *ex nihilo* of creation "fractures the deepest core of nihilism from within" and that the motif of creation (which as we will see lies for Nancy in the *ex nihilo*) "constitutes the exact reverse of nihilism" (*CW*, 71). For nihilism is the raising of the nothing as principle, whereas the *ex nihilo* signifies the absence of principle: The *ex nihilo* means the "undoing of any principle, including that of the nothing" (*D*, 24–25). It is a matter of having another relation to the nothing, another relation "to the exact place where the void opened"—and Nancy adds: "no where else but in the very heart of society, or of humanity, or civilization, in the eye of the hurricane of globalization" (*D*, 3; trans. modified)—another relation to "the empty heart of the void itself" opened by the death of God (*D*, 3; trans. modified). It is therefore a question bringing forth this "nothing of the world," whose characteristics Nancy reveals, for one senses that it is in this nothing that the cross destinies of globalization and world-forming are at stake, as well as the question of contemporary nihilism; a nihilism whose hard knot would be "fractured" by the nothing of the *ex nihilo* of the creation of the world.

5. Nancy thus specifies that the world is a dimensionality without origin, founded on nothing, an "archi-spatiality" or a "spaciousness of the opening" (*CW*, 73), that is a "spacing of presences" (always plural and singular).

6. On this point, I take the liberty of referring to my "Derrida and the Ethics of the Im-possible," *Research in Phenomenology* 38:2 (2008), pp. 270–290.

7. "A world without representation is above all a world without a God capable of being the subject of its representation," Nancy writes (*CW*, 43–44).

8. The world, not grounded on any principle, is a *fact*; it is only a fact (even if it is a singular fact, not being itself a fact *within* the world). It is not founded in reason, or in God. It is the fact of a "mystery," the mystery of an accidental, errant or wandering existence. The world is neither necessary nor contingent, if contingency is defined in relation to necessity. Rather, it would be beyond or before necessity and of contingency, an absolute fact. It is possible to free the facticity of the world from the necessity-contingency conceptual couple by considering this fact of the world "without referring it to a cause (neither efficient nor final)" (*CW*, 45). The world is

a fact without cause and without reason, it is "a fact without reason or end, and it is our fact" (*CW*, 45). We are thus called, in this thought of the world as absolute immanence, to take on this facticity without reason of the world, as well as its non-sense, or rather that its sense only lies in such a fact: "To think it, is to think this factuality, which implies not referring it to a meaning capable of appropriating it, but to placing in it, in its truth as a fact, all possible meaning" (*CW*, 45). The world is a significance without a foundation in reason. The world is without reason, and is to itself its entire possible reason.

9. Jean-Luc Nancy, *Being Singular Plural* (Stanford: Stanford University Press, 2000), p. 15. Henceforth cited as *BSP*.

10. An analysis pursued in a discussion of Gérard Granel's text, "Essay on the Ontological Kenosis of Thought since Kant," in the chapter "A Faith that is Nothing at All" (*D*, 63–74).

TWO

NO OTHER PLACE TO BE

Globalization, Monotheism, and Salut *in Nancy*

Christina M. Smerick

> Conditions are in place for a delirium that would propagate itself in proportion to the wasteland of sense and truth that we have created or allowed to grow.
>
> —*Jean-Luc Nancy,* Dis-Enclosure

Jean-Luc Nancy opens his text, *Dis-Enclosure: The Deconstruction of Christianity* with a warning and a plea, which we find echoed in his other recent text, *The Creation of the World* or *Globalization.* Nancy has engaged questions of community and the world throughout his writings, but in these latest texts, one is struck by a sense of urgency. Although one has reason to be concerned with the current state of affairs regarding religion and violence in the world, Nancy is not merely wringing his hands, but indicts philosophy as part of the problem, in part because philosophers tend to view themselves as separate from the religious hysteria of our times. We tend to think of the field of philosophy as thoroughly "secular."[1] What exactly is this danger that lurks not merely in the "re-turn"[2] of religion, but perhaps in philosophy itself? Where is it located? How are we, thinkers all, to find a way *out*?

The following work is informed by these questions. As Christopher Watkin rightly noted in his review of *La Déclosion* (*Déconstruction du christianisme,* 1), Nancy has not provided a "detailed working through of the relation between the West, monotheism, and Christianity."[3] This is, therefore, a first sketch of this relation. Specifically, I engage in a reading of Nancy that interrogates his own interrogation of monotheism and Christianity, for I find that, in these structures, Nancy uncovers both the delirium against which he warns, and a hope toward which he turns. In the following, I admit to bracketing a similar critique of ontology, which is addressed extensively in other works by Nancy. Instead, I focus on the theological "branch" of metaphysics. I aim to trace Nancy's critique of Western monotheism and his turn to (not re-turn to, and not embrace of) Christianity, in order to shed light on the paradox present in his analysis, whereby Christianity (as the exemplar of Western monotheism and Western thought) provides both delirium and hope for the world. Through this reading, we may better understand how we may cast "light on [reason's] own obscurity, not by bathing it in light, but by acquiring the art, the discipline, and the strength to let the obscure emit its own clarity" (*D*, 6).

Jean-Luc Nancy continues the Heideggerian tradition of reading metaphysics as a search for both a ground and exemplar of Being—in other words, as both ontology and theology. Nancy provides a complex criticism of this tradition: Western metaphysics, in the guise of both monotheism and fundamental ontology, has founded itself on a necessary myth, suggesting that there is a Beyond that orients the world, as well as a universal ground that supports it. This myth has had vast repercussions. Regarding the theological, it suggests that the world is One opposed to or guaranteed by some Other One (and thus, Western metaphysics is fundamentally monotheistic). Therefore, even as it is not the case that there is a beyond, we act *as if* there is, and we formulate categories, political and economic theories, religions, and values that reflect this myth. Even as modernity has secularized this myth, the results are the same and the consequences of such formulations are concrete and real: The West attempts, via war, foreign policies, and the media, to spread its universalist message to the globe, and thus to encompass and indeed to swallow the globe, incorporating it into itself and becoming it. Globalization is not merely an economic situation regarding trade and popular culture. Globalization is making One of the world, which is not-one. Western theology contributes to this myth by insisting upon the dichotomy of Creator and created, establishing two categories, the latter of which includes the entire "world." As such, globalization is a Western creation with ties to monotheistic religion.

On the other hand, Nancy reads Christianity in particular, as "self-deconstructive" (*D*, 35).[4] What is ironic about all monotheisms, and Christianity *par excellence*, is that such constructs actually establish or accommodate a "world without God"—a world in which God is beyond the world, and thus in a sense absent. Particularly in Western philosophy, we find proofs of a God who is so beyond and other to the world that He has "gone missing." At the heart of what seems to produce the Western mindset, which itself produces globalization, there is a restless deconstructing that accommodates the absence of God.[5] Christianity exemplifies this self-deconstruction in monotheism via the Incarnation, and thus becomes, Nancy argues, a "religion without religion." The question thus arises: Is this "religion without religion" hopeful, or a harbinger of globalization? How are we to counteract the universalizing tendency of the West, a tendency promoted by Western Christianity, such that we may continue to be in and with the world as we constitute it and it constitutes us? Nancy's hope is an exhausted one: He hopes for the exhaustion of values, all of which are grounded in a unicity that the West seeks to impose on itself and others. In recognizing that this world and only this world exists, that it is its own meaning, and that there is no absolute transcendent place or time that allows it to be, we may be able to allow for the plurality that is, rather than aim for a unity that should never be. One is reminded of Gianni Vattimo's "weak thought"[6] in Nancy's "hope": It seems that the only hope for us is a thinking that empties itself, that recognizes the nonuniversal nature of its very principles, and thus does not seek to an-nihil-ate difference, but rather to "become other than itself."[7] Nancy's hope is that we may be saved from hoping for reconciliation, a collapsing of different into same. This hope may be found in the very source of globalization itself: Christianity as an emptied religion.

Therefore, I aim to bring together in the following sections two themes that resonate throughout Nancy's recent work: globalization and Western monotheism. I begin with his critique of the "West" as a self-referential category and as a political movement. I then introduce his analysis of monotheism and his hope regarding religion, both of which are found in *Dis-Enclosure*. What emerges is a story of the provenance of the West, and a gesture toward the future. Finally, I make more explicit the connection between Nancy's writings on Christianity and his geopolitical concerns, expressed in *The Creation of the World* or *Globalization*, as well as a number of his other works.

In *The Creation of the World*, Nancy examines the relation between human beings and the world, although the word "relation" already implies a false duality: Human beings make the world, "work" the world, and thus the world is the "product of human beings." Nancy also argues that even as the world is a "product" of human beings, human beings are products of the world. The relationship is not unidimensional or even directional, but rather involves a multiplicity of spacings that allow the "being singular plural" of the world as such. Accordingly, the question then arises, "what is the human being insofar as it is *in the world* and as it *works* the world?"[8] The Western mindset, up to this point, has answered this question by asserting itself as that which is "universal" and "rational" *par excellence*, thus implying that the nature of the human being, as well, is rational and universal. For the West, unicity is the goal and the locus of power. Universality is a

Western ideal, rooted in a monotheistic (single-God) worldview. Thus, the real situation in which we find ourselves—as beings who exist as singular *only* in the plural—is at odds with the dictates and goals of the "dominant" civilization or culture in the world. The West, as it spreads itself via economics, politics, war, and so on, strives for that "new world order" described by the first President Bush. It seeks to establish a unicity of power and value. Globalization's roots lie not only in the scientism of Newton, or the philosophical idealism of Kant or Hegel, but in the monotheism that predates them all. Thus, any examination of the problem of community, and the related problem of globalization, must address monotheism and, in particular, Christianity. This understanding is justified and exemplified by the spread of Western "civilization" such that there would no longer be any non-West. Ironically, this position annihilates the identity the West wishes to claim as its "own," because in this conglomeration, the West overcomes its "other"; it no longer has to recognize that it is a position among positions, that there is some doubt as to its certainty (CW, 32). Acting on a belief in universal Reason, Western civilization has sought to annihilate difference; however, the West only holds its identity when there is an Other to overcome. This dominance has led not to a Hegelian advancement of sociopolitical reason ("The convergence of knowledge, ethics, and social well-being") but to a "domination of an empire made up of technological power and pure economic reason" (CW, 34). In short, "The West has come to encompass the world" (CW, 34). One cannot imagine oneself to be the savior of the world if one absorbs the world and is now nothing other than the world (just what sort of savior the world needs will be left to the latter sections of this chapter). It matters little whether one reads this dominance and suffocation as economic, religious, technological, or cultural: As long as the goal of the West is to establish itself as universal, it is annihilating.

The West, with its myth of universality, produces an *immonde*,[9] an "unworld" such that there is no longer the possibility of making a world (*faire monde*) within its definitions and constructs. Globalization as a unifying discourse will destroy the "world-making" (*mondialisation*) that is the making of sense in a plural world. This world-forming or sense-making requires lateral space, the space of differentiality. A globalized world is no longer a world, as it no longer has the space reserved for difference or for "being-in-common" either. Thus, the West cannibalizes the world even as it seeks to spread its vision of a brave new one.

Therefore, the West is in a state of war, but not in a "war of or between civilizations," but rather a war against itself, a civil war. The conflict between, on the one hand, the West's glorification of its own ideality as a rational universality, and the injustice created by this supposedly universal morality, is part of what causes this internal strife: "Monotheism indeed represents the unity and the internal contradiction of this civilization at war with itself" (*WM*, 52).

Hence, the crisis about which Nancy is "Cassandra" (*D*, 5). Whether or not the West is becoming more or less "religious," the same universalizing concepts that are found in monotheism drive its mode of being as a "civilization." We are busy creating a world in which we cannot live as singular beings-in-common. Nancy does not argue that somehow "being-with" (which *is* the world and is the sense of the world) will disappear, but it becomes more difficult to have that "sense" of "being-with" *appear* as a proper way of being. Perhaps Nancy does suggest a real threat to our "being in common": He calls where we are heading a "spiritual deluge," a "conflagration." One feels the flames lapping at one's feet while reading the introduction to *Dis-Enclosure*. Hell is coming, he suggests, unless we start thinking about how we are to be saved from this incineration produced by our desire for oneness. Nancy does not suggest a "salvation"—or certainly not the sort of salvation the Western mentality has come to expect (no spit-curled Superman will fly in from another world, no spirit penetrates flesh in order to redeem it for eternity). In fact, those sorts of rescue fantasies may be what destroy us, for they suggest a power play by some Other who will save us all, and thus they collapse again into dominance and unity. "*For, if the 'common' is the 'with,' the 'with' designates the space* lacking *all-powerfulness and all-presence*."[10] Consequently, although Nancy does not offer a way for the world to be rescued, or to save itself, he does express a hope: "For the same to cease to confront the same, there is but one means: it must become other than itself" (*WM*, 53).

As early as his essay "Of Divine Places,"[11] Nancy offered a critique of religion and monotheism with regard to community. He writes, " 'What is God?' will perhaps turn out to have been the necessary but unanswerable question in which the god set about withdrawing"(*IC*, 110). Nancy argues that monotheism is not just a conflation of many into one, but is a radically different attitude toward divinity. (In *Dis-Enclosure*, he likewise argues that monotheism does not replace many with one, but rather replaces people [immortals] with a principle.) In monotheism, God is first identified with Being itself. From a monotheistic perspective, we now "talk God" whenever we talk about anything at the limit of understanding, be it subjectivity, history, the Other, and so on. Anything that seems to lurk at the limit of our being, and thus could be construed as Being, we discuss as if it were the God of monotheism, and God disappears rather than appears in this fragmented discourse. Nancy's point is that monotheism is, at its heart, an appeal to a kind of universalism that grounds and forms the world-as-One. Therefore, any theory, be it scientific or philosophical, which seeks out this same "Oneness" performs the same essential activity as theology. In both cases, the thinker seeks out the universal standard or ground of all being. Nancy asks whether "any discourse on God can deviate . . . from that of . . . onto-theology" (*IC*, 133). This "*immonde*" discourse is the discourse of the West.

However, in "Of Divine Places," we see that Nancy states that our thinking regarding God is moving beyond the typical onto-theological structure. A mode of thought exists today, Nancy argues, that "ventures out where God no longer guarantees either Being or the Subject or the World" (*IC*, 122). There can be no "return" to God-as-One. "[God] is not unnameable in the metaphysical sense of that being that is inaccessible to all names . . . including the name of being itself, according to an unbroken tradition that is the very tradition of onto-theo-logy" (*IC*, 117). God now lacks a name altogether. In "our day," we no longer treat any name of God as sacred. "It is the sacred itself that is lacking, wanting, failing, or withdrawn" (*IC*, 120). "The lack of sacred names is the *à-Dieu* of the sacred. An *à-Dieu* from the depths of its *withdrawal*."[12] In *Dis-Enclosure*, Nancy echoes this argument by referring to Gérard Granel's work; he suggests that it is not a God who is absent, but the *divinity of the absence*, that functions (*D*, 62):

> The death of God is the *final* thought of philosophy, which thus proposes it as an *end* to religion: it is toward this thought that the West will have ceaselessly tended. . . . To have done once and for all with a constantly recurring error: *being is not God, in any way*. . . . Being is the being of the god, as it is the being of every other being, but the god is not the god of being (that expression would have strictly no meaning; the god is always . . . the god of man). (*IC*, 128, 131)

It is via this withdrawal that Nancy discards or dis-poses onto-theology. "No god" does not imply "atheism" because atheism is simply the other side of the coin of theism. By "no god," we do not substitute something else in God's place (science, etc.). What Nancy means by "no god" is that "God's place is really wide open and vacant and abandoned" (*IC*, 137). This kind of abandonment and "presence of no god" would be a "suspension" where we no longer have the presence of a subject, but rather "the presence to an entire world" (*IC*, 137). Again in reference to Granel, Nancy lays out the possibilities of interpretation: "Either God empties himself of himself in the opening of the world, or God sustains himself as being, by himself, subject and substance of the world. It is not at all the same 'God' here" (*D*, 70). It seems clear that Nancy would rather consider the former, and recognizes the latter as part of the real danger religion currently poses for or to the world.

Staying with the first formulation, then, we can return to *The Creation of the World* or *Globalization*, and see how Nancy develops this withdrawal or absence. He states in this work that mono-theism or a-theism is:

> thus a complete metamorphosis of divinity and origin. Nothing is given any longer, except that alone which is still given. . . . It is the gift offered by the unique God, but if this gift is still given from one side . . . , it cannot be reduced to that state: it is more properly *giving*, it *is the very act of gift* and in this act the singular history according to which the human being . . . is a partner more than a simple recipient of divine action . . . is engaged. (*CW*, 70; my emphasis)

This is not a negative theology, nor a discourse about "a" nothing or "The" nothing. The space between finite singularities is the "event of being." It is not temporal—not about "provenance"—but spatial: a "spacing of presences"—which are *plural*. They do not emerge from a *prior* presence, because this sort of thinking goes against both his resistance to a temporal construct *and* to a kind of fundamental ontology that he tries to deconstruct: "nothing exists unless *with*" (CW, 73).

Thus, Nancy argues that all monotheism is self-deconstructive because it recognizes, albeit on a subterranean level, a *necessary* removal of "God" from the world. A unified and absolute God is a God who has removed Himself from immediate presence to us, and thus in a significant way monotheism is an a-theism (*D*, 35–36). This is the irony in or of Nancy's reading of monotheism: the very requirement posed by a single-God creates, at the heart of monotheism, a void, an emptying-out—a space. Even more ironically, it is this "nothing" that is our salvation.

***

> Christianity is by itself and in itself a deconstruction and a self-deconstruction. . . . In other words, Christianity indicates, in the most active way—and the most ruinous for itself, the most nihilist in certain regards—how monotheism shelters within itself—better: more intimately within itself than itself, within or without itself—*the principle of a world without God*. (*D*, 35; my emphasis)

The question remains as to why Nancy prioritizes Christianity in his analysis of monotheism in general. We have seen, up to this point, that monotheism and the West are mutually intertwined; that Western metaphysics and monotheism produce the same sort of discourse that shapes the West's attitude toward the world, an attitude that seems to result in globalization—a making-same of difference, a unifying practice that is annihilating. However, we have also seen that Nancy finds, at the heart of monotheism, a "self-deconstructive" movement that seems to destabilize the very foundation Western monotheism wants to establish. Furthermore, Nancy sees this self-deconstructive element to be present most strongly in Christianity. Therefore, in this section, I turn to Nancy's most recent work on Christianity in order to understand how the very structure that seems to produce the nightmare—globalization—is also the structure that produces hope.

Nancy reads the history of Christianity as the philosophizing of a religion: Christian philosophy has rendered God absent, and Christian dogma has located that absence in a human being. Christianity thus moves from a religion among religions to a kind of "thinking about meaning and the guarantee of meaning" (*IC*, 138). A "man-god," abandoned by God, is the "totally secular divinity of humanity" (*IC*, 139). In Christianity, we have a non-paganism that nevertheless posits an incarnate god. Thus, it creates a space occupied by a man-god who is a single substance with two natures. "The god appears entirely in man and man appears entirely in God" (*IC*, 139).[13]

Nancy provides a brief commentary on Incarnation, entitled "Verbum caro Factum," in *Dis-Enclosure*. He notes that the current fashion with regard to the Incarnation is to view it (heretically, I might add) as a sort of spirit possession: The spirit, interior and invisible, penetrates a body that is represented and represent-able (*D*, 81). One finds this kind of articulation present in most American Protestant churches, for example, which are not exactly loci of careful theology. This rather Gnostic soul–body dualism finds itself articulated in the exemplar of such a dualism: the Incarnation. It is the human condition writ large.

However, in the creedal version of the doctrine of the Incarnation, one does not find such a possession motif. There is no penetration. Rather, something *became* flesh—it did not "enter" into it. There was a non-difference between flesh and. . . . And we will leave the ellipsis there. Furthermore, doctrinal Christianity expands and "intensifies" the Incarnation by suggesting that not only was God a man, but that God-man was born of a woman (Nancy here gives a plug to the political correctness of the Church fathers, who made sure that both sexes are represented!). Of course, Nancy has his own articulation of the Incarnation, and once again we find that at the root of a hearty monotheism, full of universalist dogma, we have an absence, a withdrawal, a gap. In the Incarnation, Nancy argues, God puts himself outside himself—and this understanding of God can be found, dogmatically, both in the story of Creation and in the doctrine of the Trinity. "In this sense, the Christian god is the god who *alienates himself*. He is the god who *atheizes himself* and who *atheologizes himself*" (*D*, 82). Of course, this is the doctrine of kenosis, of God emptying Godself by becoming human. In the Incarnation, God atheizes himself, such that there is "no founding presence. . . . The body of the 'incarnation' is therefore the place, or rather the taking place, the event of that disappearance" (*D*, 83). In the Incarnation, in God-becoming-man, God disappears from sight, a man is glorified and anointed, and the world is exposed to itself—not to an outside space, not to something that is Other, but *to the Other that is itself*.

Thus, God incarnate is not paganism—a revival of the immortal gods who were present with us and had being, but were not Being. Rather, God incarnate is a "spacing." By becoming human, God disappears. In the Incarnation, Christianity has at its very heart the withdrawal of God, the dissolution of the "other world" above, and yet at the same time a "with" (for there is a "with" in "withdrawing"). This is the "with" of absence.

When God disappears completely in the man-god, one can no longer talk about an "act of presence." One cannot talk of faith as adherence to a set of propositions—we have seen already that the religious discourse surrounding the one God does not allow for such a model of premise and conclusion. Rather, there is "faith as its own work," as Nancy puts it in "The Judeo-Christian (on Faith)." Faith cannot convince itself; faith has nothing to believe. Faith is the "*praxical* excess of and in action" which opens the possibility of the subject to be more than herself (*D*, 52).

In the latter essays of *Dis-Enclosure*, then, one finds the hope that Nancy often keeps close to the chest. Using the Epistle of James, well known for its "faith without works is dead" motif in contradistinction to Paul's argument that faith is all one needs, and the works of Nietzsche, Nancy sketches out the hope that may be found in the midst of terror.[14]

In James' Epistle, Nancy finds a deconstruction of religion in a text from the New Testament that was written well before doctrines concerning Christology were formulated by the nascent Church. In this letter, one finds no systematic theology—in fact, apart from a few mentions of Jesus, one would be hard pressed to read this as an explicitly Christian document. Nevertheless, in this work Nancy uncovers a description of faith that he distinguishes as deconstructive. He states, extrapolating from James, "it is false to the point of absurdity to see in a 'belief,' for example, in the belief in redemption by the Christ, that which characterizes the Christian; only Christian *practice* is Christian, a life like that *lived* by him who died on the cross" (*D*, 52). He even goes so far as to say that this is Nietzsche's position as well. Therefore, faith in James is not "demonstrated" in works, it is *monstrated* in works. There is *only* the work. Therefore, in a canonized text, one finds an expression of faith that does not rely upon adherence to a premise, but instead advocates a living-out, a faith that comes from outside and opens us, without ever guaranteeing or proving or even establishing an outside from which to come (*D*, 55). Before there was *doxa*, there was the deconstruction of it, in the midst of the sacred texts that supposedly ground the *doxa* in the first place. Thus, from these few words depicting Christ in the Epistle of James, Nancy draws far-reaching conclusions concerning withdrawal, appearance, and the inappropriation of salvation. He states, "The messiah exhibits the withdrawal of that with which he is anointed. This withdrawal is not a sacred separation: it is, quite precisely, the withdrawal of the sacred and the exhibition of the world to the world" (*D*, 58). It is in or for this withdrawal, this space, that "salvation" is possible. Nancy finds an elaboration of this sort of "salvation" in Nietzsche.

Nietzsche calls for a "revaluation of values," thus gesturing to a value that is "absolute," immeasurable, or incommensurate with the economy (in this case the moral economy) of the world. Nancy reads this as a "withdrawal"—in place of a principle by which we measure things, we have an absolute value, empty in that it cannot conform to our reasonable ways of thinking. Nancy indicates that Nietzsche puts forth the figure of Christ (or of the Antechrist[15]; Nancy is unclear at this point) who "introduces" this "withdrawal." Nietzsche's "redeemer," of course, does not insist on adherence to doctrine or to a god; for this redeemer, faith is not adherence but *act*, and nothing but act. This reinforces Nancy's interpretation of the Epistle of James. In both works, Nancy underlines the notion of a content-less faith that ad-vocates nothing, but that is in and of the world, and is oriented to the void at the heart of being-with (a necessary void, in that it is an opening-up that allows being-with to be). For Nietzsche's redeemer (or Nancy's, as this is his scan of Nietzsche), existence is being *in* the world and having the experience of something "outside" the world, without there being another world outside this one to which to refer. In other words, faith, or redemption, is an opening up of the world *in* the world. Nancy tellingly describes this as both "wound and grace."

Therefore, the kind of salvation indicated by Nancy, and maintained in the face of criticism from Derrida and others, is a salvation that saves nothing, except that it saves us from believing in other worlds, worlds we fantasize about escaping to if we could just believe correctly. The latter description of faith is what Nancy finds so dangerous and inflammatory in the current "spiritual deluge." We need to be saved from belief, particularly belief in salvation. He who is "saved" in this manner experiences a value that cannot be measured in this world (for it is, if nothing else, the value of a void), and so he "withdraws" from the system of valuation that the world promotes while at the same time remaining utterly within the world (because there is *no other place to be*). "This *évenir* opens *within* the world an *outside* that is not a beyond-the-world, but the *truth* of the world" (*D*, 79).

As such, in his posthumous response to Derrida, Nancy describes salvation as "only of the sole, of the single, yet the sole or the single is *desolate* par excellence: devastated, deserted, given over to a total isolation (*desolari*)" (*D*, 99). Both he and Derrida refer to the eulogy as a "salutation," which opens up arenas of meaning via "*salut*" (which can translate as both "salutation" and "salvation"). A eulogy salutes the one who is gone, gestures toward the one who cannot respond. Nancy sees in this gesture an opening, an acknowledgment, of the abyss that opens and encloses, limits and makes possible, such gestures.

There is no dialectic in the eulogy by which we manage, through saluting the abyss, to convert the abyss into presence, grief into joy. Nancy goads religions for being ready to "gobble up salvation" via a turn to an in-credible re-turn (*D*, 101). However, Nancy suggests that not even religion truly engages in such an act of bad faith—that Christians who watch their loved ones die, for example, do not wait in childlike wonder and without grief for the inevitable and painless "passage" to another life. While "religions, like metaphysics, never cease promoting a salvific beguiling and reassuring consolation" (*D*, 101), this consolation is not a simple continuity; no one, not even those who believe in an afterlife, deny death. As such, and in line with his arguments elsewhere in *Dis-Enclosure*, Nancy insists that faith need not be a naive belief that one is going to be happy one day, but is rather that which addresses "that which comes to pass" and as such annihilates "every belief, every reckoning, every economy, and any salvation" (*D*, 101). In faith, one is addressed to the "other *of the world*," not an other world. The moniker "God" is simply the alterity without remainder that is, and is of, the world. The dead one does not return, but there is the raising up of the salute, the elevation of the call, the "discourse of prayer" that is the final goodbye at the funeral. This is what Nancy calls "resurrection"—this raising up of the salute. When there is nothing more to be said, this is when the salute "stands up and addresses":

> But let us say, simply, that without supposing God or salvation, we never lack, dead or alive, a language by which eternally, immortally, to salute ourselves, the one the other, the ones and the others. Such a salute, without saving us, at least touches us and, in touching us, *gives rise to* [suscite] that strange turmoil of crossing through life for nothing—but not exactly in a pure loss. (*D*, 103; my emphasis)

CONCLUSION

I have sketched out, via reference to a number of Nancy's works, the complex and simultaneous hope and doom that intersect his writings about monotheism and the West. Current "continental" philosophical discourse from Wittgenstein forward has thrown itself into the impossible, attempting to articulate, via tangents, poetics, word-play and gestures, the realm of "what cannot be said." In this, Nancy is in good stead. As he continues to work his way through the ideological and historical aspects of the West in its philosophical constructs and in its religious fervor, Nancy has attempted to both warn us and to goad us into *act*. I offer here, by way of conclusion, some very tentative summaries, recognizing that, for Nancy, this must be a work in process.

Although the world seems gripped by terror in its most obvious, violent forms, Nancy is more concerned with the terrors of ideas—the repercussions of ontological constructions that attempt to explain the world via a reference to a beyond or a ground. Although we may stare wide-eyed at our televisions as the play of gore and violence is performed, Nancy looks underneath to the structure that grounds and validates such bloodshed. In short, the structure is "Western," a belief in a universality that must make same what is different, that must rationalize the world, and thus suffocates us as the space between us is squeezed. The West is fighting itself, to be sure, but that does not make the real cost any less.

Thus, a greater terror than the obvious bloodshed is the structure of understanding that undergirds it. Western monotheism insists, even in its atheistic projects, upon a universal world order grounded in a singular understanding of the human being and the world. Nancy reads this as a "death-drive" in which we hasten our own doom by pushing for a world dominance of sense that annihilates "sense-making." Globalization is this world order and this death-drive. Thus, there is a link between his critique of religion and his critique of the current political/social climate. In both critiques, Nancy demonstrates that monotheism's underlying beliefs, metaphysics' ultimate goals, and the West's drive to domination are intertwined, or draw from the same set of assumptions about the world's monovalency. This emphasis of the "one" over plurality; this notion of an idea (be it of God or utopia) that can and should become the only sense of the world, is the danger against which Nancy writes.

Yet, rather than remaining in the role of doomsday prophet, Nancy fulfills the other prophetic function: that of gesturing toward what must be thought in order to provide a way "out"—a way out that is ever more *in* this world. He urges us to recognize the abysmal heart of the same monotheism that constructs such a monovalency. When one interrogates Christianity thoroughly, space opens at its center: God disappears, and we are alone, with only each other. Thus, although up until now Western monotheism and civilization has emphasized the singular and total over the plural and empty, one can nevertheless find, precisely at its roots, an opening up of the world in the world. One does not find another world, even if monotheism posits such a world. Instead, one finds only this place and this space. Rather than reading Nietzsche against the Christian tradition, then, Nancy reads him into it, or it into him: Nietzsche's empty redemption can be traced not to some "hearty atheism," but to Christianity itself.

Nancy's warning also contains a call. If we can remember or recover a sense of being-with that does not seek to blanket the world in immanence, but instead gestures toward "absolute excedence [*excédence absolue*] of sense and passion for sense for which the word *sacred* was but the designation" (*D*, 5), perhaps a civil religion may emerge from our current state of emergency, a civility that requires neither purging flame nor miraculous salvation. If we can engage in a making of sense that does not presuppose it nor insist upon a single sense, and do so in politics, in philosophy, and so on, then perhaps we will allow ourselves to be "exposed to . . . a transcendence *inside* the world."[16]

I will let Nancy have the last word:

> The lesson is very simple, as always, but the task is awesome. We, we others, have no lesser task than that of understanding and practicing the sharing of sense—of the sense of the world, no less. That doesn't mean dialogue and communication, which drag themselves listlessly along like saturated significations and the latest conventional chit-chat, but it wants to say—or no longer even *wants* but simply says—something other, for which the proud and solitary word [*parole*] is worth as much as mutual conversation: that **the truth of sense is properly nothing but its being shared**. . . . And there we have, if I still dare use this word, an ethics for our time—and more than an ethics. (*D*, 128; my emphasis)

NOTES

1. Nancy writes, "Philosophy (and science with it) has managed somehow to intimidate itself with its proclaimed exclusions of a religion from which it never ceased, underhandedly, to draw nourishment . . ." Jean-Luc Nancy, *Dis-Enclosure: The Deconstruction of Christianity*, trans. Bettina Bergo, Gabriel Malenfant, Michael B. Smith (New York: Fordham Press, 2008), p. 5. Henceforth cited as *D*.

2. Nancy rightly points out that this is not a simple "return" or repetition at all, but something new.

3. Christopher Watkin, "Neither/Nor: Jean-Luc Nancy's Deconstruction of Christianity," *Research in Phenomenology* 37:1 (2007), p. 142.

4. One could question Nancy's use of the term *self-deconstructive*, in that the "self" may be redundant. Nevertheless, it is his phrase and so I use it here.

5. Questions can and should be raised here as to why Nancy privileges Christianity over the other "monotheisms" of the West. Several arguments can be

made, all of them tentative. First, Christianity is certainly the dominant historical religion in Western Europe and the United States (even if it is not in practice). As such, when Nancy is engaging in a critique of the West, he turns to Christianity as the dominant historical force in the arena of religion. However, I would also, again tentatively, argue that Nancy finds something at the base of Christianity (namely, the Incarnation) that seems to most fervently gesture toward the "void" or disappearance of God most strongly. In any case, I would argue that what Nancy is most concerned about regarding monotheism is something inherent in all of them: this push to universality. However, it may be that, ironic as it sounds, the hope that Nancy finds also at the heart of monotheism is a hope most directly "uncovered" by Christian doctrine.

6. Since the search for an Eternal Foundation of Truth has been abandoned, "weak thought" is defined as interpretation from within an entirely historically situated position. Rather than performing "strong thought," in which one insists upon the objective truth of one's position, weak thought recognizes the violence inherent in such strength and works to overcome it, not through parallel shows of dominance, but through refusing to play the objectivist game. See Gianni Vattimo, *After Christianity* (New York: Columbia University Press, 2002), p. 24.

7. Jean-Luc Nancy, "War of Monotheism," trans. Amanda McDonald, *Postcolonial Studies* 6:1 (2003), pp. 51–53, here 53. Henceforth cited as *WM*.

8. Jean-Luc Nancy, *The Creation of the World* or *Globalization*, trans. François Raffoul and David Pettigrew (Albany: SUNY Press, 2007), p. 39. Henceforth cited as *CW*.

9. *Immonde* usually means base or vile, but, in this case, means "un-world." I would suggest a totalizing immanence is also present in this term.

10. Jean-Luc Nancy, "The Confronted Community," trans. Amanda McDonald, *Post-Colonial Studies* 6:1 (2003), p. 25; my emphasis.

11. Published in Jean-Luc Nancy, *The Inoperative Community*, trans. Michael Holland (Minneapolis: University of Minnesota Press, 1991). Henceforth cited as *IC*.

12. One is reminded in this formulation of Kierkegaard's understanding of God's love; in *Dis-Enclosure*, Nancy references Pascal as saying that God is not simply the "hidden," but that which wants to hide. This withdrawal, in Kierkegaard's work, creates the space necessary for love. God "so loved the world" that he disappeared into it, preserving our freedom and created the space required for it.

13. This reveals an interesting bias on Nancy's part: Christianity's theological constructs begin, for him, in and with Church Doctrine; Christianity seems to have its origins (if we can speak of such things) not in the person of Jesus, but in the Council of Nicea. This ignores, then, three-hundred years of debate and a multitude of alternative constructions of the Incarnation. As I have argued elsewhere, in this way Nancy seems to remain a "good" Catholic! Watkin raises a similar concern in his review of *Déclosion* when he writes that "we are entitled to ask *which* Christianity Nancy is deconstructing."

14. In particular, Paul makes his case for faith over works in Romans, chapter 3: "For we hold that a person is justified by faith apart from works prescribed by the law." He continues, in chapter 4, to argue that Abraham's faith, not his actions, are what made him great. *HarperCollins Study Bible*.

15. The translator notes that Nancy remains with the French "Antechrist," in which "ante" or "anti" implies priority, or "before" rather than "against." See *D*, 180 n. 2. Given Nancy's continued suggestion that Christianity contains deconstructive elements before it is even constructed, this conceit of Nietzsche's, reformed but not reneged by Nancy, becomes palatable. It is entirely Nietzschean, of course: the notion that the effect precedes the cause.

16. Ignaas Devisch, "Being Mondaine: Jean-Luc Nancy's Enumeration of the World," *Cultural Values* 6:4 (2002), pp. 385–394, here 388.

THREE

CHRISTIANITY'S OTHER RESOURCE

Jean-Luc Nancy and the Deconstruction of Faith

Alfonso Cariolato

das Ende glaubt uns
den Anfang

—*Paul Celan*

The deconstruction of Christianity is the latest subject of Jean-Luc Nancy's thought. And as "latest," it displaces his previous work *from behind* (*de retro*), bringing that previous work toward an unforeseeable future. This deconstruction of Christianity is not only a task of dismantlement taking place within monotheism itself, it also aims at retrieving what the philosophical tradition put to the side or translated a little bit too quickly from the theological into philosophical terms. In the case of Christianity, indeed, it is a matter of following the complex rhythm of *dis-enclosure*, which, on the one hand, reopens Christianity to its "outside" (the unnamable "god," *ho theos* in the singular, of Plato and, beyond him, the philosophical tradition) and on the other, *dis-encloses* reason to what the Enlightenment sought to exclude, that is, the triple theological virtue "faith–hope–charity." We can say then that the deconstruction of Christianity is the place in which thought opens itself and lets itself be traversed by what it cannot master, in the direction of an atheism that nevertheless maintains the exigency that thought relate itself, in this world, to an alterity without conditions or substance. If in the entire work of Nancy thought is put into play not as an abstraction, but as the experience of that which offers and disposes itself, then the deconstruction of Christianity—which comes to the fore but is not *new* to Nancy's thought—opens thought to that which seemed inaccessible to philosophy itself. In fact, paradoxically it is against the incommensurable as such (that which is without dimension, without history, without common measure, and which should not be confused with any god or Ideal) that we measure the rigor of thought.

I follow here the philosophical stakes of Nancy's interpretation of the first theological virtue, faith, in order to bring to light what I would call the "ethos of finitude," which—to say it with Nancy, a reader of Heidegger—is nothing but the "ek-sisting of existence itself."[1]

***

1. If there is something like an *exigency* of the deconstruction of Christianity, it is *our* time that must express it. Nothing else—and no one else—can do it. Because it is not a matter (and it could not be a matter) of a philosophical "option" (supposing that philosophy would still be a matter of options) nor even of an "idea" or an "opinion" on Christianity (i.e., a judgment). Hence, the difficulty, or better, the *impossibility* of deconstruction. What does it mean, then, that it must be our time that expresses its exigency? The deconstruction of Christianity happens perhaps (or has always already happened) like a singularity in cosmology, that is, as a point in which thought itself bends back upon itself; beyond any established content, we must reassess its strength and its impact. That it is now the time to make all of this evident must be understood in a double way: First, it means that deconstruction is not the result of any "will" and, thus, second, deconstruction as such *happens* and is always already underway.[2]

Above all, we must emphasize Nancy's Hegelian approach to the deconstruction of Christianity. If indeed, as Hegel himself says, "the subject is this: that which gives to itself its own being-other (*Andersseyn*) and that which, through its negation, returns to itself, and thereby produces itself,"[3] then Christianity is a *subject*. Nancy writes, "Christianity is less a body of doctrine than a *subject* in relationship to itself in the midst of a search for self, within disquietude, an awaiting or a desire for its proper identity" (*D*, 38).[4] Deconstruction, for its part, reveals itself through the detours (or *as the* detour) of a system, of a Christianity that relates itself to itself by determining in each instance the being-other. Moreover, Christianity comes back incessantly into itself, negating and affirming itself in this negation, trying to draw anew from its own origin in order to reestablish, reformulate, or retrace again its necessity, and therefore its identity. Its own origin remains nevertheless unreachable because Christianity—like any monotheism—is itself the result, the effect, or the composition of different traditions (particularly the Greco-Roman and the Hebraic ones). On the other hand, its end remains undefined and indeterminate in its multiple variations, taking the form of an awaiting for the return of the Lord, a history that tends infinitely toward an event that never arrives, an opposition to historicity, or a variety of messianic readings. This is why it is still a matter of the unforeseeable and of the surprise.

2. There still remains the difficulty (and this difficulty is at the center of deconstruction) of thinking Christianity as subject, that is, as a process that *understands* all its different determinations and is lived from these determinations. This indefinite structure—that is, the problematic and presupposed *commonality* of the different Christian experiences, doctrines, traditions, and religions—marks the very definition of Christianity, a structure (defining itself as indefinite) that matches almost perfectly that of the West. Basically, deconstruction takes the risk of considering Christianity as a *destiny*, and thinks it (or rather shows Christianity as it thinks *itself*) *from within*, if it is true that, as Nancy writes,

> [D]econstruction . . . is itself Christian. It is Christian because Christianity is, originally, deconstructive, because it relates immediately to its own origin as to a slack [*jeu*], an interval, some play, an opening in the origin. (*D*, 149)

To put it succinctly, the "destiny" of Christianity is nothing less than the "destiny" of the West. In the same way as "destiny tries out its destiny (*Geschick versucht sich an Geschick*),"[5] as Heidegger writes, it is history itself (or what remains of it) that in its effective deployment (*Geschichte/Geschehen/Geschick* and not *Seinsgeschichte*), in its uncertain but irreparable concretion and concretization, constitutes the *fate* of the West. The West is really Christian, but it is also the *destinal* place where the *logos* imposes itself to excess, that is up to the point where it is only about itself. Deconstruction touches on all of these questions (and many more) in trying to think them together through as set of very complex movements. If, with regard to the *logos*, the emancipation of reason succeeds in giving a sense to the world while enclosing this sense as *outside* of the world, this will have at least two consequences: On the one hand, it will only be on the limit of this closure that the ulterior possibility of sense will be able to be opened, and, on the other hand, reason, in imposing itself absolutely up to the point of spinning without results, will bring about the waning of all content or value as such (this is incidentally one of the aspects of nihilism diagnosed by Nietzsche). There remains then the world as it is that no sense can achieve, let alone exhaust. There remains, then, the "Open" (*das Offene*, Hölderlin's word) beyond any concept, image, or form, to which thinking must measure itself, and also that from which the origins of philosophy cannot be separated, that is, the political or, better, *being-with*.[6]

3. Yet, Christianity belongs to this process because it carries (as do, in a certain way, all monotheisms) a message of detachment from the world and its destitution. This results in the annihilation of all worldly values as well as a radical reconsideration of reason itself (with its disparate and contradictory effects, but this is a sign of the importance of the question). Indeed, Christianity expresses first and foremost the necessity of relating oneself from within the world to the outside *of the world*.

All this lead Christianity never ceased (despite everything and in many different ways) to point to the *other (of the) world*. Nancy writes,

> Christianity assumes, in the most radical and explicit fashion, what is at stake in the *alogon*. All the weight—the enormous weight—of religious representation cannot change the fact that [*ne peut pas faire que*] the "other world" or the "other kingdom" never was a second world, or even a world-behind-the-worlds, but the other of the world (*of every world: of all consistency tied up in beings and in communication*), the other than any world. Christianity can be summed up, as Nietzsche, for one, knew well, in the precept of living in this world as outside of it—sense that this "outside" is not, [or] not an entity. It does not exist, but it (or again, since it) defines and mobilizes ex-istence: the opening of the world to—inaccessible alterity (and consequently a paradoxical access to it). (*D*, 10)

Here is the point of juncture between reason and Christianity, and also the last characteristic of the history of the West, always in an unstable equilibrium between an awaiting and a fulfillment.

Yet the closely linked "death of God," the retreat of the divine, and the eternal return (normally taken to be the antithesis of the Christian interpretation of time), as they find their formulation in Nietzsche, all come together—beyond specificities and differences proper to each—on at least one point, that is, the attention paid to the world that remains beyond any choice between the "true world" and the "appearing world." And this world is nothing other than what it is (a tautology that, in any case, remains more or less unexpressed during the entire history of philosophy) and it is even *willed* as such: *amor fati* being the love of *this* world.

All of this—this is the true stake or risk of deconstruction—does not necessarily stand in opposition to Christianity. On the contrary, there would be a link developing in two directions at the same time. If it is true that

Western reason has effectively appropriated certain moments of Christianity, even at the cost of repressions, distortions, and transformations, it is equally true that Christianity itself, as monotheism, unseats reason exactly at the point where it has reached its metaphysical peak. In particular, Christianity "opposes, as much as it comforts, the reign of the premise" (*D*, 24).[7] This means that with the idea of *creatio ex nihilo*, even though it is always inflected and explained as the relation between premise and consequences of the premise, Christianity posits—as the *ex nihilo*—the possibility of thinking a contingent existence without ground, without cause, without reason, or in short of thinking existence, Kant would say, as *absolute position (Setzung) of the thing*, something that will be at the center, according to other modalities, of Schelling's positive philosophy.[8] Even though, on closer examination, already with Spinoza (even though he denies the *creatio ex nihilo* because "no substance can be produced or created [*produci, vel creari*] by something other than itself"[9]) we find ourselves outside of the metaphysical relation between premise and consequences, or between cause and effect, because for him substance is existence itself taken as *causa sui*, that is, as nothing but existing as absolute, unconditioned existing. Modes are, therefore, not the *consequences* of the premise, but "modifications of substance, or that which exists in, and is conceived through, something other than itself [*substantiae affectiones, sive id, quod in alio est, per quod etiam concipitur*]."[10] The examples could be multiplied because there is an entire movement, an entire tremor that runs across Western philosophy and disrupts from within, as it were, the prevailing metaphysical apparatus and this, of course, happens even in the works of thinkers who contributed to creating this apparatus.

This is why (the task of) deconstruction is not only the happening of "something Christianity may not as yet have freed" (*D*, 149); it must also each time put the philosophical tradition into play again. The dismantling of Christianity necessarily implies a *self-deconstruction* (the same thing *and* yet something different) not only of Christianity itself, but also of philosophy. There is no deconstruction that would not also be a *self-deconstruction*, and there is no *self-deconstruction* that does not have deconstructive effects beyond itself.

4. But, coming back to the ambivalent relation of Christianity to the premise, one must add that this relation not only signifies that monotheism—as Schelling already wrote—leads to atheism because any divine presence withdraws from the world and all remaining presence can only be the cause of idolatry but never of faith (see *D*, 32). With Christianity, in a more or less latent and/or obvious way, as well as in all the folds of Western thought itself, the possibility of a nonmetaphysical—yet-not-completely other in relation to metaphysics (we cannot divide, dissociate, or even *rely on* [*se*

fier à] decidable oppositions: Such is the question that torments Derridean deconstruction, among others, from within). Here is where the reconsideration of singular existences, and therefore of their partitions as existents, plays itself out.

Of course, one must constantly emphasize the fact that Christianity (beyond the different Christian religions) is nevertheless—taking into account the force of the dogma of incarnation—the religion of a presence without remainder, of God in history, of consubstantiation, of transubstantiation, of Real Presence, and so on, with all the onto-theological and political consequences that follow. The theologico-political element brought to light by Carl Schmitt is nothing other than, in a certain way, the permanence in the secularized modern world—and therefore in the form of an absence—of the necessity of some (by now unreachable) full presence as the ground of the community. Here, deconstruction distinguishes itself clearly from other readings that, on the contrary, take precisely Schmitt's political theology as their point of departure to explicate not only the political, but also the economic and juridical stakes of the contemporary world, by letting it almost take on the role of the Heideggerian *Geschick*—a move that risks trapping Christianity in too rigid a conceptual web. Nancy, unlike Schmitt (and Karl Löwith), does not consider politics (and history) as a secularization of theology. To approve of the exit out of the theologico-political schema, which at bottom imprisons history and politics in an already deployed sense, signifies posing the necessity and hence the possibility of rethinking *ex novo* the very concept of the political and of rethinking it starting from the excess of sense to which Christianity points, even if ambivalently. It is this incommensurability, this exposition of community to the essence of available sense, that opens a space for the arrival of a sense to come.

5. This *step beyond* (pas au-delà), if I may say it this way, of deconstruction not only consists in believing that Christianity cannot be reduced to a specific structure or content that would reproduce itself through time according to different modes, but also that Christianity bears in itself that which drives Christianity outside of itself. Hence, a possibility *within* Christianity (I repeat and emphasize here in its generic *being-subject*), which carries Christianity beyond itself toward that which is neither Christianity *strictu sensu* nor the West, without being for all that something already determined.

Deconstruction incessantly relates itself to a gap, which is impossible to grasp or to say, within the system according to which Christianity can continue to take shape, that is, to the in-itself, which is always concealed and hence *outside of (any) self* around which any Christian determination constructs itself. The deconstruction of Christianity means letting the disassembled components of the construction be taken up by the vertigo of the unattainable origin, and therefore by an absolute sense, that is, by what has been called the Open (neither a common nor a proper name, neither concrete nor abstract, and yet a name—a name of the without name). Indeed, the Open or sense is nothing determinate but, to speak in the language of Kant, consists in a sort of transcendental structure uncoupled from a notion of subjectivity. Or better, it is not really a condition: to say "condition," indeed, is already to say too much, since sense cannot be expressed or formulated in laws or principles. It is a matter here of the "unconditioned" (*das Unbedingte*), that is to say—as Kant writes—of what is "absolutely not to be met with in Nature, i.e., in the world of the senses, though it necessarily has to be assumed."[11]

Deconstruction, like all *philo*sophy for that matter, therefore touches the unconditioned while it is in turn touched by it (or better, deconstruction is shaken through and through by it as by a quake or eruption). Here lies perhaps the exigency expressed by the time which is ours, discussed above: We relate once again to the incommensurable without which there can be no thinking. But, that being said, we cannot forget the decisive feature of this statement: The incommensurable—and therefore the unconditioned—is *nothing* and we can do nothing with it. It is neither something given, nor a principle, neither a ground, nor a cause, neither a being, nor a God—and yet, in some way or another, *it is*.

Here, reason and Christianity come into contact without intermingling. Reason confronts Christianity by becoming that which is continuously stretched toward that which has no conditions. Christianity confronts reason by being a vocation and a faithfulness to the absolute. Indeed, "Christianity designates nothing other, essentially (that is to say simply, infinitely simply: through an inaccessible simplicity), than the demand to open in this world an alterity or an unconditional alienation. However, 'unconditional' means not undeconstructible. It must also denote the range, by right infinite, of the very movement of deconstruction and dis-enclosure" (*D*, 10).

This marks as much the exit out of a rationalism that makes of itself its own end, as the exit out of the religious considered as a set of dogmas and institutions, without leading into an irrationalism on the one hand, or negating Christianity on the other. Deconstruction is not destruction, but a disassembling, whose starting point and end is an unconditioned alterity, of the system of Christianity beyond God as the *Summum Ens*. Reason is engaged in it as a thinking of the limit, that is, from and toward its own "passion" for the unconditioned.[12]

6. But then, as Nancy writes, it is the event of Christianity itself that happens as deconstruction. This also means that what comes to be thought by way of an inherently deconstructive Christianity is not "the new form

(*Gestalt*) that has immediately arisen" (Hegel) and that would have to be understood, explained, or recognized. This cannot be the case because Christianity does not stand in front of us as a fixed and stable form or as a set of significations to be "taken *en masse*." It is not a matter of putting Christianity at a certain distance and of relating to it as if it were an "autonomous mass," and it is useless to try to do so (*D*, 149).

Deconstruction, if it is not destructive, disassembles the figure or follows its excess, opening possibilities that can in turn be called "figures," but only in a problematic way. Deconstruction does not then take up Christianity as something completed, which could merely be interpreted or delved into in a different way. Rather, it is a matter of the advent itself *prior to* that advent taking on a determinable form. For deconstruction, this constitutes the (free) *necessity* of thinking: "a gesture of an opening or reopening in the direction of what must have preceded all construction" (*D*, 176–177, n. 8). And it constitutes the urgency of deconstruction and thought as such.

In 1923/1924, Heidegger had already talked about *Abbau*, "dismantling," emphasizing later in *Being and Time* the necessity of a "destruction" (*Destruktion*): "this hardened tradition must be loosened up, and the concealments which it has brought about must be dissolved [*der Auflockerung der verhärteten Tradition und der Ablösung der durch sie gezeitigten Verdeckungen*]."[13] Thus, it is a matter of loosening up (*Auflockerung*) the hardened terrain of the tradition and also dissolving (*Ablösung*) concealments (*Verdeckungen*) produced by this tradition itself.

7. Here is an opportunity to observe that in this case Heidegger explains "destruction"—which alongside "reduction (*Reduktion*)" and "construction (*Konstruktion*)" is a constitutive moment of the phenomenological method[14]—by means of a soil metaphor. It is perhaps on that basis that we can delineate the difference between Nancy's deconstruction of Christianity on the one hand and the destruction, dismantling, disassembling (*destructio/Zerstörung/Destruktion/Abbau*) carried out by Luther, Heidegger, and Husserl on the other, as these are incessantly evoked in the search for a genealogy of the concept of deconstruction. Nancy's deconstruction (like that of Derrida) puts into play the very notion of terrain on which something is constructed, that is, the notion of a ground that would remain identical and identifiable above and beyond all its historical forms.

We must therefore understand the deconstruction of Christianity—which does not aim at *grounding* any *question anew*—from the perspective of the Heideggerian *Verwindung* and/or, as Nancy proposes, the Hegelian *Aufhebung* (*D*, 143). Indeed, both these concepts and the gesture of deconstruction have in common an attentiveness to the thing that *realizes* itself, that comes to form itself out of itself, that becomes a thing (*res*) through its emergence out of nothing (*rien*), whereby thinking finds "another resource" beyond all will, dialectic, or method (*D*, 143).

It is then a matter of thinking the event of the thing and of sense by resting—this is the inherent difficulty of thinking—in the surprise of its happening. In particular, the interrogation of our (existential and political) Christian origins implies letting ourselves be touched by Christianity as it exceeds itself and/or distends itself to what exceeds it. From this point of view, it is a matter each time of another *appropriation* and another *sublation*.

8. To think means to take care for the absolutely unintelligible weight of things (*pensare*, *pendere*, which produced in French *penser*, to think, and *panser*, to bandage) not in the direction of what is defined and known, but rather toward what Kant called a "finality without end." The latter is not related to the beautiful by chance because art is the place where the sensible escapes all external finality. Therefore, it is a matter of a gaping openness.

It is a matter of bringing out that which Christianity contains and carries within its system, of course, but not as something that it would already be, that would thus only need to be brought to light. Put otherwise, following Christianity in its distantiation or estrangement from itself (i.e., from what has been constituted as tradition, myth, or belief) up to the point where it understands itself as the announcement of an "*infinite end*," as *absolute kerygma*, that is, as an announcing that announces nothing but the announcing itself (see *D*, 150–151). In this way, deconstruction no doubt brings the internal process of Christianity to its radical end, a process that began with Protestantism, but also implicates in different ways Catholicism and the Orthodox Church. But this is not all because it is first thought that measure itself (once again, but not within the onto-theological apparatus) directly with the category of faith, that is, with an unconditional faithfulness, which constitutes not only the sign of the *homo religiosus*, but from now on also of all men and women in their incommensurable being-with. It is exactly here that deconstruction discovers itself as immediately practical and political (to use a traditional lexicon)—or, as the thought of the *absolute effectivity*.

9. If it is in the dimension of the singularity in common that the explication of the "logic of what [James] calls faith" must be understood, the deconstruction of Christianity is well-rooted in Nancy's previous work (*D*, 51 and *passim*). In *The Inoperative Community*, Nancy was already speaking of a community of finite beings, and therefore of a community *of* finitude (because only "finitude 'is' in common"[15]), which is not a work to be produced, but is the exposition of singular existences constituted (distributed, placed, spaced out) by their *sharing* and thus given reciprocally to *others*; not a fusion but

the passage from one to the other, a passage that delineates singularities and exposes them through *com-pearance*, *dislocation*, and *interpellation*. This results because what happens is only the communication of finitude, and hence partition itself. Community falls short of any project, effort, or will, and its sense can be found in an "originary or ontological 'sociality' " made up of the exposition of finite beings (*IC*, 28). It is therefore transcendence that resists infinite immanence (i.e., any form of communion and all the violences of subjectivity), while the *un-worked* and *un-working* (*désœuvrée*) activity in question consists in "incompleting its sharing" (*IC*, 35) or "not to let go of sense *in* common [*ne pas lâcher sur le sens* en *commun*]."[16]

Yet, the (deconstructed) faith of monotheism, detached from onto-theology and hence absolutely different from religious belief, which is a certainty of a presence, is "faithfulness to an absence and a certainty of this faithfulness in the absence of all assurance" (*D*, 36). It becomes what we could call the absolute dis-position of the ethos of singularity (an ethos of inadequation without being one of lack) by means of which the characteristics of transcendence of the finite being expose themselves (in Heideggerian terms, *In-der-Welt-sein* and *Mitdasein*) and the intensity of an existence condemned to excess affirms itself (in Nietzschean terms, the child who plays) by negating all worldly value.

The deconstruction of Christianity with its analysis of faith (and also of love, which I do not discuss here[17]) consists in the putting into question of the very relation of reason with the *alogon*. And this within a vast perspective, which is, as we have seen, at the same time the perspective of the West (which is the civilization, composed of many decompositions, of the "Judeo-Helleno-Christian") and that of the *cum* or of the communion, whose emptied center (or heart) is contained in any *com-position* (see *D*, 44).

10. In Christianity (and in other monotheisms, but each time in a different way), the notion of a confidence, full and without reserve, that is, of an unlimited devotion or assent, affirms itself as the condition that defines and characterizes it, while at the same time surpassing it. But it is not a matter of a confidence in a notion that would be the outcome of a knowledge or of a truth absolutely independent of reason. Faith is confidence in the revealed Word (*logos*), the "true word." As John says, "the truth will set you free" (8:32). Yet, if we separate out the truth from metaphysics and from the hypostatization proper to Christianity in its historical manifestation, both of which present a common characteristic of positing a full presence without remainder, faith is only "*the adhesion to itself of an aim without other*" (*D*, 152).

An act of faith is therefore a question of an adhesion without content, a kind of empty adherence, or even the contact (if we can say so) of existence with its *being outside of itself*. That which Christianity designates as faith is the *lived faithfulness* toward the inappropriable and inadequate, which is existence itself. There will be neither an exclusively intellectual nor a sentimental immediacy of the sort for which Hegel criticized the Romantics, but the experience (I would say the physical or corporeal experience, but one that is nevertheless not closed in on itself in a materialist identity) of a void of sense, and therefore of the faithfulness to this void. This experience will be identical to concrete existence.

In a similar way, Kafka, in the fourth of his *Oktavhefte*, argued that there is an inexhaustible faith in the simplicity of living. The Heideggerian *Zu-sein* and analysis of *Entschlossenheit* responds no doubt to the same consideration (see *BT* §§ 4, 9, 60–62). But we would also have to recall what Kierkegaard wrote in his *Journal*, that is, that faith is "immediacy or spontaneity after reflection."[18] This is the case because in the act of faith, understanding and sensible intuition, interiority and exteriority, immanence and transcendence seem paradoxically intertwined.

11. A *logic of faith* "separated as much from envy as from renunciation" concerns first of all the existing and acting in the world (individually and politically) in their absence of ground (*D*, 51). It is not a coincidence that Nancy, in his analysis of the category of faith (*pistis*), along with the *poiesis* and *praxis* that characterize it, appeals mainly to The Epistle of James, which he reads through the word of "the other Jacques" (i.e., Derrida). He does appeal neither to Paul, although Paul's concept of *kenosis* plays an important role in Nancy's reading, because for Paul, faith is grounded first and foremost in the Gospel and in the figure of Jesus Christ (see Romans 10:8–9), nor does he appeal to John, even though for him there exists a close link between faith and love, but always only in relation to the concrete life of Jesus (see John 3:16). For James on the contrary, even if his position is not necessarily opposed to that of Paul or John, the mediation through Jesus "remains at a certain distance" because what is at stake is "directly, a certain relation of man to holiness that becomes an image in him" (*D*, 47). It is worth emphasizing as well that the Epistle of James can be read as a genuine metonymy of Christianity, because, as Spinoza noted in the *Tractatus theologico-politicus*, "James . . . confines religion to a very few elements [*totam doctrinam religionis . . . paucis admodum comprehendit*]."[19]

It is obviously not possible to analyze here Nancy's dense reading of James. I shall content myself with briefly enumerating some ideas that point in the direction of the question of the resemblance (*homoiôsis*) of man to God, and the indication of a faith without fixed content. Attested since *Genesis* 1:26, the resemblance of man to God means, outside of its onto-theological interpretation, which considers God as the Supreme Being, resemblance to the nothing of being. In a certain sense, this way of speaking is close to that of the Mystics, in particular Meister Eckhart. If, as James says, God is the giver (1:17), then *homoiôsis* can be understood apart from *mimesis* as a "logic of the gift" in which "as the other James [*Jacques*] enjoys thinking, . . . the giver abandons him- or herself in his or her gift" (*D*, 49).

One can find here a genuine ethos disposed by faith, which will become even more explicit in James' defense of works against the possible misinterpretation of Paul, since—contrary to the other logic, that of envy (*phtonos*) and of the desire of appropriation, that is, the logic of lack—giving is absolutely free, without being a sacrifice or an *askêsis* (see *D*, 48–51). Faith is therefore the fidelity to life in the world as if one were outside of the world, without this "outside" being anything determinate (a beyond, another world, God). Yet, there is no gap between faith and works since there can be no faith apart from works: "Instead of works proceeding from faith, and instead of works expressing it, faith here exists only in the works: in works that are its own and whose existence makes up the whole essence of faith" (*D*, 51).

If faith is not knowledge, but resides entirely in a *praxis*, that is, in the practice of *erga*, of works (the meaning of *poiesis* for James, which as Nancy remarks, differs from from Aristotle), that are only effectivity or existence (we could say the *existing existence* opened by the "free decision"[20]), then faith is the expression of the very *excess* of *praxis*. This excess makes possible the "becoming oneself" beyond oneself. Faith is the dis-position of the finite being, in a certain way, to be faithful to what happens. There is no freedom without confidence, without entrusting oneself to the absence of sense in the search for sense. It appears therefore that the *delving* that *deconstruction* is, which is a possibility of Christianity, touches on what we could call an "ethics of finitude," whose concern is the exposition to the *alogon*, and therefore, the gift (*don*, *kharis*) and aban*don*ment. This is why the "the perfect law of freedom" (James 1:25, 2:12) is posited, in a dialogue with Blanchot, Derrida, and Deleuze, among others, as the basis of an interpretation of *nomos*, of the law that, beyond all sacralization, works for "the truth that does not belong to us" and that alone can set us free (see *D*, 55–56). There is no ethos without faith, or to say the same, ethics is only possible with faith as its starting point, but as a "faith of nothing whatsoever" (*D*, 73). And if in Christianity, Jesus, who is the "chief" and the "initiator" (*arkêgos*) of faith and also the one who "perfects it" (*teleiôtês*) (Hebrew 12:2), becomes the name of the appearance (*doxa*) of faith, that is, "the proper name of the inappropriable" (*D*, 57), then faith is faith in and from this inappropriable glory of the Kingdom that has already come (and the *living contact* with it).

The Hebrew word for "glory" used in the Old Testament is *kabod*, which—beyond beauty and splendor—conceals in its etymology something ponderous, heavy, and consistent (hence the sense of "prestige" and "respect" that God inspires). Therefore, glory is the reality that imposes itself with all its thickness, its *weight*, its force, and splendor: "The Heavens tell the glory of God" (Psalms 19:2). The *glory of the Kingdom* is the affirmation, the searing splendor, of the reality of *this* world in all of its aspects: A world at once global and opening onto the absence of sense. Yet precisely opened and thus, in a certain way, faithful: faithful to nothing, or to the fragile existing of all that is.

NOTES

1. Jean-Luc Nancy, "Heidegger's 'Originary Ethics,'" in *Heidegger and Practical Philosophy*, ed. F. Raffoul & D. Pettigrew (Albany: SUNY Press, 2002), p. 84.

2. Here? Now? When? It is the very space-time itself of such a happening that should be discussed, but I will not do it here.

3. G. W. F. Hegel, *Vorlesungen über die Philosophie der Religion*, ed. Ph. Marheinecke, in *Sämtliche Werke. Jubiläumausgabe*, XV, ed. H. Glockner (Stuttgart: Frommann, 1928), p. 450. Translation is my own.

4. Jean-Luc Nancy, *Dis-Enclosure: The Deconstruction of Christianity*, trans. Bettina Bergo, Gabriel Malenfant and Michael B. Smith (New York: Fordham University Press, 2008), p. 38. Henceforth cited as *D*.

5. Martin Heidegger, "Anaximander's Saying," in *Off the Beaten Track* (Cambridge: Cambridge University Press, 2002), p. 254.

6. Contrary to what one could think at first sight, this reference to the political, that is, to the political implications of the deconstruction of Christianity, does not constitute an abrupt leap into another domain. The deconstruction of Christianity can only be in certain respects, as I will try to show, a practical thinking. We could equally say that the profound calling of deconstruction is to put into question the traditional partition of philosophy as it was fixed from Aristotle onward. Deconstruction remains absolutely unintelligible if we detach it from the ontology of the common or of "community" as it has been developed in the recent years with different results and in different modes; I am thinking here in particular of a certain reading of Bataille, of certain works of Nancy himself, of Blanchot, Rancière, Agamben, and so on. The evidence from which we start is that being-with, even though it is not synonymous with the political, measures itself against the end of its onto-theological (Platonic, Christian, Hegelian) foundations and therefore relates itself—I would say immediately, that is both without any mediation and without delay—to its own exterior limit, which is not a pregiven, pre-established border, but something that must each time be defined. Thus, politics is not anymore the place of the realization of a determinate essence. On the contrary, it is continuously pushed beyond itself. This means that it is intimately *touched*, and shaken, by the *excess* that the *logos* brings to itself. It is with this that (the possibility of a) politics must from now on measure itself.

7. See also Jean-Luc Nancy, *The Creation of the World* or *Globalization* (Albany: SUNY Press, 2007) and "Ex Nihilo" in *La pensée dérobée* (Paris: Galilée, 2001), pp. 187–188.

8. As Nancy writes, "In the first place, we might say that the *nihil* is posited. Perhaps this is the only way seriously to get out of nihilism" (*D*, 24).

9. B. Spinoza, *Ethics* in *The Chief Works of Benedict de Spinoza, vol. II*, trans. R. H. M. Elwes (New York: Dover, 1951), p. 56. (Book I, Prop. XV, Note).

10. Ibid., p. 45 (Book I, Def. V).

11. Immanuel Kant, "What real progress has metaphysics made in Germany since the time of Leibniz and Wolff?," in *Theoretical Philosophy after 1781* (Cambridge: Cambridge UP, 2002), p. 382.

12. See Jean-Luc Nancy, *Philosophical Chronicles* (Stanford: Stanford UP, 2008), pp. 4–6.

13. Martin Heidegger, *Being and Time*, trans. J. Macquarrie & E. Robinson (New York: Harper and Row, 1962), H. 22, p. 44

14. Martin Heidegger, *Basic Problems of Phenomenology*, trans. A. Hofstadter (Bloomington & Indianapolis: Indiana UP, 1998), § 5, pp. 19–23.

15. Jean-Luc Nancy, *The Inoperative Community*, ed. Peter Connor (Minneapolis: University of Minnesota Press, 1991), p. 27; trans. modified. Henceforth cited as *IC*.

16. Jean-Luc Nancy, "Of Being-in-Common," in *Community at Loose Ends*, ed. The Miami Theory Collective (Minneapolis: University of Minnesota Press, 1991), pp. 1–12, here 11–12.

17. Except to recall that love, like faith (which both come into contact without intermingling) exists only in the inadequation, excess, and passivity that characterize, as a sort of blind spot, thought itself (and existence).

18. *Søren Kierkegaard's Journal and Papers*, ed. H. V. Hong and E. H. Hong (Bloomington & London: Indiana University Press, 1967–78), vol. II, § 1123 (VIII^1 A 649, 11 May 1848).

19. Baruch Spinoza. *Theologico-Political Treastise* in *The Chief Works of Benedict de Spinoza, vol. I*, trans. R. H. M. Elwes (New York: Dover, 1951), p. 163 (Chapter XI).

20. See Jean-Luc Nancy, *The Experience of Freedom*, trans. Bridget McDonald (Stanford: Stanford University Press, 1993), p. 163.

FOUR

DECONSTRUCTION AND GLOBALIZATION

The World According to Jean-Luc Nancy

Martin McQuillan

Who shall be happy if not all?

—*Trevor Griffiths*

WORLD WEARY

This epigram is the question that Trevor Griffiths gives an imprisoned Georges Jacques Danton in his play *Hope in the Year Two*.[1] It is the unanswered demand that has organized progressive politics and the desire for social justice since the French Revolution. This line from Griffiths' play forces itself to the surface of my thoughts whenever I am given cause to reflect on the question of so-called "globalization."[2] We might call it an unanswered demand because in essence it is not answerable, at least not in any straightforward sense. If it can be answered, simply, then its answer only opens itself on to the ruin of a subsequent question, "and how?" Griffiths' drama concerns the rational kernel of the irrationalism of revolutionary Terror as Danton awaits execution (or it may be a decoy actor substituting for Danton, in case his supporters attempt to free him). Griffiths is aware of the substantial difference between the performance of this question, even the "theatricalization" of this question, and the immense, perhaps impossible, task of addressing it in a constative idiom. The open-ended question, as a structure of hope, contrasts with the violent arbitrariness of the revolutionary calendar that at once inscribes the possibility of change and its ruthless, hopeless suppression, in a comedy of teleologies: *plus ça change*, as Danton might have said. To attempt to answer this question head-on would be to hope against hope, and who has the resources for such labor? As such, I leave it here as a guide for the inquiry that follows. After this spectacle of imprisoned Jacobin rationality, I would like to organize my thoughts on globalization around another, perhaps more philosophically inflected question that necessarily precedes that asked by Griffiths' Danton: Who today will defend reason?

Everywhere reason is in eclipse as a consequence of what we have learned to call "the return of the religious." Theocracy holds sway in the capitals of Iran and Israel, Pakistan and Palestine, and the Orthodox "borders" of Europe, while the White House plays host to Pentecostalism and the "Born Again," Anglican bishops sit in the British House of Lords, and through the doors of the Vatican, Roman Catholicism exercises its global reach. Islam, Hinduism, and Buddhism can lay claim in one way or another to forty-seven percent of the world's population.[3] At this time, who can say that a Western idea of rationality has conquered the globe? Furthermore, who today would have the resources to defend reason? Reason as a principle value of modernity was surely bankrupted by the projects of colonialism and communism, running aground with Maoist excess and the recent, seeming collapse of the creditability of unfaltering progress through Western capitalism. Would it be reasonable to defend reason today? The classical idea of reason that has predicated the work of philosophy since Athens is regularly and quite rightly questioned by philosophy itself as being wholly unreasonable for its exclusions and unenlightened presumptions. Even if one were able to equate neatly reason with the secular and with science, which given the history of reason is in no way possible, one would have to say that today reason is in crisis. Shoveled up by theory, ruined by psychoanalysis, poured on by religion, by-passed by new genetic engineering, with a maximum United Nations estimate of twenty percent of the inhabitants of the earth identifiable as secular or atheist, we have good reason today to be concerned for the future of reason.

This is an especially pertinent worry in so far as the question of reason today cannot be separated from the question of what is called, for want of a better word, "globalization." Because this present phase of "globalization" emerges as the most recent conceptual product of a history of a Eurocentric modernity, then the business of "the globe" and the question of "reason" are closely connected. In fact, one might consider that what we take to be the unity of this world is an effect of what Kant would call the "regulative Idea of reason." As such, what is called "globalization," as the planetary domination of a certain Western model of thought and technology, is to a degree predicated on such a unifying ideal and an idea of unification. Now, there is little doubt that this word "globalization" is the nominal effect that disguises an ideological operation whereby the activities of so-called "free trade" are expanded across the globe while the benefits of such trade remain firmly in the hands of the privileged and wealthy "West." However, this description is not without its complications. Globalization, as the making of a world market, both extends the dominion of what we must provisionally call "Western nations," while at the same time transforming the conditions of sovereignty, which undermines the significance of both the Western model of the nation-state and any unified sense of the "West" itself. One could demonstrate this in very precise ways in relation to what is presently called in an unhelpfully vague way "the credit crunch." There is a distinction to be made between the first recession in the planetary economy that began in 2008, based on the new global market, and the singular but over determined problem of the evaporation of trust. This loss of confidence in the international wholesale money markets was the result of losses incurred by Western financial institutions on credit derivative products related to the U.S. mortgage market (and the wider practice of the securitization of debt-based assets) and the recapitalization and part nationalization of Western banks that has resulted from this. However, what is emerging from this situation is a realization that the Western nations that lead the first phase of the development of this global economy are now indebted to and therefore reliant on so-called Eastern nations such as the oil-producing Middle East and China. In this sense, one should be wary of exactly how "global" the development of globalization really is and how far the Western genre of economic privilege itself is being displaced given that this arrangement only allows a relatively select few additional countries an augmented status through their own operation of an essentially Western model of capitalism. Nevertheless, a transformation in the architectonics of global hegemony is taking place as capitalism readjusts itself in order to carry on its self-producing work. For example, the status of the dollar as a global reserve currency allowed the United States both to "bail out" its economy and fund its military budget. However, this same trade has resulted in a mutual dependency among the U.S. economy and that of China and other non-Western investors. This realignment of capitalization looks to result in what social scientists refer to as a "multipolar" world in which Western privilege and exceptionalism are held in check by mutual dependence on the health of emerging economies. This will have several consequences for geopolitics. First, American political economy must now take account of the wishes of its non-American creditors. Second, these creditors will come to demand an increased role in global sovereign decision making, such as representation on the Security Council of the United Nations or as executives of the World Bank. In turn this will limit the scope of Western exceptionalism and in particular the ability of the United States to act independently in relation to foreign policy and trade agreements, notably, perhaps, in relation to its previous unequivocal support of Israel. Accordingly, the White House may consider the reserve currency status of the dollar to be no longer a benefit but a hindrance to the country and some other unit (such as the Euro, Chinese Renminbi, or an at-present speculative world currency unit) will emerge to take its place with all this will imply for the global political economy. Although Chinese financial institutions and global bodies remain relatively underdeveloped, this situation will exist only as a possibility. However, these are the transformations already under way on the global scene that the Western nation-states are incapable of opposing.

When one begins to scratch the surface of this idea of "globalization," one can immediately see how the concept works to offer an idea of unity that in no way exists on the ground. The conditions of the current global economy remain markedly divided between those who profit from the expanded conditions of a world-wide market and those who continue to be exploited by it. In this sense, "globalization" renames a familiar problem that has had several guises over the history of the world since at least Rome. One could also say that as a term *globalization* also presents us with the restatement of a familiar difficulty, namely the universalization of a European ideological parochialism through metaphysics. Philosophy must attend to globalization because "the world" as such is a philosophical idea with a considerable genealogy, one that is closely connected to the fate of this difficulty called "reason." The West evolved not through the overcoming of the dark night of faith by reason in the Renaissance and Enlightenment, but rather through the construction of the idea of a world that emerges from within the thought of these and subsequent periods. One might consider here Kant's cosmopolitanism, Hegel's thinking of empire and the universal, Marx's world market and the production of humanity, Heidegger's being-in-the-world and poverty of world, and so on. If deconstruction has some leverage to bring to bear upon the issue of globalization, it might begin its work by questioning "the regulative Idea of the world that authorizes that world in advance," as Derrida writes in the "The 'World' of the Enlightenment to Come (Exception, Calculation, and Sovereignty)."[4] At the same time and in the name of all the heterogeneous rationalities that would seek to question the present hegemonic formulation of globalization, it will be equally necessary to disarticulate the relation between the idea of the world and reason within this philosophical inheritance.

In this chapter I consider the tripartite arrangement that connects reason to religion and globalization. I do this through an account of two books by Jean-Luc Nancy, *The Creation of the World* or *Globalization* and *Dis-Enclosure: The Deconstruction of Christianity*.[5] Immediately, one should comment on the difficulty of translation in both of these titles. The first in French is *La création du monde* ou *la mondialisation*. For all the reasons that we shall see, *mondialisation* is not translatable as "globalization" and Nancy includes two prefaces to the French and English editions stating this—so why not leave the French as it is? I suspect this mistranslation is the result of a "marketing decision" whereby English-language publishers are exceptionally reluctant to include non-English words in book titles. In fact one might say that the willful mistranslation of *mondialisation* is undoubtedly a result of the globalization of publishing. The second book in French is *La Déclosion (Déconstruction du christianisme, 1)*. "Dis-enclosure" is a poetic invention to render the untranslatable in translation. This is not an issue, but there is all the difference in the world between *Déconstruction du christianisme* and "The Deconstruction of Christianity." This is what Derrida takes to task in *Le toucher*.[6] In a nutshell, as I have argued elsewhere,[7] there can be, for Derrida, no such thing as "the deconstruction of Christianity" for two reasons. First, the tradition of the *destructio* is a Christian concept that defines the very modality of Christianity as an impulsion beyond itself; any deconstruction of Christianity would first have to untie itself from its own Christian presuppositions. Second, to speak of "the deconstruction of Christianity" implies not only a fixed idea of what Christianity is but also implies a pre-set idea of deconstruction as arriving from the outside to act on a definite Christianity. Derrida chastises Nancy here when the latter methodologically speaks of there being no "the sense of touch" ("*il n'y a pas 'le'*..."), preferring his unconditional formulation of touch, if there is any, "*s'il y en a*." For Derrida "the definite or defining article is already engaged or required by the discourse that disputes it," while Derrida's own deconstruction points to the conditions of possibility as the impossible itself: "'there is no *the* deconstruction of [*the*] Christianity [*'le' christianisme*],' because there isn't and never has been either a 'the' deconstruction or a 'the' Christianity," says Derrida (*OT*, 287–288). This is a very powerful criticism of Nancy's "deconstructive methodology," as Derrida characterizes it in *Le toucher*, but I am not sure that Nancy's own *La Déclosion (Déconstruction du christianisme, 1)* says precisely this. Although the improvised talk at the University of Montpellier in 1995 recorded, transcribed, and then published in *Études philosophiques* in 1988 bears the title "*La Déconstruction du christianisme*" (subsequently translated into English as "The Deconstruction of Christianity") Nancy says in a footnote in *La Déclosion* that this refusal of revision is intended "as a witness to the first moment in a questioning" (*D*, 188). This earlier essay itself acknowledges that deconstruction is "shot through and through with Christianity" and that the gesture of deconstruction in relation to history and tradition is one that is found in neither Kant nor Husserl, but is "only possible within Christianity" (*D*, 148). Subsequent chapters written after the publication of *Le toucher* in 2000, such as the central text, "A Deconstruction of Monotheism," given in Cairo in 2001, are notable for their use of the phrase "a 'deconstruction of Christianity.'" As we shall see, this all has consequences for any reading of Nancy on globalization, as well as the relation between reason and religion.

VIRTUALLY CHRISTIAN

What lies behind Derrida's comments on Nancy's use of the "*il n'y a pas 'le'* . . ." as a modality of deconstruction is the more persistent criticism in *Le toucher* that it is not possible for Nancy to affect a deconstruction of touch by continuing to use the archaic, Western category of touch with impunity. It is not possible to speak of touch and all its attendant figures (the body, corporeality, the hand, etc.) in the way that Nancy does without becoming contaminated by the metaphysical inheritance of these terms:

> Now, Jean-Luc, that's quite enough, give this word [touch] back, it's prohibited, you hear. Leave it to the ancestors, don't make any compromises with it, don't let this *megalovirus* contaminate you, and once and for all stop using this incredible vocabulary, this concept nothing can really vouch for, these figures without figure and therefore without credit. Don't keep pretending, as they do, don't make believe, stop acting as if you wanted to make us believe that there is something one could call touch, an understood thing itself about which we could pretend to agree, and say something new, in the very place where, in touching upon the untouchable, this thing remains untouchable. Touch is finitude. Period. Stop at this point. Haven't you yourself said "there is no 'the' sense of touch"? Knowing you, I don't think this objection will stop you, I tell myself. (*OT*, 138–139)

On the one hand, this is the same lesson that Derrida has been handing out since "Structure, Sign and Play," namely that there can be no displacement of a concept that does not draw itself into the whole history of that which is being opposed. This situation is systematic to metaphysics and one can give oneself up to it in ways that are more or less knowing, or more or less in keeping with expectation. The question I have concerning "a 'deconstruction of Christianity'" is how one negotiates this relation with respect to something that one would wish to oppose very much on the grounds of, shall we say, "reason." My question to Nancy is, can one use this ancient term "Christianity" without consequence? How can one speak of Christianity and not be drawn into the history of Christianity and have one's argument be determined by it? The answer that suggests itself here is that one cannot and should not even try to "oppose" Christianity in this sense, or at least one should not believe that there could be any position with regard to Christianity that was not already contaminated by this megalovirus. As such, where does that leave us when we ask the question, "Who will defend reason?"

In certain respects, Nancy's book on globalization is a corollary to the wider work on Christianity, so I propose to start with *La Déclosion* as an attempt to understand the world according to Nancy. The original Montpellier lecture lays out the basics of Nancy's argument here. For Nancy, a certain idea of the West and Christianity are inseparable. For this reason, "globalization" and Christianity are intertwined. Derrida offers the neologism "globalatinization" to describe this important relation.[8] The present scene is said by Nancy to involve an experience of the "de-Christianization" of the West that continues to place the West in the shadow of a retreating Christianity. Thus, for Nancy, "to deconstruct Christianity is to accompany the West to that limit [of sense], to that *pass at which* the West cannot do otherwise than let go of itself in order to continue being the West, or still be something of itself beyond itself" (*D*, 143). One might characterize the transformation of the West's privileged place within the global market, both an augmentation of that privilege and an erasure of it, as such a pass whereby the West advances itself in its own retreat as something of itself beyond itself. Accordingly, the question of the present phase of globalization remains closely tied to the fate of Christianity. In this de-Christianized West, for Nancy, citing Luigi Pareyson, "the only Christianity that can be actual is the one that contemplates the present possibility of its negation." Conversely, "the only thing that can be actual is an atheism that contemplates the reality of its Christian origins" (*D*, 140). In this way, Nancy proposes in later texts that monotheism itself is a form of atheism in which the existence of God is determined by the retreat of God as presence. He writes, "not only is atheism an invention specific to the West, but it must also be considered the element in which the West invented itself as such" (*D*, 14). That is to say that in the passage from *mythos* to *philos*, the gods are precisely no longer a worldly presence: Greek-Mediterranean culture begins with the disenchantment of God and the invention of the world as such.

However, Christianity does not occur merely as philosophy, even if its history is closely tied to the historical formation of philosophy. Nancy puzzles over Enlightenment philosophy's condemnation of Christianity and insists that Christianity should not be treated philosophically as a primitivism, but rather as an historical "collaboration and confrontation of 'reason' and 'faith'" (*D*, 8), for the history of philosophy is not just a matter of philosophy. For Nancy, atheism is co-terminus with theism and so we might say that the future of reason cannot be separated from the fate of religion. In fact, Nancy identifies the unified idea of reason that predicates the universalization of the West as globalization (through techno-science, democracy, popular culture) with the culture of humanism, and it is this humanism that is bankrupt. Nancy variously describes it as being "in its death throes" and opening itself "onto inhumanity" (*D*, 2, 30). Hence, for Nancy, the West can no longer be called the West because it can no longer acknowledge "itself as holding a vision for the world" (*D*, 30). I am not sure if this is entirely true. It just so happens that humanism's current vision is one that Nancy does not care for. Having recognized the monotheistic provenance of rationality, Nancy looks to what he calls "a 'deconstruction of Christianity'" for a new understanding of the West in globalization:

> And thus, we must ask ourselves anew what it is that, without denying Christianity but without returning to it, could lead us toward a point—toward a resource—hidden beneath Christianity, beneath monotheism, and beneath the West, which we must henceforth bring to light, for this point would open a future for the world that would no longer be either Christian or anti-Christian, either monotheist or atheist or even polytheist, but that would advance precisely beyond all these categories (after having made all of them possible). (*D*, 34)

In *La Déclosion*, Nancy never announces what this resource might be, although he hints toward it in his final line, when he when that what remains for us today is "neither cult nor prayer, but the exercise—strict and severe, sober and yet joyous—of what is called thought" (*D*, 157). That is to say, reason. But Nancy suggests several times that such reason is not a nihilism that is "the lapse of sense" (*D*, 122). Rather, for Nancy, Christianity is itself nihilism because it is ceaselessly engaged with the death of God and is ruined by its own opening of monotheism as the retreat of God. Now, although one can recognize that Nancy has no investment in the credulous or confessional, so-called "organized religion" as the management of politics and culture, and one can agree with Nancy up to the point of his identification of the Christian provenance of the West and philosophy, I would like to retain a commitment to a certain idea of so-called "nihilism." Where Nancy seems to call for a *revendication*, to use Brecht's term, of the resources of thought within Christianity as a response to the crisis of the West and reason within globalization, I would insist on a characterization of our modern period and the value of our present as nihilist. Of course, as Nancy acknowledges, Nietzsche was both the "only Christian" and a "good

European," but I have always felt close to Roland Barthes' late embrace of the French translation of Nietzsche: "I believe that nihilism is the only possible philosophy for our current situation," he writes. "But I must immediately add that I do not confuse nihilism with violent, radically destructive behavior, or—on a deeper level—with behavior that is more or less neurotic or hysterical. Nihilism is a type of reflection and utterance (because problems must always be framed in terms of language) which demands an effort of intelligence and a certain mastery of language."[9] "Nihilism" in this sense is not a lapse of sense, but a more-than-critical deconstructive vigilance regarding the grounding of that sense as value and its numerous mystifications. But equally we cannot embrace "nihilism" in any eager or easy way. Let us say, rather, nihilism if there is any, if there has ever been any.

This I think is the nub of a disagreement with Nancy. In *La Déclosion*, Nancy comments on Blanchot's association of atheism with writing in *The Infinite Conversation*. Of course, for Nancy, "the community of thinking that connects [Blanchot] with Bataille and Adorno, Barthes and Derrida" is one in which the full presence of sense is related to an understanding of God as a principle. Nancy's counter-argument would be that the invention of monotheism at once gives birth to atheism and retains within itself the ruin of a second, secretly held atheism. Hence, he is able to suggest that writing for Blanchot and his fellow travelers is:

> the movement of exposure to the flight of sense that withdraws signification from "sense" in order to give it the very sense of that flight—an élan, an opening, an indefatigable exposure that consequently does not even "flee," that flees flight as well as presence. Neither nihilism nor the idolatry of a signified (and/or a signifier). This is what is at stake in an "atheism" that owes it to itself to deny itself the position of the negation it proffers, and the assurance of every sort of presence that could substitute for that of God—that is, the presence of the signifier of absolute signification or signifiability. (*D*, 86)

Nihilism here for Nancy seems to stand at the opposite and equal end of a binary, as an insistence on presence as a substitute for God. This is also his characterization of humanism, so something must be mis-attributed somewhere. What interests me here, philosophically speaking, is that the defense of reason within the de-Christianization of the West is not so much about the existence of God herself or the retreat of a supreme being, but rather concerns the existence of being itself. On the one hand, one must acknowledge that the idea of God sits at the heart of all Western thinking, as the metaphysical technology that binds sense to presence. On the other hand, it is the task of a deconstruction of such thinking both to recognize this and to move us on from it without going around it. One might say, to paraphrase Nancy, that a defense of reason today would involve neither denying an atheistic critical nihilism nor returning to it either. This leads us toward the resources of atheism as the constitutive element that makes all the categories of the West possible: a different kind of reason as Nietzschean madness.

In this sense, Nancy points his philosophical compass in the wrong direction. If there is no treatment of traditional categories that are not already contaminated, I would rather begin with the resources of nihilism, if there are any, than those found in Christianity. Nihilism is not just a phase in the history of Christianity, anymore than Christianity is merely a phase in the history of paganism, whose tropes and figures it appropriates—at least not if we are to retain a working sense of history in its traditional progressive, worldly, and epochal sense. This disarticulation of the idea of history is a question we will unfortunately need to park for the moment.

I am not sure that I wish to "open a future for the world that would no longer be either Christian or anti-Christian, either monotheist or atheist, . . . but that would advance precisely beyond all these categories." It is necessary to defend atheism as part of a wider defense of reason. We ought not to give up so easily on a certain deconstruction of Christianity that would require an equal and complementary critique of Christianity. I do not agree with Nancy that "Christianity is no longer recognizable" as "fundamentalism" (*D*, 141). Reading Nancy's version of Christianity, I fear that he has lead a very sheltered life, indeed I equally wonder about his reluctance to extend his deconstruction of monotheism to a consideration of Judaism and Islam. It should be possible to imagine an atheism that did not substitute God for the promise of presence without having to retain the trace of God as the counter-curse against presence. This would be a critical nihilism, a deconstruction, that had the appearance of an atheism that would ruin the principle of God of metaphysics, while also putting its own faith to the test in a ceaseless contestation of all theologies, onto-theologies, and negative theologies. For his part, Nancy might respond that his deconstruction of Christianity is precisely a critical atheism. But to my mind, Nancy's defense of a displaced reason as the hidden resource of Christianity looks very much like Žižek's attempted reclamation of the "virtual content" of terror as a virtue.[10] The same difficulty persists in Nancy: What is the difference between such a virtual content and Christianity itself?

Monotheism thus remains untouched in Nancy's schema. Although the atheist must give up his or her pure atheism and acknowledge his or her own onto-theology, the Christian, by acknowledging the absence of God, does not have to give up very much because God is already absent in Monotheism. Post-Christian Christianity remains very much as it was. The "absentheism" of Nancy's deconstructed monotheism is still just monotheism. I want to say to Nancy, "now, Jean-Luc, that's quite enough, give this word [Christianity] back, it's prohibited, you hear. Leave it to the ancestors, don't make any compromises with it, don't let this *megalovirus* contaminate you, and once and for all stop using this incredible vocabulary, this concept nothing can really vouch for, these figures without figure and therefore without credit. Don't keep pretending, as they do, don't make believe, stop acting as if you wanted to make us believe that there is something one could call Christianity, an understood thing itself about which we could pretend to agree, and say something new." I am particularly vexed by the notion that a deconstruction of Christianity would involve a movement beyond the categories of Christian and anti-Christian, theist and atheist, or even poly-theist, because here I do not recognize the logic of deconstruction. The difficulty is that while in general a deconstruction might "methodologically" seek to move a conceptual order beyond a binary structure, these categories are not binaries. What does the term "anti-Christian" mean here? Who is encompassed by this label? Secularists, perhaps, but they are more than merely "anti-Christian"; they are anti-theist *tout court*. And does this term, anti-Christian, refer to Buddhism, Hinduism, Judaism, and Islam as well? It is not meaningful to describe these religions as anti-Christian unless one wishes to work with a particularly reductive understanding of them; one might just as well describe Christianity as anti-Islam. This will not do. These religions are theisms, whether monotheist or polytheist, and in this way they do not fall into the "atheism" that is set up here as opposed to theism. The anti-Christian and the atheist, then, if one holds onto these categories provisionally, are not terms of equal conceptual weight. One can no more give up the category "woman" in a deconstruction of sexual difference or give up on reason in a deconstruction of humanism than one can abandon atheism in a deconstruction of Christianity. The atheist has already recognized his or her Christian inheritance (both as "crusader" and the "great Satan") and is nevertheless being asked by Nancy to give up most in this scenario in favor of the resources of "thought," which they are quite (un)comfortable with already. Ultimately, and this "ultimately" may be a large part of the problem, Nancy's so-called deconstruction of Christianity, provocative as it is, retains a kernel of monotheism as the basis of a world culture. What's more, given the monotheism he feels most at ease discussing—"the form of which [he is] the least incapable of speaking, since it is that of [his] culture as a Frenchman and a European" (*D*, 33)—Nancy's *Dis-Enclosure* works relentlessly against itself to reinscribe the centrality of the Christianity it purports to deconstruct.

I accept the European and Christian inheritance of globalization, international law, human rights, and even capitalism. However, something else is also required here: first, a recognition of the pagan Roman and Greek origins of Christianity itself as European (i.e., a recognition of the pre-origins of monotheism); second, the deconstruction of the spurious onto-genesis of Europe and philosophy as Greek *tout court*; and finally, the thinking of a Europe beyond not just Christianity but monotheism as such. Undoubtedly, this is not an easy task. Given what we have said above concerning the idea of God that haunts every name in the West, it might in principle be impossible, at least on Western terms. However, this impossible atheism is not something to renounce in order to advance beyond the categories of Christian and anti-Christian, theist and atheist. Such an overly hasty move leaves Christianity and atheism un-thought, and they continue to lie before us as the ground for a deconstruction yet to come. It may well be that such an impossible critical atheism will look very Christian in orientation, just as one might say that Nietzsche's opening of the *nihil* is itself Christian. However, as a strategy and style for deconstruction I would wish to retain it as an example of the "*s'il y en a*," Christianity if there is any, pointing to the condition of possibility of Christianity as the impossible itself.[11] I am much more persuaded by Nancy's late reference to a possible "deconstruction of property—that of man and that of the world" (*D*, 161) as an opening of the "eclosure of the world" by the West, than a future beyond atheism. I welcome the impossible atheism of the future as the *arrivant* of its own *parousia*, not as a reassuring presence, but as the refusal to reinscribe mystification within the deferred imminence of the social bond.

NANCY'S CREATIONISM

Here we touch the nub of what Nancy thinks he is doing in a deconstruction, which is also a salvaging of a minimalist faith beyond both confessionalism and humanism. In order to attend to this particular reading of Nancy, I return to the difference between the hidden or virtual resources of Christianity and Christianity itself. If there is no difference that makes any difference, then Nancy's arguments are positively a salvaging of Christianity. If there is a notable difference, then this may have important consequences for what might be thought concerning globalization: "Reason" may be only an idiom of something like "Late-Christianity." Nancy, offers an example of what he has in mind in *The Creation of the World*. "Creation" is a category he introduces belatedly in *La Déclosion* in the final paragraphs of the final chapter, "Dis-Enclosure," in which he speaks of dis-enclosure as "a new departure for creation" (*D*, 160). *Dis-enclosure* is the translated term to suggest the opening up of a previously demarcated space, set by boundaries between the world and the heavens, between man and God. This opening is at once a deferral of the imminent presence of such boundaries and their inscription in retreat. This arrival, which is not an arrival, is the situation that Nancy characterizes as the still insistent question of *parousia*, that is, an opening of any sense of a self-enclosed world of men speaking to men, as humanism would have it. One wonders if it is really necessary to reclaim the resources of Christianity to challenge such a formulation. However, Nancy attempts to do precisely this.

As with Derrida, for Nancy the counter-conjuration to the Anglo-Saxon insistence on "globalization" is the French term, deliberately mis-translated in the title of his book, "*mondialisation*," which means "world-forming" in the sense of a world of people (*tout le monde*) in preference to a global market. A preference for the French is also a refusal of the globalizing gesture that translates everything into English, "globa*latin*ization," which acts as the suppression of any alternative world formation. In the face of what seems to be for Nancy the universal and unified threat of the so-called "Anglo-Saxon model" of capitalism (some time would have to be taken to unpick the silences and erasures in this hyphenated conjunction [*trait-d'union*]), Nancy calls for a new mobilization of the trope of "creation." He pointedly argues that " 'Creation' is a motif, or a concept, that we must grasp outside of its theological context" (CW, 50). For the reasons suggested here, I think any such grasping anterior to the theological history of "creation" would be impossible, but let us move on from here. Nancy explains his term:

> If "creation" means anything, it is the exact opposite of any form of production in the sense of a fabrication that supposes a given, a project, and a producer. The idea of creation, such as has been elaborated by the most diverse and at the same time most convergent thoughts, including the mystics of the three monotheisms but also the complex systems of all great metaphysics, is above all the idea of the *ex nihilo*. . . . The world is created from nothing: this does not mean fabricated from nothing by a particularly ingenious producer. It means instead that it is not fabricated, produced by no producer, and not even coming out of nothing (like a miraculous apparition), but in a quite strict manner and more challenging to thought: the nothing itself, if one can speak in this way, or rather *nothing* growing [*croissant*] as *something* (I say "growing" for it is the sense of *cresco*—to be born, to grow—from which comes *creo*: to make something merge and cultivate a growth). In creation, a growth grows from nothing and this nothing takes care of itself, cultivates its growth. (CW, 51)

On the one hand, Nancy's point is that there is nothing outside the world and the "self" is given from nowhere. There is only the world and the immanent space-time of the world for us to attend as the creation of that world. Fine, this is not an argument for theism. However, I worry over Nancy's seeming rapid agreement with the mystics of the three monotheisms. I am tempted to ask, what all of them? "The *ex nihilo* is the genuine formulation of a radical materialism, that is to say, precisely, without roots" (CW, 50). This would truly be radical since the whole idea of the radical, political or mathematical, relates to the Latin *radix* meaning "root." This is radicalism without the radical. Nancy's creationism is not intelligent design; it is the exact opposite: "the rose grows without reason," as he quotes Angelus Silesius (CW, 47). And the growth of the world is a similar "without-reason" [*rien de raison*]:

> Thus, we can now clarify what we said earlier: if the world-becoming (detheologization) displaces value—makes it immanent—before, world-forming displaces the production of value—making it universal—the two together displace "creation" into the "without-reason" of the world. And this displacement is not a transposition, a "secularization" of the onto-theological or metaphysical-Christian scheme: it is, rather, its deconstruction and emptying out, and it opens onto another space—of place and of risk—which we have just begun to enter. (CW, 51)

This other space is the "dis-enclosed" world without reason as an absent ground.

There is a decision to be made here before endorsing Nancy. First, if the question of *mondialisation* is understood as a production without production, what is Nancy calling "creation"? I am suspicious of the characterization of a growth that "grows from nothing and this nothing takes care of itself." Such cultivation always relies on another and comes about as the hybrid growth of two spliced organisms. My preferred metaphor for development would be *creole* rather than *creo*.

Second, although Nancy wishes to make the point that free-market capital is akin to Silesius' rose, "without-reason" or ground (CW, 50), I worry about the disappearance of the producer in Nancy's schema, not as a defense of "wealth creation" or the rights of property, but as a recognition of the real conditions of production that determine the diverse material and heterogeneous experience of lived globalization today. The producer prospers when his presence goes unnoticed. This is why, as Marx and Engels recognize, all ideology is religious in its operation. The *ex nihilo* cannot but help retaining the necessity of a producer: *for nothing comes from nothing*, even as Nancy would like to fold that producer back into the immanence of the without-reason. As in his non-fundamentalist Christianity, it would seem that Nancy needs to familiarize himself with the facts of life, the real conditions of production and reproduction. Even the croissant is a seedling that relies on culture to grow (an Islamic as well as a symbol of Christian France). If, as Nancy suggests in *The Creation of the World*, "our task today is nothing less than the task of creating a form or a symbolization of the world" (*CW*, 53), then this is also the task of resymbolization. That is the patient deconstruction and turning around of meanings as a poetic invention through reading and paleoonymy: the deconstruction of property, and of metaphysics, and of the name of God, all of which might rightly call the producer for what he or she is, but none of which can simply dis-enclose her or him from the future. The question of "the producer" is no doubt vexed, but one does not need to adopt a vocabulary and analysis of a Marxian-type to suggest that the self-production of the chain of production in no way negates the role of the producer. What is required here is not the creation of an *ex nihilo* without producer, but the recognition that production as such is always only ever a reproduction. In such a scenario the producer remains, standing within the act of production, which may or may not produce itself, but in which the producer remains a part. Even in an automated regime of global domination through technology, which would be the end of every human author, there would still be a producer who produced, as all production and reproduction implies. Every system of production and reproduction, as a predicate of productivity itself, presupposes a producer even if he or she does not own the means of production. In cases where the surrogate (re)producer does not own the fruits of his or her own labor, the idea of the producer still remains in place. Nancy characterizes this as the retreat of the Creator. But, as with his reading of monotheism, the Creator remains in the end because she or he was never there in the first place.

A deconstruction of the idea of property, if there is any, requires an understanding of the producer, reproducer, and ex-appropriation. Such a labor-intensive deconstruction would not necessarily happen *ex nihilo*, or even in seven days. Rather, there would have to be a long experience of evolution as infinite perfectibility that is also a radical materialism with long roots. This investigation of the meaning of production is also a production of meaning as an unconditional rationalism that in the name of reason makes a struggle within the West over the meaning of the West. Perhaps this would even be a contest within capitalism over the ambiguities of capitalism in the name of an impossible atheism that opened the world formed by humanity beyond all humanism and every God. My worry over Nancy's "creationism" is not that he is wrong to say that the sense of the world is only ever the sense of the world. No, in placing the future of that important thought in the hands of an interpretation determined by a figure whose history so radically denies the worldliness of sense, we risk entering a world without-reason with non-sense. This is precisely not an adequate defense of reason. Just as Nancy's deconstruction of monotheism imagines the end of monotheism while leaving monotheism intact, so too the *ex nihilo* proposed here imagines the disappearance of the producer while maintaining the need for the producer by the redrawing of boundaries that do nothing to remove the necessity of drawing. Let us not pretend that "creation" or even "pro-creation" is something we can all agree upon. Rather, let us say of Nancy's invention, "creation" if there is any…

The task of the creation of the world is *mondialisation*, and a world formed as we would wish it to be, "in man's own image," as the penny catechism has it—isn't this another humanism? Therefore, I would like my creation to be without the myth of creation, even the virtual content of creation. I propose the alternative trope of evolutionary deconstruction, which would enlighten the future through the uncovering of the genealogical sedimentation of the West. My reading of Nancy here comes from *The Creation of the World*'s "*Urbi et Orbi*." In a subsequent text, "Of Creation," he acknowledges, "'creation' is the most disastrous of concepts":

> I only use the word *creation* here in a preliminary or provisional way, reserving the hope of being able to transform it. In the end, this word cannot suffice for it is overdetermined with and overused by monotheism, although it also indicates in this entire philosophical context the wearing out [*usure*] of monotheism itself . . . and even if, furthermore, I do not know what word could replace it, unless it is not a matter of replacing it but of allowing it to be erased in the existing of existence. (CW, 67)

Nancy is ultimately a man of the world. He has the good sense to recant this particular deconstruction of Christianity. However, his conversion on the road to Damascus is not quite complete in this second essay. He wishes to retain a purpose for his creation as "the exact reverse of nihilism" where nihilism "corresponds to the accomplishment of onto-theology according to the logic of a 'bad' infinite of presupposition" (CW, 71). "Creation" involves by contrast a "'good infinite,' or actual infinite" of a null presupposition, which begs the questions of whether the null presupposition is itself an infinite presupposition and how one might tell a good infinite from a bad infinite, when there is only infinity? The "ex" in *ex nihilo* is, says Nancy, "the ex- of ex-istence that is neither produced nor constructed but only existing [*étante*]. . . . And this *ex nihilo* fractures the deepest core of nihilism from within" (CW, 71). At this point, Nancy seems to want to have his cake and eat it too. The whole justification for Nancy's creation without a producer is that the world is "neither given nor posited, the world is only present: the present of the day in which it exists" (CW, 71). This is and is not true: There is only a present, but such a present presupposes both a past present and a present to come. There would be no present as such without this classic metaphysical formulation. But for Nancy the presence of today "neither differs nor is derived from any other presupposed presence, any more than from an absence that would be the negative of a presence: *ex nihilo* means that it is the *nihil* that opens and that disposes itself as the space of all presence." Nancy thus can never be done with the *nihil*. His creationism is a profound nihilism because it must ceaselessly engage with the opening and emptying of the nihil. Nihilism, like any "ism," if there are any, could only ever be an ex-nihilism in the sense that Nancy wants to use the prefix "ex." A great labor of reading Nietzsche, Derrida, Blanchot, Bataille and others in this epoch of the deconstruction of value would be required to demonstrate this, but let me say that nihilism never is and never was the closed system that Nancy needs it to be.

I am also not sure that in an understanding of world-formation I would want to abandon either the future (the idea of the world to come) or the historical past as quickly as Nancy does here in favor of an eternal or infinite present of non-presence. This question is tightly bound to what Nancy thinks he is doing with Derrida's *différance*, which also seems to be the model for his retreat of monotheism. This would constitute another chapter of considerable length. In brief, Nancy imagines that the *ex nihilo* and *différance* are one and the same as the generating structure for the presentation and nullity of ontological difference. This situation for Nancy is "the disposition of the world" (CW, 73). He moves on from Derrida's famous statement on *différance* to say that "the infinite is finite," hollowed out in its own withdrawal, which is also the opening through which finite singularities dispose themselves. For Nancy, "the infinite as nothing (in-finite = no thing) passes into the finite" (CW, 72). This is an extremely complex procedure that is difficult to do justice to here, but I would suggest that Nancy's *ex nihilo* is not the same as Derrida's *différance*. Nancy always wants to read the radically finite trace as a trace of the infinite in its withdrawal, as in the case of the motifs of Christianity. However, as Bennington characterizes it, in Derrida "the always finite opening of the finite itself [is] (infinitely) finite, or more properly . . . [is] neither straightforwardly finite nor infinite."[12] I am not sure that the infinite is "no thing"; even zero is not "no thing." The possibilities of world-formation may in Nancy's view be infinite, but the world itself is not: the world is rather a great many things that are in themselves finite and finitely opened as infinitely finite, being neither straightforwardly finite nor infinite. For this reason, *différance* does not simply imply the absence of a producer or generation since it is not an infinite dis-enclosure of space, which would itself be just another form of closure. Equally, globalization cannot be straightforwardly displaced by *mondialisation*. On the contrary, our experience of the world must reflect a complex opening of one onto the other, something like a *globalatinization*.

Let me return in conclusion to my earlier question, "who today will defend reason," and answer it through the lesson to be learned in reading Nancy. I suggest reason, if there is any, if there has ever been any, would be a good idea. That is to say, reason must continue to lie before us as the future of a world of an enlightenment to come beyond every God and every humanism. What might the fate of Christianity and of reason mean for Danton in his cell? To be sure his question, "who shall be happy?," might be thought of as Christian in scope. However, a properly "undeconstructed" or "undeconancystructed" Christian response might say that no man can be happy in this world, only in the next. In this sense, Danton's Enlightenment politics is a radical departure from an idea of the enclosed world determined by Christianity. Only with a future for reason (*Hope in the Year 2*) comes an idea of the world that would be unconditionally dis-enclosed. Equally, what might the fate of Christianity and of reason mean for the present phase of globalization today? One welcomes the Christian President Obama's early defense of science and the return of American global leadership on issues such as reproductive technologies and the distribution of prophylactics in the global treatment of AIDS, although to be certain much work lies ahead of us. This is a different kind of bailout of American credit-worthiness, as a currency without reserve, in the absence of a God we might be able to begin again to trust. Such trust in American values is not a creation that will take place in seven days but in a multipolar, multifaith world, it might yet represent the best chance for another "reason," another Enlightenment, and another formation of the world.

NOTES

1. Trevor Griffiths, *Hope in the Year Two*, first performed in 1995 as *Who Shall be Happy?*. See *Trevor Griffiths: Plays 2* (London: Spokesman Books, 2007).

2. This text was written in the week of the G20 summit in London, April 2009.

3. Source, United Nations Statistics Division, http://unstats.un.org.

4. See Jacques Derrida, *Rogues: Two Essays on Reason*, trans. Pascale-Anne Brault and Michael Naas (Stanford: Stanford University Press, 2004), p. 121.

5. Jean-Luc Nancy, *The Creation of the World* or *Globalization*, trans. François Raffoul and David Pettigrew (Albany: SUNY Press, 2007). Henceforth cited as *CW*. Jean-Luc Nancy, *Dis-Enclosure: The Deconstruction of Christianity*, trans. Bettina Bergo, Gabriel Malenfant and Michael B. Smith (New York: Fordham University Press, 2008). Henceforth cited as *D*.

6. Jacques Derrida, *On Touching—Jean-Luc Nancy*, trans. Christine Irizarry (Stanford: Stanford University Press, 2005). Henceforth cited as *OT*.

7. See my "Toucher I: (The Problem with Self-Touching)," *Derrida Today* 1:2 (Nov. 2008), pp. 201–211.

8. See Jacques Derrida, "Faith and Knowledge: the Two Sources of 'Religion' at the Limits of Reason Alone," in *On Religion*, ed. Jacques Derrida and Gianni Vattimo (Stanford: Stanford University Press, 1988).

9. Roland Barthes, *The Grain of the Voice: Interviews 1962–1980*, trans. Linda Coverdale (New York: Hill and Wang, 1985), p, 155.

10. See, for example, Slavoj Žižek, *Virtue and Terror*, ed. Maximilien Robespierre (London: Verso, 2007).

11. In contrast to Nancy's deconstruction, see Martin Hägglund, *Radical Atheism: Derrida and the Time of Life* (Stanford: Stanford University Press, 2008).

12. Geoffrey Bennington "Handshake," *Derrida Today* 1:2, (Nov. 2008), pp. 167–184, here 182. In this article, Bennington has gone some way to accounting for Nancy's appropriation of Derrida's *différance*.

PART TWO

EXPOSITIONS OF ONTOLOGY, OR A POST-DECONSTRUCTIVE REALISM

FIVE

NANCY'S MATERIALIST ONTOLOGY

Anne O'Byrne

When he insists that the world—our world, the world we create—is the world of bodies, Nancy fleshes out his thought that the world is the resolution of fact into sense; the world is the never-ending resolution of the fact *of bodies* into the sense *of bodies*. Thus, we can begin to grasp the radical reach of his materialism.[1] Nancy cannot be described as a materialist in the manner of the Epicureans or of Engels, and although he would reject any attempt to reduce our bodies to mere matter, it is nevertheless his commitment to the insurmountable materiality of bodies that gives his ontology its weight and makes it unique. Yet what can that materiality mean? What sense is there in a materialism developed in the context of Cartesian dualism, or a thought of material being that inherits the abstractions of Heidegger's fundamental ontology, or an understanding of material bodies that echoes Bachelard's materialist rationalism, or a post-Christian materialist reading of incarnation? More to the point, what can be the meaning of a materialist ontology that bears the mark of all of these?

In Nancy's hands, the meaning this materialist ontology turns out to rest on the displacement of meaning and his determination to locate sense in the world of material bodies, a world that must constantly change thanks to the mortal passing away and natal newness of bodies. Given that his concern is with bodies rather than matter as such (if we can even conceive of such a thing), and given that fact and sense are engaged in a creative, worldly mutual resolution, Nancy provides us with an ontology in motion.

EXTENSION, NOT *RES EXTENSA*

In such an endeavor, Descartes seems a particularly unlikely interlocutor. Yet Nancy's *L'extension de l'âme* [The Extension of the Soul] (C, 136–144) is an essentially materialist re-reading of Descartes' dualism that provides an important insight into Nancy's understanding of the materiality of the body or, as we will see, the body–soul union. All materialisms can escape reductive monism by virtue of the place allotted within them to the nothing as the opening for indetermination, and we have seen that Nancy's thought of the *creatio ex nihilo* relies on a conception of the material world as being shot through with God in the form of the nothingness that lies between. This particular engagement with Descartes is an occasion to work through that structure again in explicitly material terms. Nancy's starting point is the thought that thinking substance does indeed share in the essential attribute of matter, that is, extension. He quotes Descartes' correspondence with Princess Elizabeth of Bohemia:

> But, since your Highness notes that it is much easier to attribute matter and extension to the soul that to attribute to it the capacity to move a body and to be moved by it without having matter, I suggest that you feel free to attribute this matter and this extension to the soul; this is no more than conceiving it as united with the body.[2]

After all, Descartes reminds Elizabeth, this is what we do all the time in the course of our lives. It is only in the context of a very particular sort of epistemological quest that the mind turns only on itself, preoccupied with the certainty of its knowledge and the task of ascertaining truth. Yet even then, as soon as it avails itself of sensation, the union of body and soul is manifest and then immediately realized when we turn from philosophizing to action. With that turn the union becomes effective and all the less open to being known, at least with regard to the clear and distinct knowledge on which Descartes relies.

It is not that the two substances are erased or circumvented or collapsed. Instead, it is a matter that they be allowed to emerge as epistemological devices rather than as metaphysical givens. Descartes deploys the thought of substance in the *Meditations* in the service of the clarity and distinctness of ideas and, in order to serve their epistemological purpose, *res extensa* and *res cogitans* must be rendered utterly distinct. When he later encourages Elizabeth to think of them as sharing the defining attribute of matter, we are not witnessing the dismantling of the Cartesian universe, but only the necessary lapse from philosophical, meditative withdrawal into the lived world. In that world, we experience ourselves as an ensemble of body and soul in a way that has something of the clarity of thought but also much of the murkiness of sensation.

If God is the being for whom knowing and being are one, and we are beings for whom there is always a gap between what is known and what is, Descartes' struggle was to identify the contours of that gap from the point of view of knowledge. His aim was to develop a method for training our thinking to refrain from affirming anything it cannot clearly grasp, thus narrowing the scope for error. Yet this scope will never be entirely closed, not least because what we encounter most readily in our efforts to know the world—our bodies—are not simply objects of knowledge. Nancy writes:

> The body knows itself as a soul, or as intimately united with soul. But the soul knows itself as what is extended, not across the body but along the body's extension. . . . The soul is extended right along what is extended, not as a content in a container (nor as a pilot in a ship) but as the extension of the unextended, through which the thing extended (or the body) is known in its union with what is unextended. (C, 139)

Thus, the body presents a locus of resistance and impenetrability, but not by simply being opaque.[3] Instead, it displaces the oppositions of clarity–obscurity, subject–object, passivity–activity, and self–other and is, rather, the space for experience. Knowing may be the province of the mind and sensation may be the province of the body on Descartres' account, but experience is derived from the union of the two. "[T]he soul doesn't experience the body, any more than the body does the soul. But someone experiences, and the 'one' of this someone is altogether justly the indistinct motion of this "experiencing" (C, 144). If mind and body belong in the order of substance, their union is of the order of relation (C, 141).

After all, these substances share a characteristic that makes relation possible; both are susceptible to movement. When Descartes conjures the image of animal spirits that race through our limbs or when he describes the trembling of the pineal gland, he is offering ways of understanding that the world is both "a totality of extended emotion and moving extension us and extended emotion" (C, 142–143). We are exposed, and exposition is "the indistinctly corporeal and incorporeal movement of that which is extended in an indissociable double sense: which is endlessly divided [*partagé*] into impenetrable *partes extra partes* and which endlessly penetrates and is penetrated as *extra*-position in itself" (C, 143).[4] This is a materialism that shows us thought moving to and beyond its limit in matter in a way that eventually allows us—singular, plural, corporeal, natal beings—to emerge *as* sense.

Ian James grasps the thrust of this reading of Descartes clearly when he describes Nancy as taking the terms *soul* and *body* and using them to explain the movement of sense and embodiment in his own ontology. James writes, "In the body which feels, walks, sleeps, and eats, sense or soul is extended, the awareness of a meaningfulness conferred upon sensation is itself sense or soul, and it is in the extension of the sensible or animate body that the union of body and soul occurs."[5] I would add that, as a form of materialism, this is necessarily a finite thinking. Material does not confound itself with its own meaning, and the world of bodies does not run the risk of taking the fact of its being to be identical with the sense or meaning of being. As Nancy writes in *Birth to Presence*, the body has the same structure as mind, but it does not presuppose itself as the reason for that structure.[6] In the union of body and soul, body encounters the sense of sensation while the soul runs up against the obdurate and complex materiality of bodies, confronting there its own limits and thereby its own hubris.

The world is not itself a body or body as such, but is rather the world *of* bodies; it is both *for* bodies and *made up of* them. Put another way, the material world does not occur as mere matter; we do not experience extension as the unbroken surface of the world. As Gaston Bachelard points out in *Le matérialisme rationnel*, a genuine "materialism of matter" must be informed by the enormous plurality of different materials.[7] In the same way, Nancy argues in *Being Singular Plural* that the ontology of being-with must be materialist "in the sense that 'matter' does not designate a substance or a subject (or an anti-subject) but literally designates what is divided of itself, what is only as distinct from itself, *partes extra partes*, originarily impenetrable to the combining and sublimating penetration of a 'spirit' understood as a dimensionless, indivisible point beyond the world."[8] Matter spaces itself out as the plurality of bodies that present their many surfaces, different volumes, and differentiated bodies to the touch of our bodies. They are together and we are in the midst of them, all essentially with one another. This differentiation is not the result of the imposition of a principle of individuation or the application of any form or structure that is not itself material. It relies only on materialism's capacity to reach the limit of matter in the nothing which, for Nancy, is the "with." "[The 'with'] really is, 'in truth,' a mark [*un trait*] drawn out over the void, which crosses over it and underlines it at the same time, thereby constituting the traction and tension of the void" (*BSP*, 62).

According to this materialist ontology, bodies are exposed to one another across the void and this is how being is exposed. Nancy points out more than once that he conceives of beings in all their material variety—"inanimate, animate, sentient, speaking, thinking, having weight, and so on" (*BSP*, 84) or "stones, plants, nails, gods . . . and 'humans'" (*BSP*, 3)—but, just as Dasein is fundamental to Heidegger's ontology, we turn out to occupy a position of privilege in Nancy's exposition of being. Singular bodies are placed or disposed in relation to each other, impenetrable to one another in the sense that each occupies a place to the exclusion of all other bodies. They are also impenetrable in the sense, mentioned above, that no body yields to the advances or indeed the glance of spirit that approaches or looks down from a point of view that is exterior to the world, that is, exterior to the being-together of bodies. As a result, a body is only approached or seen or touched by other bodies. There is no way to talk about being and being-with in the third person, no way to say that "it is" or "there is . . ." or indeed "I am." Instead, the only term for the being of bodies together in the world is "we are." Turning again to the language of Descartes, Nancy writes, "The truth of the *ego sum* is the *nos summus*; this 'we' announces itself through humanity for all beings 'we' are with, for existence in the sense of being-essentially-with, as a Being whose essence is the with" (*BSP*, 33).

This material being is all that being is. Being happens through a natal spacing—posing, disposing and exposing—of our bodies as well as according to our natal mode of being in time, which I explain below. Moreover, material being is and is in relation according to our natal mode of relation. It is not that there were no stones or fish, fibers or breath (*BSP*, 3) before there were humans, but rather that what existed without us could exist only factically, and not intelligibly. Without our being there to expose being as shared, that is, without our being there to say "we," the fact *that* fish and fibers *were* could not emerge as the problem of facticity, which is to say, as the demand for sense. By saying "we," we open up the distinction between the fact that we beings are and what that fact means; we open up the world as the infinite movement of fact and sense towards one another and we expose the singularity of finite beings as plural singularity.

What this means in terms of temporality is that we are bodies that come to be and pass away according to the specific rhythm of "being born, dying, open, closed, enjoying [*jouissant*], suffering, touching one another, swerving" (*C*, 65; trans. modified). The syncopated temporality of our birth means that we are always running to catch up with ourselves, always struggling to make sense of the fact that we already are. Additionally, even as birth sets us into relation, it is also our coming to be as singular beings. Heidegger begins his existential analytic with the remark that the being in question is "in each case mine [*je meines*]."[9] Nancy's version of this "each time" is the singular birth to presence of each of us. Being is each time me—existing, material, extended me. What drives his singular plural analytic is not the groundlessness of Being but rather the thought that every being, every singular coming-to-presence, every singular exposition, is itself groundless.[10] Each new coming is the origin; the world begins its turn each time with me (*BSP*, 19); the creation *ex nihilo*, creation after no model, happens with each one of us.

This is neither an individualistic nor an anthropocentric (or even zoo-centric) ontology. Even as I speak in terms of *my* birth, it is with an appreciation of the attenuated mineness that is at play in that specific phrase and of the singular plural existence of any "I." At most, it is fundamental in the sense of providing *a* starting point for ontology, but it does so as a point of access to the Being of beings, not as a foundation on which all ontology can be built. As Nancy writes,

> The simplest way to put this into language would be to say that humanity speaks existence, but what speaks through its speech says the whole of being. What Heidegger calls "the ontico-ontological privilege" of Dasein is neither its prerogative nor its privilege: it gets Being on its way, but the Being of Dasein is nothing other than the Being of being. (*BSP*, 17)

In terms of natal spacing, birth sets us in place, disposes us among and with other singular material beings. Our coming to be—that is, the birth that has already taken place *as well as* the birth that is always taking (*BP*, 23)—is always a coappearing, not least in the sense that we are looking at the world almost as soon as the world sets eyes on us. Yet exposure happens earlier and more intimately, as Nancy allows when he addresses exposition as *expeausition*, folding *peau*, French for skin, into a word that otherwise suggests the work of vision. We are *ex-peaused*, skin to skin and flesh to flesh from the earliest moments of our existence, when we come to be as finite beings with and within another singular finite being. Those earliest moments happen in our mothers' bodies but in the mode of being-with as well as within, *partes extra partes*. Our spatial, extended existence means that we are at a distance from one another. Even as our bodies will later reach out and touch and entwine, they will nonetheless remain in a relation of exteriority; our natal spacing is the fact that this is the case right down to the touch of the fetus and the maternal body. This, even before the enunciation of "we," is the exposure or exposed sharing that gives rise to what Nancy terms the prelinguistic mutual interpellation of singularities.[11] Even in the womb, touch separates as it brings together; material being is originally shared out (*partagé*) even as it is most intimately shared (*partagé*).[12]

ON THE THRESHOLD OF FINITUDE

The tools Nancy offers for thinking natal spacing come not in a consideration of the maternal–fetal body relation but through an analysis of the (not unrelated) sharing that happens in sex. Lacan pronounces that there is no sexual relation ("*Il n'y a pas de rapport sexuel*") but Nancy's response, in *L'« il y a » du rapport sexuel* [The "there is" of sexual relation], is that sex is the relation that reveals relation as such while simultaneously revealing us as finite, in-finite beings who are always coming to be.[13] In a gesture towards the relation between sex and birth (or, more accurately, between the sexual relation on the one hand and the relation of parents and children on the other), Nancy acknowledges this coming to be as happening out of the generative sexual relationship that is the origin of each of us. Lacan was right if the claim was that there was no such *thing* as the sexual relation; this no-thing-ness between a couple is the ground for the pleasure that exceeds their relation, and, occurring as procreation, it is the nothingness at the ground of each life. The essay provides for a material but also essentially *generational* ontology in which we move toward and beyond one another.

Sexual relation is already an odd term. As Nancy points out, it has a legalistic or medical air and is a strictly physical or physiological objectification of something more appropriately designated by verbs. Just as we must understand being as a verb if ontology is to be kept in motion, sex, as the revelation of relation as such and therefore of being as such, must be understood as an action rather than an object. We talk about having sex, or making love, but both terms do the work of objectification; "sleeping together" quite precisely misses the action itself. The French word is *baiser*: As a noun, it means "a kiss"; as a verb, it is best translated as "to fuck."[14] Thus, the term "sexual relation" is already an attempt to convert an action into something that can be reported—related—for a medical record or before a court. The attempt is doomed to failure, suggesting that "there is no sexual relation" simply means that "there is no report or account that captures what it is that happens when a couple couples" (*IRS*, 17). It is not that all accounts of the sexual relation must fail because of some lack in language; the ontological point is that the sexual relation is not a thing at all.

When Nancy writes that relation is "of the order of what the Stoics called the incorporeal" (*IRS*, 21), he is not retreating to a version of spirit or *res cogitans*. He is rather restating the materialist insight that what happens between bodies is precisely not-bodied. The incorporeal—for the Stoics, this consisted of the fourfold of space, time, emptiness and the said—is what makes it possible for bodies to distinguish themselves. Without it, there would be an undifferentiated material mass. We have seen that distinction separates and makes relation possible, nowhere more clearly than in the sexual relation.[15] Nancy writes, "The sexual is not an example of the category 'relation'; rather, in the sexual, relation has its integral/integrated extension and exposition" (*IRS*, 26). He does not claim this ontological privilege of sex as originary, but rather points to its capacity to reveal our finitude and also our infinity; "[w]hen one makes love, one poses or exposes relation *as such*" (*IRS*, 51).

The two terms—"relation" and the "sexual"—do not coincide but are understood together. Citing Aquinas, Nancy argues that relation is "accidental, that is, itself related to some substance or subject that it is itself not. . . . In other words, on the one hand relation and separation of subjects are the same thing, and, on the other, this same thing is sameness itself as differing/deferring itself" (*IRS*, 24). Thus the logic of relation is neither a logic of identity nor a logic of constitutive loss (*IRS*, 25). It is a logic that instead owes something to that other Lacanian axiom "that there is no all at all." Relation and the sexual share this differing/deferring structure (which is also, as I argued above, the structure of creation). The sexual is no more substantial than relation. Rather, Nancy writes:

> [T]he sexual is its own differing and its own distinction. To distinguish oneself as sex or as sexed is precisely 1) what makes sex or sexed-ness, 2) what makes sexual relation possible and, 3) what does not create its own entelechy or end. For no-one is man or woman without remainder, no more than anyone is homo- or heterosexual without remainder. (*IRS*, 27)

This is neither to reify sexual difference, nor simply to multiply sexual differences. Once again, it is a matter of displacing the thought of thing and substance and setting relation in motion:

> The difference of sexes is not the difference between two or several things, each one subsisting for itself as one (one sex): it is not like a difference between types or between individuals, nor is it a difference in nature or degree. It is the difference of sex insofar as sex defers itself. (*IRS*, 30)

Understanding this *différance* in terms of desire means grasping a *movement* of difference that is not driven by loss. There is no object of desire, Nancy argues, in the sense that what is desired is not a static, autonomous thing. He writes, "What desire desires is not objectified, is not placed before it, over against it, but instead is a part of the desiring movement. . . . It is neither a lost object nor the subject of a quest, but the projection itself, the throwing, the sending, the address" (*IRS*, 35). This is what is revealed in the Freudian analysis of the tension of desire and pleasure, or, in Nancy's terms, the infinity of desire-pleasure, "which is the infinity of sex deferring itself" (*IRS*, 35).

According to the Cartesian schema, infinity forms a pair with finitude: there is the infinite thinking substance (God) and the finite thinking substance (the ego). Finitude on this model is a state of lacking the scope of the infinite; it is the state of having boundaries beyond which lies all that infinity has and finitude lacks. At the same time, these boundaries make finitude complete and graspable in a way that infinity is not by virtue of infinity's having no end. The French is "*fin*"; the verb "to finish" is "*finir*." *In-fini*, an adjective, can thus be read as *not finished*, more readily suggesting an on-going temporal state than the spatial infinity that comes to mind with Descartes. Rather than finitude being a small space carved out in the great expanse of the infinite, what is finite is what is over and done, while what is infinite is endless. It is not that the infinite is not yet over, but rather that it is not the sort of thing that is ever over. It goes on; it keeps moving.

If *finition* is the process of finishing, of adding the final touches to something as the finishers employed in the fashion industry or in construction take care of the *finissage* of a garment or a building, giving it a finished look, then *infinition* is the eschewing of that, the refusal of that final polish, the refusal of the boundary where we would be obliged to stop. It is unfinishing that renders something in-finite. It is also where sex and relation come together again.

> [T]here is sexual relation in force everywhere relation finds itself in play . . . that is to say, everywhere where something is in play that we could call an *actual infinition* [infinition en acte] of two, or more than two, finite realities turning towards one another, opening to one another the intimacy of their infinity. Nothing can define jouissance and relation better than the *intimacy* of the *infinite* and the *infinity* of the *intimate*. (*IRS*, 44)

Relation is incorporeal but it occurs between bodies. There is no better image for this than the one produced by Plato in Aristophanes' speech in the *Symposium*: humans are originally half-people, each of whom was once attached to another as part of a single rounded body with four arms, four legs, two sets of genitals, and so on (190d). These half-people were finite realities created by the cut of Apollo and then tweaked and arranged by Hephestus, their genitals and heads rearranged until they were finished off. But built into them—into us—is a propensity to turn to one another, exposing to one another the deepest, most intimate parts of themselves, the parts that shows their *in*finition, their lack of finish. This is the intimacy of the infinite and the infinity of the intimate.

It is not a matter of the bad infinity that involves being forever stuck in a dead end, the infinity Nancy describes in Christian terms as the infinity of the missing object. Instead, this is the good infinity of—again in Christian terms—the rising subject, the actual infinity that applies to the act because the act always surpasses, exceeds, and undoes itself. It is of the essence of sex that it exceeds itself; this is the sense of its infinity (*IRS*, 39). Relation, thanks precisely to its finitude, punctuates that infinity, interrupting it, giving it pause, shaping it, and finishing it off. After all, what happens when Aristophanes' half-people fuck? If they were originally cut from one of the man–woman circles, they have babies and, if they came from man–man origins, they have the pleasure of sex and can go about the affairs of the city. (The woman–woman combination fades from sight [191b-e].) In both cases, relation binds them together as though to restore their wholeness but, in both cases, sex goes beyond them and their relation, generating pleasure and children. The original, complete—and therefore monstrous—circle people had no knowledge and no need of either.[16]

Insofar as we think of ourselves as complete or susceptible to completion, we are drawn on by the promise of relation, only to be undone by the excess of the sexual. Insofar as we engage in the deeply modern endeavor of approaching perfection, we engage coming to be as the experience of increasing coherence, autonomy, and certainty, as in Descartes' emergence out of the accumulated uncertainties and half-knowledge of childhood into the self-certain clarity of the *cogito*.[17] Insofar as we understand our coming to be sexual according to the same model, we dwell on the moment of determination—the "finition"—of certain sexed identities (which even Nancy acknowledges) without also appreciating the infinition of those identities exposed in sex. Making love is an action in which the actors expose their own infinition, "on the threshold of finitude" (*IRS*, 51). Once we also grasp that we come to be—which is also to say, come to be sexual—*sexually*, we see that it is an essentially natal finitude.

Despite their shared structure, the excess of pleasure and the excess of fertility have nothing to do with one another; they need not coincide and the one need not be superimposed on the other, since pleasure is not the generative force and the child is not the product of pleasure. They stand, rather, as two distinct figures of the incalculability and un-relatability of excess, figures that, if anything, seem to avoid knowing about one another at all (*IRS*, 42). Yet, much as pleasure ignores fertility and much as the child avoids recognizing herself in the relation of her parents, it remains the case that we each come to be out of a sexual relation and the infinity that is exposed—not brought about—when we make love has its origin in the fertile sexual relation from which we emerged.

BIRTH *EX NIHILO*

When philosophy has attended to this emergence, it has construed it in terms of distrust (Descartes), conflict (Hegel), anxiety (Heidegger) or love

(Oliver).[18] I have been arguing, using Nancy's work, that the sexual relation is, in any case, infinite in the sense of *unfinished* and *unfinishable*; moreover, it is materially so and this is what has yet to be made concrete. We emerge within and out of our mothers' bodies. As we saw above, Hegel writes of the soul's emergence and Nancy discusses the status of the child in the mother. Now we must approach the same question in the most material, embodied terms. Nancy argues that the child in the mother *is* only insofar as it is in another. The fetus is never part of the maternal body, but it cannot differentiate itself from itself; it *is* only insofar as it is acted on. Yet what would it mean for a fetus to differentiate itself from itself, even as it has its being in another? What would that look like? How would we recognize it?

Mark Taylor argues that the work of differentiating ourselves gets under way in our bodies' attempts to create immune identity, though he notes at the same time that this attempt often fails.[19] The function of our bodies' immune system is to identify foreign elements—bacteria, viruses, transplanted organs—and to mount a defense against attack. The fetus is differentiated *by* the maternal body, but this can happen only because what is produced there is a new body that is genetically only half-related to it. Sexual difference and sexual reproduction mean that what comes to be in the womb is immunologically different from the maternal body that puts it in place and constitutes its place. From the point of view of the maternal immune system, how does the fetus escape detection and rejection as a foreign entity? The answer appears to lie in the placenta, the point of contact between the bloodstreams of fetus and maternal body. The placenta is generated from the fetus' genetic material and is a place remarkably lacking in the markers that would alert the maternal body to the foreignness of what she is carrying. Thus, the fetus is indeed differentiated by and from the maternal body but in such a way that, immunologically speaking, the womb is a relatively neutral space where the fetus begins the work of learning identity in the original chaos of difference.[20]

According to Taylor's analysis, the relation between the maternal body and fetus cannot be considered originary. It is not the forum in which the relation of self and non-self has its first expression because "the body is [already] inwardly divided,"[21] as when the immune system that is meant to defend against intrusion attacks the body itself. The capacity to distinguish between self and non-self is not innate, and must be acquired. "One's immune system does not seem to recognize the epitopes on molecules and cells that are part of one's own body. . . . Self-tolerance is . . . something the immune system 'learned' in embryonic life by either eliminating or 'paralyzing' all lymphocytes that would produce self-recognizing antibodies."[22] This makes the *auto*immune response originary or, as Taylor puts it, "the auto-immune response is antecedent to both self-unity and self-identity." But this is like saying that God is the creator of time and existed before time. Just as *before* has no referent in the absence of time, *auto*immunity has no referent when there is as yet no self. More precisely, then, the immune/autoimmune response is functioning before it can begin to learn the difference between self and non-self and before it can learn to tolerate self. This is also to say that it functions before its functioning can be differentiated into immunity and autoimmunity.

This is not a question of an initial moment of confusion or a distinctly fetal condition. If it were, medicine would know little about it given the relative invisibility—advances in medical imaging notwithstanding—of the fetus compared with the availability to vision of—not to mention the therapeutic demands made by—child and adult bodies. How then do we know about this aspect of fetal life? Rather than a case of Hegelian mantic knowledge, we have to think in terms of the Heideggerian "whence?" The question of origin is an echo of our coming to be; the fact that autoimmunity remains common in adult bodies is the echo of the original chaos of immune/autoimmune responses. Grave's disease, Reiter's syndrome, rheumatic fever, systemic lupus, rheumatoid arthritis, Crohn's disease, myasthenia gravis, multiple sclerosis, and insulin-dependent diabetes are all autoimmune diseases common enough to indicate that the learning, once it is under way, very often remains incomplete. Taylor writes, "Though it seems impossible, the body is simultaneously itself and other than itself."[23]

Thus, when the relation fetus and maternal body is specified as the first forum for identity formation, it is as the immunological forum created by the fetus itself as a product of sexual difference. Maternity and paternity together determine the child as new and unknown. Maternity, in addition, requires the opening of a space within the woman's body that is not precisely her body but that nevertheless marks her as a maternal body. Having shared in the generation of difference, the maternal body withholds its identity in order to make possible the development of another identity in the course of the fetal struggle to discern self and non-self. It is a struggle that is not resolved at the moment of birth and may never be resolved. Autoimmune diseases manifest themselves at every stage of life and are a concrete instance of what Nancy calls the passing of identity. Moreover, the details of the functioning of immunity/autoimmunity before and after birth suggest a continual passing that does not begin in a conflict between self and other, self and mother, but in a space that is formed within and by the maternal body and configured as an immunologically privileged space by the joint efforts of the fetus—itself a strange amalgam of maternal and paternal identity—and the maternal body. The material that goes to make up the fetus's body and the placenta is provided by the maternal body: the form it takes and, in particular, the immunological nonidentity of the placenta, is determined by the maternal–paternal combination that is the new fetus. The space thus formed is where differing and deferring of self and non-self gets under way; it is the nothing out of which we are born.

CONCLUSION

The world is created *ex nihilo* and, once we understand the world as the world of bodies, this is another way of saying that we are born out of nothing. Birth does not stand for or stand in for the creation; birth *is* the creation of the world. Bodies—natal, growing, changing, aging bodies—are always coming, always something other than entirely present and this lays at the root of the Nancian impulse that everything is possible (*BP*, 197). It is also the source of our responsibility for creation and for being creative. This is far from being an exhortation to fertility[24] because, as Nancy writes in *The Sense of the World*, "[t]hat which is born in birth is not, first of all, a product or the engendered term of an author or parents, but precisely *being* insofar as nothing posits it and insofar as all exposes it, always singular being" (*SW*, 155). There is no accounting for the fact that we are here; there is no sense to our being here, *other than our being here*. This is what Nancy identifies as the responsibility of sense. If, as I claimed at the beginning, the world is the resolution of fact into sense and sense into fact, it is we who resolve, and we do all that that word connotes by dissolving, transforming, harmonizing, deciding on and deciding for our being here in our finitude. We do it infinitely.

We do not do it willy-nilly. Being is not a state but an activity and there are distinct and competing ways of being a world of bodies; Nancy identifies the globalized version and the world-formation version, a distinction François Raffoul and David Pettigrew make clear in their translators' introduction to *The Creation of the World* or *Globalization*:

> On the one hand, there is the uniformity produced by a global economical and technological logic—Nancy specifies, "a global injustice against the background of general equivalence"—leading towards the opposite of an inhabitable world, to "the un-world." And, on the other hand, there is the possibility of an authentic world-forming, that is, of a making of the world and of a making sense that Nancy will call . . . a "creation" of the world.[25]

The resolution of fact and sense is the movement—never-completed—of the one toward the other. What I have argued here is that, as creation, it moves according to the syncopated rhythm of our natality, the beat of our generational life.

NOTES

1. See Jean-Luc Nancy, *Corpus*, trans. Richard A. Rand (New York: Fordham University Press, 2009), p. 31. Henceforth cited as C. See also Jean-Luc Nancy, *The Sense of the World*, trans. Jeffrey Librett (Minneapolis: University of Minnesota Press, 1997), p. 155. Henceforth cited as *SW*.

2. Descartes' letter to Elizabeth, June 28, 1643, quoted in C, 11.

3. We do not commonly think of bodies as impenetrable, but Nancy addresses the penetration involved in sex (e.g., although it is more than an example) using the term *intussception* from the Latin *intus* meaning within and *suscipere*, to take up.

4. For an explanation of *partes extra partes*, literally "parts outside parts," see Ian James, *The Fragmentary Demand* (Stanford: Stanford University Press, 2006), p. 143: "The structure of parts outside parts is central to Nancy's thinking of the spacing of sense and of the effraction of sense and matter that is the 'taking place' of bodies and the creation of the shared world."

5. Ibid., p. 137.

6. Jean-Luc Nancy, *Birth to Presence*, trans. Brian Holmes et al. (Stanford: Stanford University Press, 1993), p. 200. Henceforth cited as *BP*.

7. Gaston Bachelard, *Le matérialisme rationnel* (Paris: Presses Universitaires de France, 1953), p. 4.

8. Jean-Luc Nancy, *Being Singular Plural*, trans. Anne O'Byrne and Robert Richardson (Stanford: Stanford University Press, 1999), pp. 83–84. Henceforth cited as *BSP*. See also Marie-Eve Morin, "Thinking Things: Heidegger, Sartre, Nancy" *Sartre Studies International* 15:2 (Winter 2009), pp. 35–53.

9. Martin Heidegger, *Being and Time*, trans. John Maquarrie and Edward Robinson (New York: Harper, 1962), H. 42, pp. 67–68.

10. Heidegger writes in the *Beiträge zur Philosophie*, "When being is posited as infinite, it is precisely then that it is determined. If it is posited as finite, it is then that its absence of ground is affirmed," quoted in Jean-Luc Nancy, *A Finite Thinking*, ed. Simon Sparks (Stanford: Stanford University Press, 2003), p. 9. See also Morin, op. cit.

11. See Jean-Luc Nancy, *The Inoperative Community*, ed. Peter Connor (Minneapolis: University of Minneapolis Press, 1991), p. 29. See also "Verbum caro factum," in *Dis-Enclosure: The Deconstruction of Christianity*, trans. by Bettina Bergo, Gabriel Malenfant and Michael B. Smith (New York: Fordham University Press, 2008), pp. 81–84, where incarnation is described as the becoming world or flesh of the world.

12. This is also the structure of sense. See *BSP*, 2.

13. Jean-Luc Nancy, *L'« il y a » du rapport sexuel* (Paris: Galilée, 2001). Henceforth cited as *IRS*.

14. This choice is not an altogether happy one but I have not found a better option among the alternatives, which range from the archaic term *to swive* (my thanks to Tim Hyde for drawing my attention to this) to all the too familiar sex verbs in contemporary slang.

15. See *BSP*, pp. 91–92 where Nancy elaborates on the syncopation in the relationship between the presupposition and disposition of our being.

16. Their excess, rather, took the form of a violent assault on the gods. See *Symposium* 190b.

17. See the opening sentence of Descartes' *Meditations* and also Susan Bordo's commentary on Descartes' desire to shed his childhood self in "Selection from *The Flight to Objectivity*" in *Feminist Interpretations of René Descartes*, ed. Susan Bordo (University Park: Pennsylvania State University Press, 1999).

18. See Descartes' First *Meditation*, Hegel's famous Antigone analysis in *The Phenomenology of Spirit*, section 470, Heidegger's *Being and Time* § 40 and finally Kelly Oliver, *Family Values* (London: Routledge, 1997), pp. 60–61.

19. Mark Taylor, *Nots* (Chicago: Chicago University Press, 1993), pp. 214–256.

20. Derrida makes considerable use of the term *autoimmunity*. See, for example, *Religion*, ed. Jacques Derrida and Gianni Vattimo (Cambridge: Polity, 1996), pp. 42, 51, 65. But he has insisted, at least in conversation, that the term for him has nothing to do with the biological occurrence of autoimmunity. This claim is complicated by a footnote to *Religion* where he writes: "As the phenomenon of these antibodies is extended to a broader zone of pathology and as one resorts increasingly to the positive virtues of immuno-depressants destined to limit the mechanisms of rejection and to facilitate the tolerance of certain organ transplants, we feel ourselves authorized to speak of a sort of general logic of auto-immunization" (p. 72 n. 27). His resistance to the biological model is, in my view, a resistance to the mobilization of that model as determinative or originary in a way that accepts uncritically the distinction that allows biology to present itself as the real or the natural and therefore beyond question.

21. *Nots*, p. 253.

22. Jerne, quoted in ibid., p. 252

23. Ibid., pp. 252–253.

24. Hannah Arendt writes of "the aboriginal command, 'Be ye fruitful and multiply,' in which it is as though the voice of nature herself speaks to us." Hannah Arendt, *The Human Condition* (Chicago: Chicago University Press, 1958), p. 106.

25. Jean-Luc Nancy, *The Creation of the World* or *Globalization*, trans. François Raffoul and David Pettigrew (Albany: State University of New York Press, 2007), p. i.

SIX

ON INTERFACE

Nancy's Weights and Masses

Graham Harman

Elsewhere I have called for an object-oriented philosophy,[1] a project inspired by the phenomenological tradition. In Husserl, we have *intentional* objects: apples or mailboxes that form integral units for perception even though their sensual profiles shift wildly from one moment to the next. In Heidegger, with a bit of finessing, we have *real* objects: unified tool-beings that withdraw not only from theoretical description and pragmatic interaction, but from any form of causal relation at all. This dual interplay between intentional objects and their accidents, and real objects and their relations, offers a fourfold alternative to the stale Kantian rift (and equally stale post-Kantian marriage) between human and world, whose interplay is now dismally cemented as the sole topic of philosophy. Taken as a pair, Husserl and Heidegger enable a new, weird realism, in which the relation between palm trees and raindrops is no less a philosophical problem than the gap between speakers and signifieds.

Against the endless reign of humans and their written texts, object-oriented philosophy argues for a fresh return to the things themselves. A handful of partial allies is easily found in the Husserl/Heidegger tradition, in a group of thinkers I have termed the "carnal phenomenologists": Levinas, Merleau-Ponty, and Alphonso Lingis.[2] These authors are linked through their vivid attention to concrete entities such as bread, haunted houses, and parrots, and by the rare stylistic gifts through which they depict such objects to the reader. Yet there is another line of heirs descending from the school of Husserl, one not always on my personal list of heroes. Two of the most prominent figures of this alternate lineage are Jacques Derrida and Jean-Luc Nancy. My objections are worth noting at the outset because they make my admiration for Nancy's "Corpus" an interesting surprise. The subject matter of Derrida and Nancy is rarely the field of specific objects such as trees and radio towers, but often is restricted to famous books. Instead of giving crisp evocations of the life of sailboats or zebras, they prefer to enact in prose all the deferrals and impossibilities that they revel in describing. Here the poetry of the carnal phenomenologists gives way to a thicket of self-references, a mass of parentheses and puns, and an inflationary universe of footnotes. In many respects, it is the opposite of the style and content of philosophy I have endorsed.

Nevertheless, the two approaches share an obvious bond in their phenomenological heritage. In terms of intellectual DNA, object-oriented philosophy surely has more in common with Derrida and Nancy than it does with Deleuze, Badiou, Žižek, and cognitive science. Hence, the usual failure of Derrida and Nancy to take an object-oriented turn should be viewed as generously as possible, like the unfamiliar mannerisms of visiting cousins. There must be a clear point of divergence where they depart from phenomenology by an alternate exit. The problem is less about how to escape the textual labyrinths of Derrida and Nancy than about how to enter them in the first place. Luckily, there is a striking passage at the close of Nancy's "Corpus"[3] that verges on object-oriented thinking. Instead of vintage Nancy, we find an opposite stylistic excess. This is the practice (of which I have justly been accused myself) of occasionally producing random lists of intriguing objects in the hope of jolting the reader into a field of concrete entities where neon lights and wild dogs have the same philosophical rights as the human subject and all its decentered, deconstructed, post-human stand-ins. In the final sentence of "Corpus," Nancy's object-oriented turn reaches a startling extreme:

> Ribs, skulls, pelvises, irritations, shells, diamonds, drops, foams, mosses, excavations, fingernail moons, minerals, acids, feathers, thoughts, claws, slates, pollens, sweat, shoulders, domes, suns, anuses, eyelashes, dribbles, liqueurs, slits, blocks, slicing, squeezing, removing, bellowing, smashing, burrowing, spoiling, piling up, sliding, exhaling, leaving, flowing—. (*BP*, 207)

Other than the stylized shift from nouns to verbs near the end, this passage would be fully at home in the works of Lingis, although Derrida would never have written it. Here is a point of entry, then. By the end of "Corpus," Nancy sounds like a carnal phenomenologist—like Lingis charting some Pacific island landscape. Yet this is the same Nancy who began the essay in his more customary style:

> A *corpus* is not a discourse: however, what we need here is a corpus. We need a *corpus*, a *cata*log, the recitation of an empirical logos that, without transcendental reason, would be a gleaned list, random in its order or in its degree of completion, a corpus of the body's *entries*: dictionary entries, entries into language, body registers, registers of bodies. (*BP*, 189)

And this is a sentence that might have come from the pen of Derrida, but that Lingis would never dream of writing. Somehow, during the few dozen pages of "Corpus," a strange alchemy occurs that brings Nancy closer to the carnal phenomenologists than Derrida ever was. This makes his essay an ideal point of comparison with the object-oriented approach. It needs to be seen what Nancy has to say about objects, even though he rejects this word no less than Heidegger does. Nancy's term of choice is in fact *corpus*, a name for specific entities ranging from shells, minerals, feathers, and suns to items of more prurient interest.

THE CORPUS

The most refreshing aspect of Nancy's essay stems from his recurring catalogs of things. It is not typical of recent French thought to appeal to ribs, skulls, diamonds, and mosses. Or at least it is not typical to speak of them as actual bodies, rather than as figures of speech quoted from Valéry or Artaud. Although Nancy holds that literature does more justice to bodies than philosophy does (*BP*, 193), he is still concerned with these bodies themselves, not with some famous writer's passing mention of them. Although it remains to be seen what Nancy means by the bodies themselves, he has already set up shop in the most sensual zone of phenomenology. Those who label Husserl an idealist do so with justice, despite his mantra that consciousness always aims at something beyond itself. But Husserl is not just any idealist. Whereas Fichte and Hegel could only remain mute before all diamonds and moss, Husserl might easily spend a semester analyzing their appearance in consciousness. He is not just an idealist, but an object-oriented one. Plenty of action unfolds in Husserl's intentional objects, which stand obstinately before us despite every movement of negation. Husserl's field of consciousness flickers with impenetrable icons. Against all odds, Jean-Luc Nancy now joins him amidst the things themselves.

Although the opening style of Nancy's essay is overly mannered, the news here is already good. In the first two pages he asserts that bodies are nonlinguistic, autonomous, determinate, and inaccessible. As we have seen, bodies are not language: "a *corpus* is not a discourse: however, what we need here is a corpus" (*BP*, 189). What we need, stylistically, is "a gleaned list, random in its order or in its degree of completion. . . . a passive recording, as by a seismograph of bodies, of senses, and again of the entries of these bodies. . . . We need to recite, to blazon, body after body, place after place, entry by entry" (*BP*, 189). Nancy's seismograph seems to be in good working order: "foot, belly, mouth, nail, wound, beating, sperm, breast, tattoo, eating, nerve, touching, knee, fatigue . . ." (*BP*, 190). What is surprising here is that bodies are initially treated as so many independent *units*. The usual move in recent French thought is to undercut a body's presence by saying that it is contaminated from without, interwoven in a web of signs that cannot be reduced to mere indications, such that bodies are deprived of independence. Although Nancy will not entirely renounce this procedure, his random seismograms do register a certain autonomy to bodies. And this autonomy goes hand in hand with determinacy: "Two bodies cannot occupy the same space simultaneously" (*BP*, 180). Though mixing will occur, not everything mixes with everything. The blender has its limits; bodies are not *completely* contaminated.

Furthermore, Nancy concedes that we do not have access to these bodies. Or rather, we do and do not have access to them. As he puts it, the previous catalogue of bodies "would be possible only if we had access to bodies, only if they were not impenetrable, as physics defines them. Bodies impenetrable to language, and languages impenetrable to bodies, bodies themselves" (*BP*, 189). And because we do not have such access, "failure is given at the outset, and intentionally so" (*BP*, 190). But paradoxically, "a *double* failure is given: a failure to produce a discourse on the body, also the failure *not* to produce a discourse on it. A double bind, a psychosis" (*BP*, 190; my emphasis). Yet this is less a psychosis than a simple return to Socrates, despite the recent habit of using Plato's dialogues as a mascot for naïve classicism. Nancy's "psychosis" is no different from Socrates' struggle with virtue in the *Meno*: a virtue that recedes from all definition, but never entirely so. Socrates fails to produce a discourse on virtue, and also fails *not* to produce it. There is no shame in endorsing this classical gesture, which is the founding insight of philosophy in a sense that no one has succeeded in dismantling. Wisdom is not achieved, but wisdom is sought, even as it eludes us. *Philosophia* is still what we do, despite Heidegger and Derrida's endless claims to the contrary.

As a term for our dual access and non-access to bodies, Nancy selects the excellent name of *touch*. To touch something is to make contact with it even while remaining separate from it because the entities that touch do not fuse together. To touch is to caress a surface that belongs to something else, but never to master or consume it. It requires a certain space between beings, but also an interface where they meet. How can we touch something without touching it? Every Socratic definition of the undefinable faces the same problem. So, too, do the Islamic and French occasionalist traditions (only God can touch anything), and their upside-down heirs in the skeptical and Kantian traditions (only human habit, custom, or categories can make things touch). "How does one touch? . . . *Comment toucher?*" This may be the central problem in the history of philosophy because it governs all Socratic quests. "What does a word touch, if not a body? But there you have it: How can one get hold of the body? I am already speechless" (*BP*, 190). Far from it. Nancy goes on to say a good deal more, from which I choose just a few key points.

MASS AND WEIGHT

Two basic features of Nancy's notion of bodies immediately stand out. First, they are not images of some deeper original model because this would repeat the unwanted denigration of bodies found in Plato's cave, where "the body first was thought . . . as buried darkness into which light only penetrates in the form of reflections, and reality only in the form of shadows" (*BP*, 191). The corpus is not just the surface of some cryptic underlying reality; Nancy's world is not one that honors the dimension of depth, of reality copied by derivative surface. The obvious risk associated with this step is that bodies might be reduced to their currently accessible features, thereby allowing them no excess beyond their presentation here and now. For Nancy, the ontology of the self-sufficient surface is no less dangerous than that of a hidden real world. But "bodies resist" (*BP*, 197). How can they resist without being hidden, real things that lie deeper than secondary cave-shadows? Nancy's attempted solution lies in his appeal to a *process* (my term) in which bodies are perpetually still-to-come, a constant emergence. This appeal to ongoing dynamism sets out to prevent bodies from being identified with any particular represented configuration.

The appeal is neither to presence nor to absence, but to a "*birth* to presence." In his preface to the English-language collection of the same name, Nancy makes this clear: "presence in its entirety is coming: which means, not 'having come' (past participle) but a *coming* (the action of coming, arriving). Presence is what is born, and does not cease being born. Of it and to it there is birth, and only birth" (*BP*, 2). And on the same page we read, "what is born has no form, nor is it the fundament that is born. 'To be born' means rather to transform, transport, and entrance all determinations. . . . It is the same with all verbs" (*BP*, 2). And finally, "nothing will have preexisted birth, and nothing will have succeeded it. It always 'is,' it never 'is.' To be born is the name of being" (*BP*, 3). Everything that occurs is immanent in the world we know, not hailing from some depth underneath. Yet this immanent world is always a verb: churning, transforming, and birthing rather than sitting in stasis as a frozen form.

Second, bodies are not entirely isolated from one another. In an admirable pairing of terms, Nancy contrasts the *weight* that bodies exert on other bodies with the *mass* through which they concentrate in themselves. "All bodies weigh against one another: celestial bodies and callous bodies, vitreous bodies, and all others. . . . Their weight is the rising of their mass to the surface" (*BP*, 199). This might give the impression that Nancy is skillfully balancing the internal and external lives of bodies, letting them harbor a private mass that rises to view while not reducing them to their mutual weight. But the weight of mutual relations takes clear precedence; mass serves primarily as an alibi against the charge of reducing things to their interactions, which if pressed too far would dissolve them as discrete bodies. Nancy had already spoken as follows: "a body always weighs; it lets itself weigh, be weighed. *A body does not have a weight, it is a weight*" (*BP*, 198–199; my emphasis). And, "it is by touching the other that the body is a body, absolutely separated and shared" (*BP*, 204). But how can touching be responsible both for the interaction of bodies *and* for their separation? The answer is that bodies have no individual character outside their mutual touching and weighing. Nancy contends that even though bodies are "interlaced" (*BP*, 195) and mutually "engrammed" (*BP*, 202), they do not dissolve into one another (*BP*, 203). They are prevented from doing so by their mass, and thus have not yet risen to the surface. Yet this mass of bodies turns out to be little more than a traditional conception of matter: nothing determinate in itself, yet capable of becoming anything. As he puts it in "The Heart of Things," there is "the same heart for all things, for every thing . . ." (*BP*, 167). Stated more frankly,

> insofar as it is posited, exposed, insofar as it is the thing itself, every thing is *whatever*. The whatever of the "there is," or the anonymity of being, is being itself in the withdrawal through which it is the being of the thing. . . . "Whatever" is the indeterminateness of being in what is posited and exposed within the strict, determined concretion of a singular thing, and the indeterminateness of its singular existence. (*BP*, 174; my emphasis)

And more candidly still: "What marks the community of things? As *whatever* sort of things, they are interchangeable with one another. . . . One could say [that] . . . *some* thing is free to be a stone, a tree, a ball, Pierre, a nail, salt, Jacques, a number, a trace, a lioness, a marguerite" (*BP*, 186). There is no Pierre, no salt, and no lioness before they touch one another. The in-itself is a unified *whatever*, although occasional attempts are made to make each "whatever" unique, as in Nancy's unworkable attempt to draw on Leibniz without paying the price: "No thing-here is the same as another thing-here; such is Leibniz's principle" (*BP*, 181). Yet Leibniz pays for this principle of the identity of indiscernibles by injecting qualities directly into island-like monads. By contrast, Nancy's monad-free vision is one in which things gain determinacy only through mutual touch. What precedes this touch is merely "whatever," and two whatevers would have nothing to distinguish them. Hence, there cannot really be "whatevers" in the plural.

This seems to return us to the ancient pre-Socratic model of an indeterminate *apeiron* (just as with the Levinasian *il y a*, hypostatized into pieces only by human consciousness). Nancy makes a failed preemptive strike against this charge: "*hen panta*, the One-All, does not designate the 'one and the same thing' of all things but, on the contrary, the 'being the spacing of all things' of the One, which is not a thing" (*BP*, 187). Yet this does not strike at the heart of the accusation. It merely asserts that there is no shapeless One apart from the spacing between specific bodies; it does not provide for any spacing within the One itself. We are still left with a unified whatever and a determinate sphere of touching and resisting bodies. No form or determination is provided for anything outside the relational kingdom of mutual weights. Take an imagined glimpse behind the realm where bodies touch, weigh, and transform one another and you will find that they are no longer those bodies: they are merely "whatever." They are simply unformed matter.

To summarize, Nancy wants to account for the paradoxical sufficiency and insufficiency of bodies. They are self-sufficient insofar as they do not copy a real model in the manner of cave-shadows, but they are insufficient because they must be more than their current configuration in the world, under penalty of being exhausted by their presentation. His two-pronged strategy for addressing this paradox is as follows:

1. Bodies are not fixed, stable moments, but a perpetual coming-into-birth.
2. Bodies are not fully determined through their mutual contact, but each is a "whatever" capable of becoming anything else, which is precisely what prime matter means for Aristotle.

In short, process and matter are the keys to Nancy's corpus-based ontology. The common link between the two terms is clear enough. We know that Nancy does not hold that bodies can be reduced to their specific articulations here and now. Something must lie in reserve, unformatted in any sort of presence. Otherwise, bodies would always already be exhausted in the present and lose their resistance. Yet he makes the fateful assumption that whatever is withheld from representation cannot have a *form*. What he fears most is the two-tiered world of cave and sky, and allowing for hidden bodies already formed would reduce the mutually caressing bodies that we encounter to flickering simulacra in a cavern.

This evident worry has the following consequences. For Nancy, if the determinate form of bodies takes shape in a relational interplay of bodies weighing on each other, this can be countered only by a formless mass belonging to each body, but one that is also the same for all of them. And if the form of bodies refers to their adequate expression through the presence of an individual body, this is undercut only by appeal to a coming-to-birth that subverts each presence from within. In other words, when Nancy says that a diamond has form through its interaction with the bodies it touches, he is careful to add that it also remains autonomous as a shapeless *whatever* that allows it to unleash surprise and resistance to its neighbors. And even when Nancy considers the diamond as a visible form in isolation from its neighbors, this transient configuration is eclipsed, not by a veiled being of the diamond, but by an endless process of emergence, a ceaseless coming that can never be pinned down in a determinate shape.

CORPUS VS. OBJECT

All of this places Nancy at odds with the object-oriented view for which I have argued. This would not bother him because the term "object" is not one of his favorites: "knowledge wants an object, but with bodies there is only subject. . . . *The 'body' is grounds for not having any object*" (*BP*, 199). Although Nancy shares Heidegger's disdain for the word, it is for the opposite reason. For Heidegger, "object" refers to things reduced to mere representations, and hence they are too superficial to be true. For Nancy, "object" refers to an objective reality deeper than the cave-shadows, and hence is too falsely *deep* to be true. In my view, "object" is too flexible a term to waste on pejorative missions of this sort. Hence, I employ it as a positive name for the sole subject matter of philosophy as understood by Socrates and ratified by Nancy himself—that which cannot be touched and also cannot *not* be touched. This untouchable touchable deserves the name of "object." What I mean by an object is a concrete reality that has specific determination or form quite apart from its relations with anything else, and quite apart from its purely accidental way of being on the stage at any moment. Nancy shares this wish to give bodies more than their here-and-now, but he does this by appeal to process and matter, to birth and "whatever." He describes birth and whatever in such a way that they are devoid of all determination, that is, of any specific form. As I see it, this is the downfall of his theory, but also of similar theories found in Bruno, Schelling, and Deleuze, although the remainder of this chapter focuses simply on Nancy.

Nancy's return to specific bodies is refreshing when contrasted with most continental philosophy. Yet he immediately equates specificity with an overly determinate surface, and counteracts this surface with formless mass-matter and emergent birth. As we have already seen, the fact that the two always go together for Nancy, that there is no birth without something being born, and no formless "whatever" without a specific configuration of touching, does not address the real issue. It remains the case for Nancy that all determinacy of bodies is accessible, and that a whatever that withholds itself from access must be indeterminate. Why is he so reluctant to allow for *concealed* forms? The reason seems to lie in a simultaneous rejection of Plato's doubled world along with a full embrace of Kant's.

That is to say, Nancy is appalled by any model that would oppose veiled hammers to openly embodied ones, since this would reduce the embodied hammer to second-rate status. Yet he still needs some current of reality to throb beneath the immanent world, such that things will not be exhaustively representable. By shying away from shoes-in-themselves and dogs-in-themselves, he has no alternative but to endorse a formless layer of reality able to volatilize the transient determinate weights of bodies. The formless One is opposed to the formatted many, even as we hear repeatedly that the One exists only through its upsurge into the many. This aligns Nancy with a fairly mainstream consensus that dismisses individual objects as insufficient. It is said that the actual needs potentiality, or virtuality, or disembodied laws that the actual will follow as it transmutes into new states of the actual. What all such models share is the notion that there can be no hidden *actualities*, no determinate individuals apart from their relations to others, no cryptic entities. On this view there can only be relational forms, not *substantial* forms. If someone objects that substantial forms belong to a classical model of Western ontology that has been overcome, my answer is that the alternatives belong to a modernist model of Western ontology that *ought* to be overcome—a basically Kantian vision in which things are granted form only when they are shaped by some other entity. Against this model, we should pursue the paradox by which *objects* are what touch without touching. This is a paradox that spreads well beyond the bounds of human access to the world and into the fibers of the world itself, as when fire burns cotton or earthquakes topple boulders. The dilemma of touching and not-touching must always be a question of objects versus objects, not objects versus humans, formed bodies versus formless matter, or individual bodies versus global birth. What makes objects so fascinating is that they are determinate *despite* both separating and not separating themselves from the rest of the world.

Imagine that diamonds and moss are both found in some odd situation, perhaps an "Orientalist" scenario involving smugglers, headhunters, elephants, and monkeys. Imagine now that Nancy and Husserl are both on the scene and are asked to assess it. Nancy would say that these bodies all touch one another without touching, massaging each other's contours and jostling each other while somehow remaining discrete. He would not go so far as to say that they are entirely exhausted by these relations (as my allies Latour and Whitehead would wrongly say). Nancy needs some principle of excess outside the touching, under penalty of reducing all bodies to adequate presence. Yet the excess he comes up with is merely a "whatever" at the heart of things. Monkey is only monkey thanks to its touchings; what is left over is—*whatever*. Diamond is diamond only in its touchings; the diamond-residue outside these touchings is—again, *whatever*. Moss without its neighbors is—once more, the same *whatever*. This recurring term reminds us uncomfortably of the jaded speech of my fellow members of Generation X, who came of age using this dismissive word to smear everything into the same cynical pulp: "A real world? . . . Whatever."

Now contrast Nancy's account with Husserl's. At each moment, Husserl sees the diamond sparkle in different ways as he circles the scene. The monkey screeches ever more hoarsely, increasing tension in the moods of the nearby smugglers. The headhunters and elephants are witnessed in ominous approach, appearing ever larger in Husserl's field of view. Now, if Husserl wants to describe what belongs to the diamond or monkey outside their specific configurations, he will not call them *whatever*. In fact, this would be an obvious mistake. For Husserl, there is a clear difference between diamond-in-this-specific-format and diamond. We know this in the simplest of ways: the diamond undergoes numerous surface variations even as we continue to think of it as the same thing. It is our own sincerity that makes a split between the diamond and each of its transient profiles. Conscious beings subtract the accidents from a thing and vaguely sense its determinate core, even when they are hallucinating or utterly wrong. What stands opposed to diamond-in-this-specific-format is not "whatever," but *diamond*. What stands opposed to monkey-in-this-specific-format is *monkey*, not a shapeless mass of matter. This conclusion requires no gullible realist metaphysics because the real world is not yet at issue. All that is needed is a quick look at the field of perception, where bodies are *accepted* as the same bodies through countless shifting variations. But Nancy loses all sense of Husserl's tension between intentional objects and their accidental variations. For Nancy, a body is either completely determinate in its relations to other things, or it is merely whatever. Contrast this with Husserl, for whom a body (i.e., an intentional object) constantly withstands shifts in the regime of touches and weights, unless it shifts so greatly that we no longer admit it to be the same anymore. Husserl's object-oriented approach allows an intentional object to be form, not just matter, quite apart from its interactions with other perceived bodies.

Now imagine that Husserl departs, and Nancy is joined by Heidegger. It is nightfall. The humans and animals have fallen asleep, and the torch-light produces a fairly uniform glow on the diamonds. Nancy and Heidegger sit motionless in fairly stable moods, not circling the objects from various perspectives, but staring intently at one of the diamonds as an isolated individual. Both agree that the diamond cannot be reduced to its current manifestation; this would reduce it to mere presence without reserve. Yet their methods of escaping this predicament are entirely different. For Nancy, there can be no concealed diamond-in-itself, since this would reduce the present diamond to a mere shadow on a cave wall. Hence, he would speak only of an emergent process, a *birth* to presence that undercuts the claims of the diamond-here-and-now without positing a withdrawn, determinately formed diamond. By contrast, Heidegger would rescue the diamond from exhaustive presence through the familiar route of the tool-analysis.[4] For Heidegger, the diamond is irreducible to its presence-at-hand insofar as the situation does not exhaust its reality. The diamond is always full of surprises. It may have absorbed so much heat from the torches that it will scald the hand of the next person who touches it. It may be so riddled with unknown internal flaws that it shatters at the next sound echoing through the jungle. Through these surprising failures of expectation, we come to see that the diamond is something other than what we thought. In short, what lies outside the current presence of the diamond is not merely a process or a perpetual coming-to-birth. Rather, this perpetual birthing is possible only if the presence of the diamond does not exhaust its diamond-reality, which must exist elsewhere.

Returning to the more familiar case of the hammer from *Being and Time*, the tool does not surprise us with malfunction because of some form-less natal principle, but because of the difference between our previous use of the hammer and the hammer in its own cryptic, veiled, subterranean reality. What undercuts the presence of an object is not some vague process, but a *real* object not fully exhausted by its previous incarnation in relation to others. And here is the first moment where we might be accused of "naïve realism," although I would prefer to call it an *inevitable* realism, an unavoidable theory that objects have a specific structure whether we encounter them or not. As long as objects (Nancy's "bodies") are reduced to their fully determinate character here and now, there is no way to save their capacity for motion and change by appealing to a shapeless process or a uniform material whatever. At bottom this is nothing but the old *vis dormitiva* maneuver: The sleeping potion causes sleep by virtue of a sleeping-power, and bodies change by virtue of a changing-power, or *vis motiva*, that we might call by the name of "matter." But an appeal to matter does not solve the problem. The only way to account for dynamism in the world is to draw a distinction between real objects and the relational caricatures of them as encountered by other objects.

CONCLUSION

To summarize, Nancy recognizes no tension between objects and their accidents, or objects and their relations. Indeed, he does not recognize objects in my sense at all, meaning objects that are both determinate and concealed. For Nancy, bodies are fully constituted by their touching of other bodies, and are saved from this fate only by what is not itself already formatted: either natal process, or masses of whatever. His shift from the largely textual references of his colleagues to actual seashells, skulls, and balloons is a welcome step toward a philosophy of objects. But we cannot endorse his refusal to let a body have forms that are not produced in interaction with other bodies. For Nancy, anything outside the relational sphere of touching and weighing can only be a shapeless mass or a throbbing field of birth.

This weakens his otherwise fascinating treatment of touch. Recall that touch or tact were meant to address the paradoxical (and entirely classical) fact that we both grasp and fail to grasp bodies. But it now looks as though we grasp them a great deal more than we fail to grasp them. For what really escapes our grasp for Nancy is not *bodies*, but only the natal process or mass that escapes determinate configuration. But we have seen that matter or process themselves are always One, and are more than a One only insofar as they imply a spacing of discrete bodies that they themselves generate. In other words, the problem of touch is merely dissolved rather than solved. Instead of bodies that touch without touching, we have bodies that surge forth from the same unified One. Bodies are permitted to escape the genuine paradox of contact. Insofar as they are discrete bodies, they are already in contact *qua* weights; insofar as they exceed contact *qua* masses, they are not discrete bodies at all.

To repeat, what is missing in Nancy is all sensitivity to determinate objects that exist both in and out of contact. The problem of touch is the problem of finding an *interface* where determinate objects touch without touching, link without entirely linking. Nancy begins "Corpus" wonderfully by raising the problem of touch. But the recourse to shapeless mass, matter, or coming-to-birth softens the paradox to the point where it no longer exists. One horn of the bull is cleanly sawed away.

NOTES

1. See especially *Tool-Being: Heidegger and the Metaphysics of Objects* (Chicago: Open Court, 2002); *Guerrilla Metaphysics: Phenomenology and the Carpentry of Things* (Chicago: Open Court, 2005); and "On Vicarious Causation," in *Collapse*, Vol. II (2007).

2. See Part One of my *Guerrilla Metaphysics*.

3. Jean-Luc Nancy, "Corpus," in *The Birth to Presence*, trans. Brian Holmes et al. (Stanford: Stanford University Press, 1993). Henceforth cited as *BP*.

4. This claim is somewhat controversial because at most times Heidegger *does* seem to think that reality has no determination until Dasein breaks it into chunks, just as the early Levinas holds. But a strong case can be made for a Heidegger who allows for individual objects in themselves—not just in the later lecture on "The Thing," but already in the tool-analysis itself. I have made this case at length in *Tool-Being*, throughout.

SEVEN

THE SPECULATIVE CHALLENGE AND NANCY'S POST-DECONSTRUCTIVE REALISM

Peter Gratton

For too long, the thing itself (*res* or *an sich*) has absconded from the purview of philosophy. Self-styled "speculative realists,"[1] including Quentin Meillassoux, Graham Harman, and Iain Hamilton, have prominently offered a direct affront to a crucial decision contained in all manner of Continental philosophy. This decision, they argue, has been to favor ontologies that describe human access to the real, but fail to think the real *as it is* outside or beyond differential textual relations or phenomenological "access." In this way, contemporary philosophy is said to have left unquestioned a post-Kantian "correlationism" that thinks being through its givenness or human means of contact, that is, in terms of the relation between the thinker and the world. The project of speculative realism is not without its internal divisions and challenges—not least the various attempts out of the paradox of thinking the real as it outside of all thinking—but it is one I would argue nevertheless is in line with central aspects of Jean-Luc Nancy's project.

Whether discussing the world, bodies, fragments, things, the singular-plurality of being, or the "ex-scription" of writing, the question of the real has been crucial in his work. What is the weight, to paraphrase Nancy, the very reality, of a thought, if not a word? How does it incline *as* and *toward* being? Nancy argues that thinking what he calls the "areality" of "reality" is but one modus of thinking this weight. His answer to these questions comes not by marking language's failure in terms of its representational power, as if language were extant to or separable from the world. "We are attempting to grasp," he writes in *The Gravity of Thought*, "an exposition (or the sketching of an *art*) of the inappropriable gravity of meaning (*sens*). An image, a writing, a gesture, in order to stress or let weight the heavy or light features of a presence in the endless process of coming."[2] This gesture is one that Nancy delineates in terms of an "exscription" or "exposition" of *sens*, which in turn is never separable but is always reaching just up to or getting to the heart of (*à même*,[3] to use Nancy's terminology) what is. In *Sense of the World*, he writes the following:

> *World* means at least *being-to* or *being-toward* [*être-là*]; it means rapport, relation, address, sending, donation, presentation *to*—if only of entities or existents *to* each other. We have known how to categorize being-*in*, being-*for*, or being-*by*, but it still remains for us to think being-*to*, or the *to* [*à*] of being. (*SW*, 9)

In what follows, I draw together Nancy's conception of this "*à*," this "being-*to*" or "at" the things of the world, with what Derrida dubs his "post-deconstructive realism," which he uses to denote the gap that is nothing other than the unnameable relation among and between existents. The point of this usage is to think of this relation not simply as *at one* with thought, as *at one* with words—instead, as *à même* existence, or better, as thinking existence as nothing but *à même* one thing to another, and thus this "*même*" marks a small but important opening out of idealism. Accordingly, Nancy will look for a way to think of the relation of things without correlating things *as they are* to human existence, which would return us to the subject–object binary of the Kantian tradition. This aligns Nancy's work with the critiques of "correlationism" that has been the upshot of the speculative realist rejoinder to post-Kantian Continental philosophy.

In the first section of this chapter, I set out the stakes of the speculative realist project through the important work of Quentin Meillassoux, whose style of argumentation has ignited a following among those looking for methodologies (the speculation of "speculative realism") to take them beyond the supposed dead-end of recent Continental philosophy—said to be caught in interminable iterations of the end of metaphysics and its closure. We are enjoined to "get out of ourselves, to grasp the in-itself," Meillassoux writes, to "know what is whether we are or not."[4] We'll focus on the way in which Meillassoux's work gives us the means by which to intrude on and think again Nancy's corpus, in order both to skim and go to its very heart (*à même*) as part of a larger consideration of a *writing* or *exscription* that would be a passing of sense in the *res* itself and not about it.

THE SPECULATIVE CHALLENGE

Offering what he calls variously a "speculative materialism" or a "speculative realism,"[5] Meillassoux contends that phenomenology and post-structuralism have failed philosophy's oldest quest: to think the *outside* of thought and language (the *logos*), that is, the real *as it is* beyond its appearance to human beings. After so many turns in contemporary philosophy—the linguistic, the postmodern, the "theological"—speculative realists call for the return in contemporary philosophy to thinking things, objects, and the world in ways irreducible to phenomenological (in both the Kantian and Husserlian senses), structural, linguistic, and differential relations to being. We must, we are told, twist ourselves free of the endless recitations of the textual labyrinths in which Heidegger, as well as Derrida and Nancy, are believed to be caught, instead taking the "pure, literal offering" of mathematics as the means for speculation on the ontico-ontological difference.

Meillassoux argues for finding a means beyond naïve realism to "touch"—his word—"the Great Outside" ("*le Grand dehors*")[6] in order to make contact with the real beyond the simple banging of the head of the thinker on the prison walls of the phenomenal or linguistic realm. The real in this way won't be "posited" dogmatically by a "*coup de force*," but is to be "demonstrated."[7] The point, in the end, is to think a "realist" *absolute*, "a non-thinking reality independent of our access to it."[8] Meillassoux's speculative realism begins by hacking away at the crutch afforded to modern philosophy by the nomenclature of "access." Correlationism, he argues, "consists in disqualifying the claim that it is possible to consider the realm of subjectivity and objectivity *independently* of one another."[9] Whatever form of correlationism this takes—he cites the Kantian schematism, the intentional structure of the Husserlian phenomenology, and the language games of Wittgenstein, among others—it must stipulate "we can't know what the reality of the object is in itself because we can't distinguish between properties which are supposed to belong to the object and properties belonging to the subjective access to the object."[10] For Meillassoux, this has the result that the world "is only meaningful as given-to-a-living (or thinking)-being," that is, "for us."[11]

Meillassoux's speculative project begins notably not by denying the correlationist circle, whereby any given object is "always already correlated to an act of thinking,"[12] but rather by thinking through to its end the correlationist logic. Meillassoux thus *absolutizes* the correlationist relation in order to find the "narrow passage"[13] toward the "uncorrelated, which is a world capable of subsisting without being given."[14] This reality would be "absolute" for Meillassoux in the term's primary sense: a "world unbound (*delié*) . . . from all representations of the world" and thus "autonomous" of thought.[15] For Meillassoux, in order to posit any correlationism between thinking and being, one must first admit the "absolute contingency of the given in general," because otherwise one would fall into idealism's positing of a *necessary* relation between thinking and being.[16] Here it would help to outline briefly what Meillassoux takes to be the four major responses in modernity to naïve realism, which in turn will help us to formulate Nancy's contributions in the latter part of this chapter.

1. Weak correlationism: Kant is the paradigmatic case for Meillassoux because he proscribes any knowledge of the in-itself because the categories of the understanding cannot be applied in his transcendental philosophy beyond intuition. However, we can think the noumenal because we can reason *a priori* that the in-itself not only exists and is amenable to the law of noncontradiction. Importantly, for Kant, there is no sufficient reason for the correlation itself because one cannot explain *a priori* why the relation itself *is*, let alone in a given particular form (e.g., with space and time as the only forms of intuition). In order to do so, one would have to overstep the bounds of understanding into the noumenal, or that is, hurdle out of the very relation in question. In this way, the correlation between thinking and being is contingent, an ineluctable but nevertheless nondeducible fact of our existence.
2. Strong correlationism: Here Meillassoux identifies Heidegger and Wittgenstein, along with supposed "historicists" of relationality, who posit a relativism of concepts to particular places and periods of time.[17] As Meillassoux's describes it, the strong correlationist argues that we are so trapped on this side of the correlation that we cannot even *think* the noumenal as Kant argued. All we ever have is the pure givenness of the phenomenal, or, for the "historicists," that which comes to us mediated through linguistic structures.[18] This discourse of the *an sich*, he argues, is "self-limiting" and leaves the field open to "discourses of the Wholly Other [*Tout Autre*]"—discourses that for Meillassoux are "wholly other" to philosophy because they are a form of the "religious, the theological, or the poetic."[19] Here, as in weak correlationism, the relation between *thinking* and *being* is taken as contingent because there is no *a priori* ground in the noumenal (nature, God, or another ontotheological entity) for necessitating the relation of thinker, perceiver, or the speaker to being.

3. Speculative idealism: Hegel is Meillassoux's example here, although he often cites approvingly of Hegel's well-known critique of the noumenal. Hegel argues that Kant cannot *know* the boundary between the phenomenal and the noumenal without contradicting the transcendental enterprise. In the Hegelian structure of the co-implication of thinking and being, one would be right to note how little Marx turned Hegel on his head, given that Hegel already marks the "ideal" as real in and through the movement of the in-itself. This idealism is "speculative" in that it advances into the in-itself—thus the name for Meillassoux's own approach—but it remains "metaphysical" because it positions an absolute that is necessary: the correlation as the absolute *in-itself*. It is against this "infinite," absolute dialectical movement of the Idea that the modesty of the strong correlationist appears salutary. Rather than positing, as Meillassoux describes, an infinite and necessary being, the strong correlationist rejects dogmatic metaphysics while emphasizing human finitude and its inherent inability to think various grounds for being.
4. Speculative realism: As Meillassoux puts it, all of the above fail to "touch the absolute" and to do justice to the things of the world. Meillassoux's "speculative" approach, as in Hegel, is to radicalize the correlationist relation, which he describes in terms of the necessity of contingency.

Meillassoux's tact is to take seriously the correlationist's rejection of dogmatic metaphysics, which, as in Leibniz, begins with a necessary entity (God) and deduces, by way of the principle of sufficient reason, *a fortiori* necessity to all things. Without rejecting correlationism as such, Meillassoux identifies the presuppositional kernel at the heart of the correlationist stance: that the relation it stipulates (e.g., between the phenomenal and noumenal) is contingent, not least because the possibility, if not the likelihood, is held open by correlationists that the *an sich* may be absolutely heterogeneous to what appears to us (and thus the relation itself could have been very different).

This precipitate of a certain "contingency" is the Archimedes point for Meillassoux's speculative project thus far. Whereas the correlationist must take the correlation to be contingent (i.e., non-necessary) in order to consider the in-itself as "wholly other [*tout autre*],"[20] he or she cannot account for this contingency because contingency—this "touch[ing]," this "happening"[21]—can be known, whereas facticity (the systematic contingency of all relations) is unknowable from *within* the relation, according to the correlationist's own description. We can know objects are contingent as they are experienced, that is, as they are given within a co-relation: Objects come and go and their being is non-necessary. But to assert the facticity of contingency itself, the correlationist must assert as fact something that it cannot, by its own lights, know. Hence, correlationism must assert positively one *absolute* fact: the facticity of contingency, in particular, the facticity of the contingency of the relation itself.[22]

The correlationist would have to argue that the *an sich* exists but that one can only know that we have no knowledge of it. For his part, Meillassoux "maintain[s] that the in-itself could actually *be anything whatsoever* and that *we know this*."[23] This is what forms Meillassoux's ontology of what *may be*, and thus is not a realism or ontology of *what is*.

Speculative realism is thus founded on the principle that the in-itself has an independent, absolute existence and our knowledge of it extends to the necessity of its contingency, to the fact that it "could actually be anything whatsoever."[24] "We now know," he writes, "the location of the narrow passage through which thought is able to exit from itself—it is through facticity, and through facticity *alone*, that we are able to make our way towards the absolute."[25] This *positive* knowledge, this *fact* that there is *contingency*, is at once minimal and crucial. We know that everything can be otherwise, that is, that there is a non-facticity of facticity, which Meillassoux dubs with the neologism *factialité*. This absolute is not a *thing*, which would be the God of onto-theology; the "eternal principle" is rather the facticity of the contingent relation.[26] In this way, speculative realism leaves aside the principle of sufficient reason (*nihil est sine causa*), integral to the Hegelian system as well as all manner of philosophical determinisms, and argues that by working out from the form of correlationist thought, one can "demonstate" certain facts about the noumenal and access the "Great Outside" in a way not mediated by the conditions for that access.[27]

What we have, then, is an *an sich* that is "hyper-chaos" because, as Meillassoux points out, without the principle of sufficient reason, not just every *thing* is contingent, but so is every physical law. But behind all of this, Meillassoux's return to the things themselves, to the *res* of reality, reinscribes rather than contests the distinction between what things are *for us* and as they are *as such*: "There is nothing beneath of beyond the manifest gratuitousness of the given, nothing but"—this "nothing but" is all important since the "nothing but" in this sentence leaves in place the phenomenal/noumenal split—"the limitless and lawless power of its destruction, emergence, or persistence."[28]

This risks a dualism, if we can speak this way, *without* relation because at the end of the day Meillassoux's claim is that "it's possible to sincerely maintain that objects could *actually and for no reason whatsoever* behave in the most erratic fashion *without having to modify* our usual, everyday relation to things."[29] How, then, to think *together*, in some form of *relation*, the abyss separating, on Meillassoux's account, ontic appearances and the ontological "hyper-chaos"?[30] How to think the point of *contact*, however contingent, on Meillassoux's terms, *between* the "sensible" that only "exists as a subject's relation to the world" *and* the *an-sich* that is ever amenable to the "mathematizable properties of the objects . . . exempt from the constraint of such a relation"?[31]

The answer, for Meillassoux, is the ever-repeating, eternal language of mathematics, which provides "access"[32] to what "cannot be reduced to a correlate of thought."[33] As an unchanging and "eternal" symbology, mathematics provides the science of being *qua* being, the science of the absolute, giving us in turn a thinking "after finitude" and in turn a "mathematical absolute" that is the "analogue of extended substance."[34] Symbolic without being representational, the question rebounds, then, upon the point of contact, the "*à même*," between the symbol and what is:

> [W]e must transform our perspective on unreason [that is, the doing away of the principle of sufficient reason], . . . we must project unreason into things themselves, and discover in our grasp of facticity the veritable *intellectual intuition* of the absolute. "Intuition," because it is actually in [*à même*] what is that we discover a contingency no limit other than itself; "intellectual" because this contingency is neither visible nor perceptible in things and only thought is capable of accessing it, just as it *accesses* [my emphasis] the chaos that underlies the apparent continuity of phenomena.[35]

"THE TIME OF THE THING"[36]

The aporia of any future realism, speculative or otherwise, begins and ends here, where "intuition" "grasps the world," that is, where "intellectual intuition"—a pre-Kantian, Cartesian *cogitationes*? Platonic *mathêsis*? Aristotelian *noùs*?—is *right at, just at, just up to*, but perhaps *at the heart of* (*à même*) "what is." This is real; this is serious. As such, I must be careful not to get lost in wordplay as I approach Meillassoux's account, even as his project links up movements of sense (intuition, speculating, theorizing, etc.; but also, classically, all the signs of a systematic haptology: "grasping," the "contingent," "touching upon the absolute," etc.) to a rejection of any "natural," non-mathematical language as unable to "touch" the real. We would risk the worst of what Meillassoux calls a relativism or historicism, trapped in a linguistic game and a play of etymologies when what matters about the materiality of matter is the thing it-self, the thing in-itself (*Ding-an-sich*, literally, the thing *at* itself, which Nancy renders when he translates *an sich* as *à même soi*).

The task is to set out the stakes for what Nancy has called the "time of the thing" after the modernist age of representation. Meillassoux's attack on what he calls "correlationism" remains beholden to the dualism his work sets out to critique, especially when it comes to vexed problem of an "intellectual intuition" he distinguishes in order to describe how *mathēsis* makes contact with the real. What is crucial, however, is not to let this chapter serve as a rear-guard defense for the philosophers of post-structuralism, including Nancy, in the wake of newer currents in contemporary thought. We'll thus leave aside the terms with which I might be expected to bludgeon Meillassoux's work: metaphysics of presence, ontotheology, and the like. Instead, we'll follow, perhaps through the thicket of this aporia, a path he himself provides for a way out of the problem with which his project begins and ends.

Nancy's wager is that there is no *thing* in-itself, just as there is no language (trapped) in itself, and thus one could say that there is no self, no *même* that would not be *at* (*à*) something else: "existing," Nancy writes, "is right at being" ("*exister, c'est être à même*"), that is, being-there (Da-sein, *être-là*) is nothing but "*être-à*," being-*toward* or *at* (*SW*, 26–28). Thus, we could not envision a self locked into a language or indeed on *this side* of the phenomenal realm without *at least* it being-*at* the *res* of reality. Correlationism must not be superseded by a "realism" that bifurcates being between what is and what is written, or for that matter, between the chaos of what is "neither visible nor perceptible" (Meillassoux's noumenal) and the "apparent continuity" of sense experience (Meillassoux's phenomenal). Thinking through his "*à même*" of intuition, thinking through its existence "right at" what is, which is really "right at" "being-toward" for Nancy, is to rethink the starting point, the very condition of the relation, of the "right at," posited as the tipping point for any speculation, and therefore any sense (speculative, touching, or otherwise) of the real in speculative realism. As Meillassoux points out well, there can be no transcendence of Kantian intuition as such, and therefore there cannot hold any *a priori* that is not also *a fortiori*. Regarding Kant, Meillassoux argues:

> To hypostasize the subject, there exists no transcendental subject that is not instantiated right at [*à même*] an empirical consciousness, which is itself incarnated [*incarnée*]. Outside the body, there is no subject; outside the subject, there is no relation to the world [*rapport-au-monde*]; but outside the relation to the world and preceding it, there is the world—already the world [*déjà le monde*].[37]

Following this logic of "there is the world—already the world," could we not go back through Meillassoux's corpus to touch on all the points of contact *right at* (*à même*) the distinction he wishes to hold between the phenomenal and the noumenal, or between the "intellectual" and the "empirical," in order to think an intuition that would already be worldly? I want to bring Nancy into a point of contact with Meillassoux's project right (*à même*) the "*à même*" that has detained us thus far, where Meillassoux's realism, by way of its use of "intuition" as its point of "access," gives the impression of *not* touching the "touch [of] the absolute."

The question is that of "access." The point is not just to think that which is there when we are not, but also to mark an excess of sense and meaning at the heart of things (a sense overflowing to the point of nonsense, if not chaos, on Nancy's account). For Nancy, reality is that which "confronts us when we are confronted by nothing," and for him it is not a question of what is "accessible to the ego" (*FT*, 85). What Nancy ultimately argues is not that there are no things; in fact, in a line found in *After Finitude* as well, Nancy writes, "that there is something is necessary."[38] But these things have an *absolute* freedom in their *relation-to*, in their points of contact to and from one another, and thus their sense is irreducible to a given discourse about things, to a given set of significations. This is not to say that there is an "in itself" of sense *beyond* signification, but rather that there is always an excess of things in their relations-to, in their relations to each other as relations-to, and an excess of signification *itself* as a real thing. In this way, significations make *something* present, but that *thing* is never fully present, given the relationality of the singular-plurality of beings, including any supposed subjects or linguistic beings cut off from the world. For Nancy, this is an "absolute knowledge" "that is given without thinking" (*BP*, 176). This means that it is given *before* thinking in both the spatial and temporal meanings of the term, though thinking, too, is never *present* as such, since it is always in relation to things, to the things that are themselves always *à même* one another, one as the other, and one in the other (*FT*, 317).

Indeed, it is not just that this "absolute knowledge" is "given without thinking"; it is also not "given" *tout court*. For Nancy, phenomenology fails as a *logos* of the *phainomena* because it reduced appearing to mere appearance, that is, as an appearance-to a knowing subject. It fails, he writes, "to open us up to that which . . . infinitely precedes consciousness and the signifying appropriation of sense, that is, to that which precedes and surprises the phenomenon in . . . its coming or its coming up" (*FT*, 317).

Thinking, Nancy argues, thus has a responsibility to "engage" and "open itself" to the excess of sense, although this thinking is but an open response to this excess of sense over any possible signification (*FT*, 293). This is not the source for a "mystical experience" (*SW*, 15), but rather is the common "abandonment of the 'there is [*il y a*]'" (*BP*, 177) in the "co-existence of the world" (*FT*, 306).[39] Consequently, we are not "finite" in the sense that we are deprived of some sense (even if that sense, in correlationism, would be an "in itself"). For Nancy, we are, each of us, as someone and something, "infinitely finite": We are "exposed to our existence as a nonessence," as having a being "in us exposed to its own otherness" (*FT*, 27).

RELATIONS, NOT CO-RELATIONS

Ultimately, despite the difference in philosophical style and lineages, Nancy's philosophical project and that of the speculative realists are premised equally on two concomitant claims. First, after the death of God (the event of the *deus abscondus*), philosophy must follow on the trail of the *res absconda*. This means that the mundane, worldly things of this world must be returned to a certain dignity, denied to them by ontotheologies that took them to be points of references or fallen signs of a transcendent God-beyond-being. These things must also escape the gaps of a humanism that can only think the real in its rapport to the human. A "post-deconstructive realism,"[40] if there is such a thing, must avoid the paths of the ontotheological and subjective hermeticism. Secondly, it follows from this that there is no absolute point (human or God) from which to think being, no privileged point of view from "nowhere." As Meillassoux puts it, speculative realism takes account of the "loss of every privileged point of view," and in turn "the dissolution of the ontological hierarchization of places."[41] On Nancy's account, this means giving description to what he dubs the "ex-position" of the "sense of the world," an "acosmic" cosmology that would no longer be caught in the look of a *kosmotheoros*, of a "panoptic subject of the knowledge of the world" (*SW*, 38). In this way, then, the human must give up its sovereign place as the thinker of being, which makes being but an extension of humanity and its values.

But this risks an account that is abstracted of things, thus losing track of the *res* of a so-called "post-deconstructive realism." Nancy treks on territory familiar to Meillassoux's readers, arguing that there is no sense of the world that is given *from the outside*. This would treat the world as representable, instead of, as Nancy claims, an infinite happening of coming to presence, each time just this once, unique, and thus non-representable. It is thus the case, he argues, that "there is something, there are some things, there is some there—and that itself makes sense," without a need for a God.

For example, Heidegger notoriously argues in his 1929–1930 lecture course that the "stone is without world," that the animals are "poor in world," and that human Dasein is "world forming."[42] But for Nancy, the world does not only make sense "for, through, or in Dasein":

> [T]he world beyond humanity—animals, plants, and stones, oceans, atmospheres, sidereal spaces and bodies—is quite a bit more than the phenomenal *correlative* of a human taking-in-hand, taking-into-account, or taking-care-of. . . . For it is a question of understanding the world not as man's object or field of action, but as the spatial totality of the sense of existence, a totality that it itself *existent*, even if it is not in the mode of Dasein. (*SW*, 55–56; my emphasis)

Certainly, Nancy notes, one could suppose in this thinking an *exteriority* to humanity, but this is not to be thought merely as the unknowable beyond the "relation between subject and object" (*SW*, 56). For this reason, Nancy is careful not simply to place language to one side of this relation, as Meillassoux and other speculative realists are want to do. If we take there to be a circulation of sense among things, then there are in a sense (a sense that is not reductive when compared to human language) signature and singularities at work, and thus a passing of signs, even if these signatures "exscribe" their sense elsewhere from the intuition or contact of the human.

For Nancy, being is a "fragment" of the world, which in turn denotes having a signature, having a place and a taking-place that is not simply, on the Heideggerian model, a placing oneself in view of that which has been hidden away (*abscondus*). The signature is always *underdetermined* in the circulation of sense, and thus can be confused with nothing.

To take the risk of an anthropomorphism that will quickly recede, this is what we mean when we say that we are touched. Something touches us (and thus is touched by us in turn) and its affectivity passes along the signatures of one and the other with such a gravity—whether the touch is light or not does not matter—that "to be touched" is synonymous with profundity, a depth and profundity of meaning being passed along and circulated. And this is why, beyond Meillassoux's apt discussion of "touching upon the absolute," each touch (or all touching) is a touch upon the absolute, upon an infinity of sense irreducible to a signification communicated or a bit of information passed along; it is never just a simple touch. Having a sense or sensing of this touch marks a "coming to presence" "just at" (*à même*) us such it that can never be pinned down as a presented thing[43]; it can never be fully felt and thus conceptualized: A touch is always shared and distributed (*partager*), or it is nothing.

And yet, we will in turn sovereignly declare human beings as having *the* touch, as we say in English. The result is that, as Graham Harman puts it in a different context, "One privileged entity is allowed to form links where others cannot. Against this notion, I propose *the more democratic solution* of a local occasionalism or vicarious causation, in which *every entity that exists* must somehow be equipped to serve as a medium of contact between two others."[44] On this matter, as so often, Heidegger takes the less democratic approach:

> The stone is lying on the path, for example. We can say that the stone is exerting a certain pressure upon the surface of the Earth. It is "touching" the Earth. But what we call "touching" here is not a form of touching at all in the strongest sense of the word. It is not at all like *that* relationship which the lizard has to the stone on which it lies basking in the sun. And the touching implied in both cases is above all not the same as *that* touch which we experience when we our hand upon the head of another human being. . . . [B]eing a stone it has no possible access to anything else around it, anything that it might . . . possess as such. (*FCM*, 196–197; *SW*, 59)

If Nancy is right in arguing that the epoch of representation is coming to end (*GT*, 83) and that the "time of modernity is [to be] followed by the time of things" (*FT*, 317), we must register for the "test of the real," even if, on Nancy's account, "there's nothing to prove" (*FT*, 317). This, for Nancy, is the mark of our primordial exposure—an exposure that is not ours alone—to the ruptures of sense in the "movement of a presentation *to* . . . which is a rupture of presence itself" (*GT*, 63). He calls this a "responsible praxis of sense" (*FT*, 292). Every being-*toward* is *toward* another *being* that is itself *toward*. Without this circulation and excess of sense, there would only be reductive signification, that is, "mere indication" and the "denoting of things," a zero-degree of sense that Heidegger presumes to find in the rocks that do not have a world and the lizards "poor in world."

This "test of the real" surrounds the notion of "access," one that begins first with a responsibility of sense. The word "access" has its root in the Latin *accedere*, to approach or come near, but was also part of the motto of Roman civic life: *accedere ad rem publican*, to do one's civil duty and begin a public life. The responsibility today, the "more democratic approach," as Harman puts it, is very much about the public things—and how we accede to them, even if acceding to public things means questioning access itself: this is the question being proposed widely and in different ways in ecological and animal studies, which has everything to do with the publicity of public things.

Reproaching Heidegger, Nancy writes:

> Why, then, is "access" determined [with regard to the stone] *a priori* as the identification and appropriation of the "other thing"? When I touch another thing, another skin or hide, and when it is a question of this contact or touch and not of an instrumental use, is it a matter of identification and appropriation? . . . Why does one have to determine "access" *a priori* as the only way of making-up-a-world and of being-toward-the-world? Why could the

world not also *a priori* consist in being-among, being-between, and being-against? In remoteness and contact without "access"? (*SW*, 59)

As Nancy notes, the Heideggerian scene is all but feudal, if not Platonic, with its hierarchies of touch as it ascends closer to the sun, wherein "a hieratic and paternal pose fraudulently substitutes a knighting [the placing of the hand on the head] for a touch" (*SW*, 60). The whole of this antiquated anthropocentrism is "betrayed," he rightly argues, "by the expression 'the earth is not *given* for the stone." But what, he asks, if this givenness were never "pure"? What if it were preceded by what makes that gift possible in the first place, namely the distribution and sharing out of unassignable gifts "neither to be perceived or received as a 'gift' "? And what of the networks of stones and animality and—why not?—humanity passing in and through this "contact" of stone, heat, and surfaces of all kinds:

[the stone] is in contact. . . . There is no "subject" and "object," but rather, there are sites and places, distances. . . . [W]ithout this impalpable reticulation of contiguities and tangential contacts, without the place (interstice, interval, and escape) of a geared down *being-toward* . . . there would be no world. "In itself," the thing is "toward" the *other things* that are close, proximate, and also very distant because there are several of them. (*SW*, 61)

In this way, he writes, the stone isn't simply there as an abstraction, laying in wait for its encounter "by or for a subject" (*SW*, 62). The stone does not "have" the world, as Heidegger argues. But are we still naïve enough to think that we things, we *res extensae*, *have* the things of world either? The stone, for Nancy, is *toward* the world or "is the world" as "areality: extension of the area, spacing . . ." (*SW*, 62). The stone has a "liability [*passibilité*]" to sense, an area of passing through and passing along of sense irreducible, Nancy argues, to an "animism" or "panpsychism," which would figure the sense of the stone, of the things, back through the human in terms of an anthropomorphism. There is in the stone its "concrete" liability, which is also "concrete condition" of its singularity (*BSP*, 18). This liability is but another word for "accede": the stone, too, accedes to the public thing.

The stone's "concreteness" is a "real *différance*" or *différance* as real and as *à même*, circulating materially. The problem has not been, as Meillassoux argues, too much of the thinking of relation in modernity, but too little. What is called for is a thinking of a circulation of sense and materiality, that is, a thinking of an excessively real, if I can put it that way, complex of relations. This is the absolute to which we are all, one and other, one as another, liable and acceding, in the public and in common, passing along signs, *partes extra partes*, in a generalized circulation of exposure and relation. It is this exscription, this *real* writing in the passage of sense, that is the *res ultima*. Where speculative realism in Meillassoux begins and then circles back to the correlationist circle, Nancy offers a generalized and therefore public thing, an *ultimate res* that refuses to privilege any given relation over any other, thus providing a "more democratic solution" of rocks, bodies, fragments, ligaments, and an endless catalogue from there, in touch with and sharing with one another. In this way, the *an sich* is still, as rethought by Nancy as the "*à meme*" and exposure of the "*to*," the *ultima res*. It is time, then, to "learn to think *toward* the world" (*SW*, 191, n. 112). This means the absolute is not some *res absconda*, but rather is the *abscondus* of the res: the secreting and motion away from signification of things that retains a trace, a touch, of the *res* along the way.

NOTES

1. See, for example, their exchanges collected in "Speculative Realism," *Collapse 3*, September 2007. See also the editors introduction to *The Speculative Turn: Continental Materialism and Realism*, ed. Levi Bryant, Nick Srnicek and Graham Harman (Melbourne, Australia: Re.press, 2010).

2. Jean-Luc Nancy, *The Gravity of Thought*, trans. François Raffoul and Gregory Recco (New York: Humanities Press, 1997), p. 83. Henceforth cited as *GT*.

3. This is a preferred phrase of Nancy at exactly those points in his texts where he discusses the proximity (or lack thereof) of thinking and things, of words and things. This prepositional phrase, "*à même*," combines, of course, the French word for "to," "toward," or "at" (*à*) with the French adjective or pronoun meaning "the same" or the "self" (*même*), literally meaning, then, "at or toward the same." The phrase itself is otherwise all but untranslatable because it can mean "right at," "just about at," but also "at the heart of" something, although Nancy will also play on this self-distancing "right at" or "at the heart" of the self (*meme*), implied in the term (similar to literal of the English "at one"). And just as this prepositional phrase grammatically links and thus also differentiates locatively nouns in a sentence, Nancy suggests that every *at* or *towards* or *right up to* is "pre-" or before any positionality in a logic he discusses explicitly in relation to Derridean *différance*. See, for example, *The Sense of the World*, trans. Jeffery Librett (Minneapolis: University of Minnesota, 1997), p. 35. Henceforth cited as *SW*.

4. Quentin Meillassoux, *After Finitude: An Essay on the Necessity of Contingency*, trans. R. Brassier (London: Continuum, 2008), p. 27.

5. The term is Ray Brassier's (*Nihil Unbound: Enlightenment and Extinction* (New York: Palgrave Macmillan, 2007), p. 31. For an excellent overview of Meillassoux's work in *After Finitude: An Essay on the Necessity of Contingency*, see Brassier, pp. 43–86. I also offer an extended consideration of Meillassoux in "After the Subject: Meillassoux's Ontology of 'What May Be,'" *Pli*, Vol. 20 (2009), pp. 55–79.

6. *After Finitude*, p. 26.

7. "Speculative Realism," p. 420.

8. Ibid., p. 427.

9. *After Finitude*, p. 5; my emphasis. The impasses of Meillassoux's approach (up until now) are to be found in this beginning formulation. Rather than contest this supposed "independence" of one and other, Meillassoux reifies each as an "independent" realm as a means for unworking idealist and correlationist conceptions of the real, both of which, he argues, are forms of "subjectivism" colonizing the real through the export of anthropocentric categories: "One can privilege the perceptive correlation between subject and object, the intellective correlation, but also the affective, voluntaristic, and vitalist relations to the real. A metaphysical subjectivism . . . can be a vitalism, a hylozoism, a thinking of the will, or the will to power." These are forms, he writes, of thinking "that attribute to being itself certain traits of subjectivity—reason, perception, affect, will, life," that is, are forms of anthropomorphism that circle back from reality to the self. See Quentin Meillassoux, "*Contingence et absolutisation de l'un*," paper given at the Sorbonne conference, "*Métaphysique, ontology, hénologie*," February 12, 2008, p. 8. Suturing the realms of appearance (discussed in terms of phenomena and language) and the in-itself (through post-Cantorean set theory) becomes in Meillassoux a surgical difficulty more and more reminiscent of Descartes' studies on the pineal gland—apt, perhaps, given Meillassoux's avowed return to Descartes' mathematicization of the in-itself. See *After Finitude*, pp. 29–33.

10. "Speculative Realism," p. 409. Here, as elsewhere, Meillassoux rejuvenates the Lockean distinction between primary ("properties . . . belong[ing] to the object" and secondary ("properties belonging to the subjective access to the object") qualities.

11. *After Finitude*, p. 15.

12. "*Contingence et absolutisation*," p. 4

13. *After Finitude*, p. 63,

14. Ibid., p. 28.

15. "*Contingence et absolutisation*," p. 4. Meillassoux argues that science already provides a means for thinking beings outside of any correlation. Perhaps his most well-known argument is the one that opens *After Finitude*, which is his least interesting and most easily refutable one: Science provides us an account of "ancestral events," for example, the formation of the our galaxy billions of years ago, that can in no way, for Meillassoux, be a correlate to thought because it did not yet exist. In summary, he argues, a proof against any correlationist thought. But here Meillassoux is treating correlationism as but a straw man who can't tell the difference between epistemological givenness and ontological dependence. But if this were so, all correlationists would be guilty of the most facile version of the metaphysics of presence, thinking that what is not *now* present to thought would be incapable of existing, that is, what exists in some sense depends on it being known. It's also unclear why Meillassoux argues from a temporal vantage point, since there are many things, both distant and microscopic, not given to thought in terms of what is knowable (e.g., some yet unseen subatomic particle, or a galaxy not yet on view through the Hubble telescope). But, second, the correlationist simply asks is that if one is thinking or enacting a discourse around an ancestral event,

then one admit that *ipso facto* there is mediation, which is a claim far different from denying ancestral events themselves.

16. *After Finitude*, p. 54. Meillassoux argues that idealism is not the only form of thinking that proposes a necessary relation between thinking and being: "one can privilege the perceptive correlation between subject and object, the intellective correlation, but also the affective, voluntaristic, and vitalist relations to the real. A metaphysical subjectivism . . . can be a vitalism, a hylozoism, a thinking of the will, or the will to power." These are forms, he writes, of thinking "that attribute to being itself certain traits of subjectivity—reason, perception, affect, will, life," that is, are forms of anthropomorphism that circle back from reality to the self. "*Contingence et absolutisation*," p. 8.

17. "*Contingence et absolutisation*," pp. 6–7.

18. *After Finitude*, p. 43.

19. "*Contingence et absolutisation*," p. 10.

20. Ibid.

21. *After Finitude*, p. 108.

22. Hegel had begun his speculative dialectic by working through the necessity of the relation itself; Meillassoux asserts the necessity of the contingency of the relation, a subtle but all-important difference.

23. *After Finitude*, p. 65; my emphasis.

24. This is what Badiou means when he asserts that whereas Kant had set out the conditions of possibility of experience, the post-metaphysical project is to delineate the possible conditions of the world as such, with an emphasis on the multiple possibilities of such worlds, which Meillassoux dubs "pure possibility" (*After Finitude*, p. 62).

25. Ibid., p. 63; my emphasis.

26. Ibid., p. 65.

27. Meillassoux writes, "Let us agree to call *speculative* all philosophies which accord to thought the capacity to accede to an absolute, and metaphysical all philosophies which ground themselves on a modality of the Principle of Sufficient Reason to accede to the absolute. For speculation which founded itself on the radical falsity of the Principle of Sufficient Reason would describe an *absolute* which would not constrain things to being thus rather than otherwise, but which would constrain them to *being able not to be* how they are." "Spectral Dilemma," *Collapse*, vol. IV, pp. 261–275, here p. 308; my emphases.

28. *After Finitude*., p. 63.

29. Ibid., p. 85.

30. Ibid., p. 127.

31. Ibid., p. 3.

32. Ibid., p. 65

33. Ibid., p. 117.

34. "*Contingence et absolutisation*," pp. 2–3.

35. Ibid., p. 82.

36. J.-L. Nancy, *A Finite Thinking*, trans. Simon Sparks (Stanford: Stanford University Press, 2003), p. 317. Henceforth cited as *FT*.

37. "*Contingence et absolutisation*," p. 3. The body, for example, is at once a necessary condition for the transcendental, which on Kant's account is no less real than the body, which is intuited through the categories of the understanding. Logically *a posteriori*, the body points to an anterior space-time before the transcendental intelligibility in terms of space-time to which it gives rise, and thus is the condition of possibility for the transcendental understanding that can only *a posteriori* represent it (*After Finitude*, p. 26). For Meillassoux, this *anteriority* of the space-time of the body marks the leap out of the correlationist circle to a time before the categories (available in Kant at the level of his argument) that "temporalizes and spatializes the emergence of living bodies," and opens us onto a "discourse" of a past when both "humanity and life are absent" (ibid.).

38. *The Birth to Presence*, trans. Brian Holmes et al. (Stanford: Stanford University Press, 1993), p. 173. Henceforth cited as *BP*.

39. Graham Harman offers a helpful example in terms of what he calls "intentional objects": "While the real tree is always something *more* than whatever I see of it, the intentional tree is always something *less*. That is to say, I always see it much *too* specifically, encrusted with too much accidental color or from an accidental angle, or in some purely coincidental melancholic mood. Any of these details could be changed without changing the intentional tree, . . . It is not an empty *je ne sais quoi* projected onto unformed sense data, because in fact it precedes and shapes any such data. As Merleau-Ponty knew, the black of a pen and the black of an executioner's hood are different even if their wavelength of light is exactly the same. The qualities are *impregnated* with the objects to which they are attached." Graham Harman, "Intentional Objects for Non Humans," available, with the author's permission, at http://speculativeheresy.wordpress.com/resources/, p. 6.

40. The term is from Jacques Derrida, *On Touching—Jean-Luc Nancy*, trans. Christine Irizarry (Stanford: Stanford University Press, 2005), p. 46. Derrida writes, "the spacing of space" that Nancy exposes "remains irreducible to any mathematizable extension and perhaps to any knowledge—an absolute realism, but irreducible to any of the tradition's realisms." But it's also the case that Derrida refers to this realism as "irredentist," suggesting a usurpation by Nancy of a neighboring territory (the real) outside of his own.

41. *After Finitude*, p. 136, n. 1

42. Martin Heidegger, *The Fundamental Concept of Metaphysics: World, Finitude, Solitude*, trans. William McNeill and Nicholas Walker (Bloomington, IN: Indiana University Press, 1996), p. 177. Henceforth cited as *FCM*.

43. This is why Nancy argues that "sense," as touching, is an "untouchable touch," since it can never grasp the full significance of the sense, the touch, that is open among things (*FT*, 110).

44. "Intentional Objects," p. 8.

PART THREE

EXPOSITIONS OF THE POLITICAL

Justice, Freedom, and Equality

EIGHT

ARCHI-ETHICS, JUSTICE, AND THE SUSPENSION OF HISTORY IN THE WRITING OF JEAN-LUC NANCY

B. C. Hutchens

Jean-Luc Nancy's commitment to a revolutionary politics attentive to the incessant re-inauguration of justice fulfills the promise of his notion of "archi-ethics," which sets out to resist those discourses that threaten to substantialize the notion of community by means of historical ideals. Nancy challenges the Kantian and libertarian traditions of justice (broadly construed) that insist on the subordination of freedom to certain "rights," which strive but fail to appropriate the singular efforts of freedom and the incommensurable "sharing" (*partage*) that, for Nancy, composes communities.

This chapter addresses the question of the relation between the discourses of the suspension of history and the demand for justice. More specifically, I propose that Nancy's notion of the "archi-ethics" of writing is consistent with his effort to understand freedom and justice in the context of the "suspension of history." On my reading, Nancy is arguing that the suspension of history transforms the traditional paradigm of justice as an "equality of measure" with respect to the obsolete notions of the "individual" and the "community" it presupposes. What he calls "archi-ethics" arises through this transformation and serves as a form of writing that enables alternative relationships between a singularity that incessantly reaffirms itself, despite generalized individuation, through a freedom that constantly surprises and seizes itself rather than is "granted" by a political body or "taken" from a political class. A community thought in this way would be a sharing of relations rather than of substantial individuals relating atomically, and would be the mark of a justice that answers to freedom's groundlessness.

"ARCHI-ETHICS"

The expansive discourse of the "end of the discourses of history" throws into sharp relief the shortcomings of traditional ethics. Given the "death of God," the dissolution of the subject, the subversion of rationality, and the suspension of history, can one provide a discourse on ethics at all? Specifically, can there be a discourse of justice and more specifically, of the *praxis* of justice itself?

Castigating the nihilistic despair with which such questions are so often uttered, Jean-Luc Nancy has posed a provocative answer in the form of an "archi-ethics," which figures in two sweeping trajectories of his thought. On the one hand, there is the insuperable resistance writing poses to the discourses of history, and even to the "revolutionary" *praxis* that often motivates these discourses. Writing is an assertion of identity, of self-perception, in a manner that both frustrates political appropriation and reveals what Nancy refers to as the "empty truths" of democracy. Nancy often uses the notion of "exscription" to clarify this. Exscription is the act of writing that puts the writer and his or her community beyond what is written about. In all acts of writing, there is a body writing itself exscriptively, a writing body that is irreducible to the thematic body that is being inscribed by what is written. "The body is not the locus of writing," Nancy insists, and "is not what can be read in a reading."[1] In other words, in the very act of inscribing freedom, individuality, and community into discourse, the writer exscribes him or herself from this discourse. Alternatively, to write freely, knowledgably, and justly is not simply to write about freedom, knowledge, and justice, but to place oneself as a free and knowledgeable singularity and recipient of juridical consideration beyond what has been written about these matters. The writer's embodied self is shared out even as it shares in sense: Its writing is "the body of a sense that will never tell the signification of bodies, nor ever reduce the body to its sign."[2] In fact, this compromises the communication necessary for substantial community: Writing may facilitate communication, but it does not merely bring a community together. On the contrary, the very relation among writer, reader, and other writers dislocates communication, that is to say, places singularities beyond the thematic nature of the communication itself.[3] Each singular act of writing, then, resists the appropriation of the act; the writer, the communication given, and the community are related by being singular, by putting beyond writing what writing puts down on paper, that is to say, the written is irreducible to the singular.

Although this writing is disruptive of rational reduction and political appropriation, it is still a worthy endeavor to query whether there could be a self-consistent discourse of this resistance. If so, Nancy speculates, then the discourse of the resistance to discourse must be understood as if there were something akin to a categorical imperative impelling writing and calling for resistance to writing's own discursivity. Writing is the "task of sense, on condition that it not be the assumption of a sense that has already been tied up, but the response—without resolution—to the absolute injunction of having to establish ties" (*SW*, 121–122). However, writing, insofar as it is the free writing of freedom, does not merely "have" or "produce" meaning. On the contrary, it "is" sense only as an answer to this imperative, and it is in this answer that the imperative is "sense" itself.[4] Because its universal injunction prescribes no precise duty, one might propose that any response to the imperative, even withdrawal or refusal, amounts to obedience to the injunction "be free"; alternatively, freedom is freedom when it resists this imprecise prescription. The singular sense of the address is discernible as it circulates through the singularization of each writer's freedom, exposing the incommensurable sharing of community itself. Archi-ethics is an inquiry into the exscriptive movement of writing through which sense circulates irreducibly because it ceaselessly strives to enable its resistance to be political without reifying into the terms of the political binarism of "right" and "left."

On the other hand, archi-ethics responds to the question of the dissolution of subjectivity by proposing the notion of radical singularity or what Nancy calls "finite transcendence," that is, each one is different on each occasion; each "instance" of subjectivity is singular in the sense that there is no ontological ground or rational foundation by which comparisons could be drawn among them. Singularities are not comparable "individuals" collected "together" with a common essence and within the space of a closed immanence mediated by political discourses. If each singular being relates in a singular fashion on each occasion, then relations themselves are infinitely reticulated events that lack any ontological ground. More precisely, they are themselves, almost casuistically, the groundlessness of the ontological grounding itself. In other words, singular beings and their relations are neither ontologically predetermined nor rationally pre-established; rather, all such determinations and establishments are grounded in such beings and their relations. This entails that neither a community nor social relations in particular presuppose any essential properties possessed by individual subjects (citizens). Community, then, is not composed of constituent individuals who share any essence. On the contrary, any community consists of the sharing in the incommensurability of each singular being with its own mimetic perception of itself. Generally speaking, community is the sharing of singularity in the lack of any such essence or ground. Thus, as I have argued elsewhere,[5] Nancy's "community" is open (insofar as it consists of a circulation of sense through infinitely reticulated and absolutely singular events of sharing) and insubstantial (inasmuch as there are no predetermined entities or pre-established grounds by which it is rendered intelligible).

This is significant because singularity and its freedom *categorically refuse* the categorical imperative. Interestingly, for Nancy, singularity and its freedom have *always already* categorically refused the categorical imperative even before it issues toward it. Specifically, freedom persists in refusing the imperative even as it receives it; the singularity is free despite the imperative rather than in answer to it. In this sense, archi-ethics is not an "ethics of ethics" or a meta-ethics, but is rather a movement along a trajectory in which the affirmation of singularity and the sharing of community are explored in virtue of their ability to categorically refuse the categorical imperative. In this sense, archi-ethics addresses this refusal and its consequences.

In several ways, then, Nancy strives to consider the limitations of the categorical imperative. However, for James Gilbert-Walsh, Nancy's rethinking of the categorical imperative undercuts itself at the same time as it fails to displace it.[6] The imperative, for Nancy, both singularizes the recipient's subjectivity by withdrawing from it and generalizes it by preconditioning its freedom. Gilbert-Walsh is correct to note that both of these formulations of the imperative fail to make a difference on the grounds that it is not clear what motivational force any such command could have. Perhaps for Nancy the very idea of motivational force is relinquished in the name of a discourse of the resistance to the discourse of such force. True *praxis* of the revolutionary kind would be revealed in the form of a demand for justice that singularizes the demanding being and provides the condition of justice in community only if such singularization takes place. The categorical imperative, then, both interrupts always already any *praxis* that might substantialize community and exposes the condition of incommensurable sharing that is constitutive of human existence itself. The command's emptiness of all motivational content is the result of the plural singularizations it addresses (and that, conversely, address its exigency). Properly speaking, Nancy's view of the categorical imperative does not "make a difference," since this would imply a comparison of individuals (entities and states of affairs) that is at once contributive to a predetermined *praxis* of means and ends figuring as a motif of substantialist metaphysics and devoid of the shock necessary for a revolutionary politics. A categorical imperative that makes individuality significant would not permit the singularization of existents in terms of the incommensurability of sharing. The imperative "makes a difference" only in the sense of exposing human existence to its own singular-plurality. Generally speaking, Nancy offers no tenable discourse of ethics that could conceivably make a difference, but instead understands the singularizing and interruptive imperative as an analogy with a categorical imperative divested of any ethically motivational content.

The specific question I am posing in this context involves the interruption of the discourse of the *praxis* of justice by virtue of the suspension of the history of such a *praxis* and its conceptualizations. In what precise way has justice been suspended historically so that archi-ethically it is now transparent to theory that all discourses of a communal kind carry their own exigent conditions of suspension (i.e., are always already interrupted by their own constitutive *praxis*)?

BEYOND RESORBED HISTORY

For Nancy, history has been "suspended" since the Enlightenment and Romantic narratives have played themselves out in an aporetic tension that lays the groundlessness of community bare, thereby rendering us contemporaries of ourselves alone.[7] There is no "sense" in which "historical figures" are our ideal contemporaries. Nancy writes that "our time is no longer the time of history, and therefore, history itself appears to have become part of history," a time of the suspense or suspension of history (inspiring only an "uneasy expectation") (*BP*, 144). History is no longer sense, that is, a meaningful-conferring movement along a teleological or progressive path. However, Nancy is vehement that the "philosophy of history" must be redressed as a discourse of "essence without essence" or Idea, a discourse lacking the pristine consistency that would facilitate the idealization of so-called historical figures and theories about historical progress. The idea of history now obdurates the necessity of thinking the pre-originary conditions of human existence itself. It is imperative, he remarks, to think through the conditions that have enabled the "double-bind" of historical thinking: On the one hand, there is "moving history," the trajectory of subjectivity proceeding towards itself, progressing in the fulfillment of needs and the perfection of human essence; on the other hand, there is "resorbed history," the immanent reflection of subjectivity present to itself. Paradoxically, the movement of history is one that disrupts the very resorption it is thought to promulgate. Yet, this resorption creates the conditions for the mimetic identification of history that the "moving" historical subject no longer is. History always moves beyond what is resorbed: What is resorbed is no longer what history is as it progresses (*BP*, 149). In a sense, we are "outside" history, at once too inexorably imbedded in its processes to find our place in it, and identified so clearly outside of it that our existential state is obscured.

This sobering thought might impel us to accept that the meaning of "history" cannot be given *to* "history" by philosophy. History can no longer be deemed to consist of epochs whose lessons are available to social and political theories. On the contrary, history is an epoch itself, the epoch of the "establishment and enclosure of meaning as such" wherein the meaning of the myriad meanings of human endeavor is no longer disclosed to theory. That is to say, "history as meaning" has happened and what we continue to call "history" is "no longer relevant for this 'happening' as such." All that we can say of history is that "there is happening" and it is precisely in this "something happening" that we exist, either as the sense exposed to the perennial newness of each happening or as the non-sense lost to the meaning of each happening (*BP*, 153). It is *this* existence that we share: the exposure to uncertainty and the sense of its non-sense that composes community.

It is almost banal to add that the very idea of humanity too has been suspended. History is neither the expression of a human essence nor the forum wherein the tribunal of reason judges its progress. The various technological and bureaucratic means by which a "humanity" was once thought to organize and assert itself now produce dehumanizing practices and inhuman phenomena that attest to a "self-destroying mankind, [a] self-annihilating history, without any possibility of the dialectical work of the negative." We are simultaneously enthralled by the possibility of a theodicy that bestows meaning on even the most violent instances of our history and paralyzed by the evil this violence often expresses (*BP*, 144–145). The double-bind of moving and resorbed history opens the possibility that destruction is the primary referential index of the contemporary epoch. We might very well be contributing to a "culture of destruction" in which warfare results in the devastation of the very structures, the "connections, interplay, assembly and its complexity" of culture itself, affirming only the sense of destruction and thereby the non-sense of all sense.[8] Whatever extreme our horror at this burgeoning culture of destruction might reach, Nancy is insistent that no discourse of the renewal of humanity, no call for a return to some moment idealized by nostalgia, is possible.[9] Humanism presupposed a history that is now inaccessible to theory, and therefore it cannot provide tenable resources for a renaissance of human ideals. Nancy writes:

> If "humanity" must be worth something, or if Being in general must "be worth something" under the heading "humanity," this can only be by "being valuable" *singularly* and, simultaneously, in

> "being valuable" by and for and with the *plural* that such singularity implies, just as it implies the fact of the "value" itself. (*BSP*, 74)

Indeed, if one can speak of "humanity" at all now, it would be only in the sense of a plurality of singularities that would remain incommensurate with any humanistic ideal.

Although Nancy's formulation is unclear, one might conjecture that "history" and "humanity" were myths that served as social and political ideals by which communities have been held together as closed and substantial entities consisting of atomic individuals. Such communities were among the primary catalysts for the very history that is now suspended and closed to theory. Hence, with history suspended, its figural agents have been dissolved, and, by extension, so has the capacity to compose and mimetically reflect myths such as "history" and "humanity" in order to provide substance to communities. There could be no community without such myths; conversely, such myths would be inconceivable without the presumption of substantial communities (*IC*, 55–57). Yet neither myth nor substantial community possesses a transcendental reserve of sense that would enable them to survive the incessant interruptions of mythic and communal discourse.

THE FREE WITHDRAWAL FROM THE IMPERATIVE

Despite the suspension of history, Nancy maintains, philosophy continues to obey protocols as if it were replying to an ethical imperative. It is still presumed that philosophical writing, for example, responds to an ethics whose conditions an author must satisfy. Its *praxis* is self-regulated by protocols that mimetically reflect on the very identity of philosophy itself. Beyond philosophy, the imperative to write impels a *praxis* of writing that incessantly interrupts philosophical discourses. In particular, it interrupts the practical desire to be practical, subverting all efforts to crystallize philosophy into conceptual patterns vulnerable to political subsumption. In this respect, archi-ethical philosophical writing should be inspired by a literary ethics of resistance against political appropriations, especially those discourses that enable the closure community and the individuation of the singularity.

If there is distress about the absence of a viable ethics of a traditional kind, then nothing would emphasize this distress more than a demand for a renewal of an ethics no longer accessible to the fragmented discourses of the contemporary world. Perhaps theory can be receptive to a future ethics, an ethics "to-come," but our openness to such a possibility will be determined by the extent to which we are "deprived of rules, without being deprived of truth." It is necessary to let ethics withdraw from philosophical writing and to write about this withdrawal. In other words, there is an imperative to write about an "extra-discursive duty" that implies the very ethics that has been suspended. But it is also imperative to write from *within* this suspension and thereby to continue to write in resistance to the paradigms of ethics that fail to disrupt political appropriation. If there is any question as to the status (or indeed, even the possibility) of an ethics, then "one must interrogate the duty of the question" and write an ethics of this interrogation.[10]

Although the categorical imperative is traditionally understood to be a universal and unconditional command, in Nancy's view it addresses each singularity, not "as such," but precisely as a singularity. Although it is "anterior to morality"[11] as an "unreserved sovereignty of a moral absolute," the imperative in fact serves to suppress a freedom that can only free itself, properly speaking, if it withdraws from the imperative (*FT*, 133–136; 148–149). There is a sense in which freedom must refuse any duty the imperative might prescribe, must withdraw and affirm itself *despite* the imperative, and not because of its motivational force. However, because the imperative is famously content-less, prescribing no *precise* course of action, *any* response is tantamount to obedience to the injunction to be free. The categorical imperative does not provide the condition of self-legislation; it merely exposes the finitude of the singular moral agent and opens a singular space within which it is addressed. Because this space is one in which the incommensurability of the imperative and the freedom of the respondent are revealed, the duty it dictates "belongs to the structure of finitude" without providing the condition for an ethics of finitude. One might maintain, then, that finitude itself is the opening of ethics. This is so, Nancy suggests, to the limit of finitude as a spacing of ethics itself (*RP*, 40).

The subject of singularity figures in a multiplicity of contexts in Nancy's work. Here I am concerned only with the exposure of the finitude of the singular being as definitive of ethics itself in a manner preparatory for looking at the conditions for justice. For Nancy, there is only one singular Being that assumes myriad forms as singular beings between which sense circulates.[12] This is not to say that singularities have a common Being, a pre-established ontological condition, but rather that the Being they "have" is determined in their "compearing" (co-appearing) relations. Freedom is asserted by each singular being on each occasion of its sharing in such relations. Such a freedom is always a surprise and is always surprised to itself in its sharing.[13] Indeed, the "shock" of experience itself discloses to the existent the extent to which it is free despite the imperatives of duty. Cognizant of its uncertainty, freedom is the withdrawal from duty in which the singular being is even surprised that there is a world in which such a demand is placed on it. And Nancy is confident that it is precisely this withdrawal from duty, definitive of each singular human existence, that creates the "spacing" wherein exposure to others is possible (*EF*, 67–68). In other words, it is the withdrawal into finite existence, not the categorical imperative, that facilitates social relations.

If being is the sharing in the relation, not a property shared amongst *relata*, then the being of each existent, each some*one*, is nothing other than this sharing: "ipseity is constituted by and as sharing" (*EF*, 69). Freedom, then, is "mine," yet co-terminously, being is outside "me" in the multiple spacings of sharing that compose social being. However, if sharing is not determined by an ontological ground, then there is no commensurability among subjects such that their existences can be measured. Conversely, it is only insofar as there is such an incommensurability that each singular being can be so measured. Each freedom, as it were, is incommensurable with all the others, and it is in this alone, perhaps, that there is equality in the sharing in the incommensurable (and thus a standard of comparison amongst them). But because freedom is groundless, because it is an incessant assertion of surprise against the exigent shocks of existence, it is the singular being who measures its own freedom against . . . precisely nothing. In other words, each singular being measures itself against the very impossibility of its own existence being measured. Freedom is always surpassing its own expected measure, diverting from it and intentionally dissatisfying its expectations. Thus, when the singular being measures itself against its own impossible measure, it is attuned to the strumming intensity of its own surprising and surprised existence. There is nothing willful or heroic about this attunement: The singular being discovers itself in the very space of existence composed of the sharing of social relations, which is to say that, although freedom can only measure itself against the groundlessness and uncertainty of its own surprises, the standard of measure itself is lit up in the sharing that composes community. Nancy avers, then, that the "in common" and the "common measure" of the equality of this sharing is the "excess of the sharing of existence" itself. The measure of justice is the "equality of sharing in the incommensurable" (*EF*, 69–72). If subjectivity is singular, if freedom is groundless, and if comparisons between "individuals" is impossible, and if justice is possible only in terms of an indeterminate measure, then justice is a matter of sharing in the incommensurability of both each existent with its own measure and of a community with its own substantial identity.

JUSTICE AND SINGULARITY

Justice becomes necessary precisely in this "archi-originary" form of sharing wherein the humanistic paradigm of all theories of justice is supplanted by an emphasis on relations that provide singular beings with "humanity." It is a matter of constant reinauguration, not of a foundational establishment. Yet Nancy is keen to point out that there is no consequence that arises from the success of this achievement. Singular beings never cease being surprised in and by their freedom, and thus "humanity" is always at risk for dissolution in such surprises as well as in the reticulations of sharing in which they are manifest. Perhaps all one can say assiduously of "humanity" is that freedoms are shared out by and in relations among singularities. There is freedom only when the actualization of the very essential condition of "humanity" is being incessantly suspended.

In several places in his work, Nancy proposes that freedoms are not guaranteed by any juridical, political, or economic paradigms. No Kantian or libertarian view of freedom offers a viable explanation of the groundless nature of the freedom surveyed above. Indeed, Nancy remarks that freedom is a "free space of movements and meetings," as well as "external trajectories and outward aspects, before being an internal disposition" (*EF*, 75). Freedom is active in the space of sharing constituted by such trajectories prior to the formation of any "internal disposition." Society is the spacing-out of singularities along such trajectories; it consists of points and vectors of a network of relations that they constitute. That public space itself is a "spaciosity" of such relations that provides a place and a time for the provision of the measure of freedom. It is often conceived, Nancy notes, as a "circulation, reticulation, an exchange, a sharing, a localization that is at once multiple, overdetermined, and mobile" (*SW*, 104). The public space is not one in which juridical paradigms supervene given and guaranteed "rights" to freedom over the myriad burstings of freedom and the sharings of relations. Generally speaking, the singular being that takes the groundless measure of its own freedom does so along such trajectories of sharing on such spatial and temporal occasions as the public space provides. At this point, Nancy offers what is perhaps his most provocative survey of justice in his work:

> The justice necessarily in question here—because it is a question of sharing and of measure—is not that of a just mean, which presupposes a given measure, but concerns a just measure of the incommensurable. For this reason—regardless of the negotiations that at the same time must be conducted with the expectations and reasonable hopes for a just mean—justice can only reside in the renewed decision to challenge the validity of an established or prevailing "just measure" in the name of the incommensurable. (*EF*, 75)

Justice, then, is not based on a specified measure, in which all perspectives are given weight "equally" in terms of abstract principles of right and what is owed. Conversely, if each singular being can only "measure" the responsibility aligned to its freedom in terms of its groundless singular existence, and if all singular beings have only this in common, then justice would be justice to the incommensurability of each and every singular being's measure against its own groundless singularity. One might conjecture that justice comes in the form of a demand that justice be done to each singularity precisely because, in its singularity, no just measure could conceivably be imposed without disregarding the pre-originary groundlessness of each existence. Justice would be the "challenge" or the calling into question of the very right to impose "justice" in this way. The challenge Nancy provides here would necessarily be interminable, as freedom must assert itself through all its incessant and exigent surprises. If justice is understood solely in terms of exterior relations amongst citizens, then all that results is a "formal" and empty justice for "everyone" that facilitates the opening of injustice (*SW*, 108). Formal justice would bear on *every*one or *some*one, but Nancy, as we have seen, emphasizes singularity, the each one of every*one* or some*one*. A politics of justice in Nancy's sense would be an "infinite and incommensurate dimension" of singular "ones," each "subverting," in its freedom, the closure that an appropriative politics, a substantial community and a paradigm of "formal" justice would promise (*SW*, 114).

In the light of this view of justice, Nancy himself challenges (one could say "justly") the thought that freedom is a "right" that can be secured only through the implementation of measures of justice. In this case, freedom would be the end, the goal, of all just practices and discourses of justice. It would be determined as a Kantian "fact of reason" whose determination would be anticipated through the formation of rational paradigms whereby just measures could be conceptualized.[14] Justice would be nothing other than the originary paradigmatic position from which freedom could be established as a guaranteed right. Such reasoning would be circular in the sense that it would presuppose for this establishment the very freedom it proleptically determined to be an establishable right. However, Nancy vigorously defends the inversion of these priorities: Freedom is that pre-originary state always arising or unleashing itself in the incommensurability of the measures of singularity and sharing. Being groundlessly antecedent to rational paradigms that underlie the regulative ideals of justice, freedom is discernible in, on the one hand, the challenge to abstract justice and, on the other hand, the demand for justice to singularity and to the sharing of community. Roughly speaking, we would not be sufficiently rational to establish the justice we occasionally experience if we were not antecedently free. In that freedom, we are capable of asserting ourselves within (and despite) the surprise of existence and the shared trajectories of social relations.

ARCHI-ETHICS AND REVOLUTIONARY POLITICS

Nancy's "archi-ethics" of the groundless resistance to ontological reduction and his challenge to the measure of justice leads him to propose that justice is a matter of "revolutionary politics." In the absence of any discourse of history in which justice would be the incessant correction of implementations of law, the "interminability" of freedom and community is the sporadic reinauguration of justice itself. Each demand for it and challenge to it (re)creates the condition of justice in terms of the difference of singularities on each of their irreducible and incomparable occasions. Freedom is always the beginning (not an established end of the discourse and *praxis* of freedom), and in this respect can only be "taken" through the assertion of freedom itself. Hence, on the one hand, freedom is not "given" as an award or deserved right. On the other hand, it can only be "taken," not in the sense that it has been seized from others who possess it, but rather in the sense that, in trying to seize it, one inexorably expresses one's own groundless state of existence. Freedom, then, is this incessant seizing that produces that which it strives to seize (*EF*, 77). This politics of the groundless and nonderivable freedom is itself the network of such seizures of the speech that circulates sense through the public space, thereby providing a configured dimension within which sharing occurs.[15]

Therefore, Nancy provides neither a "theory of justice" nor a method for assessing competing theories. Instead, he is fixated on the groundlessness of human existence that enables justice to be in question in the first instance. Moreover, the archi-ethical imperative putting justice discursively into question is accomplished precisely because freedom itself requires it. Freedom is a spacing amongst singular beings in which all the uncertain points, vectors, trajectories, and reticulations of relation create intensities of experience that demand justice. It is not a domain untrammeled by the exigencies of existence, as rational paradigms of justice require. Justice is not a right or privilege, but the very "right" of each singularity to challenge and demand that its own singularity be attested. The fact that each singularity is incommensurate with any absolute measure of certainty (even by means of its own self-knowledge and historical role) does not preclude the possibility of justice. Rather, it exposes the very manner by which justice is possible, if, indeed, it is possible at all. On every occasion in which justice obtains, it does so precisely because of the response to the summons of a self-attesting subjectivity, and not because a "right" demands it.

NOTES

1. Jean-Luc Nancy, *The Birth to Presence*, trans. Brian Holmes et al. (Stanford: Stanford University Press, 1993), pp. 197–198. Henceforth cited as *BP*.

2. Jean-Luc Nancy, *The Sense of the World*, trans. Jeffrey S. Librett (Minneapolis: University of Minnesota Press, 1997), p. 197. Henceforth cited as *SW*.

3. Jean-Luc Nancy, *The Inoperative Community*, ed. Peter Connor (Minneapolis: University of Minnesota Press, 1991), p. 25. Henceforth cited as *IC*.

4. Jean-Luc Nancy, *The Experience of Freedom*, trans. Bridget McDonald (Stanford: Stanford University Press, 1993), p. 107. Henceforth cited as *EF*.

5. Benjamin C. Hutchens, *Jean-Luc Nancy and the Future of Philosophy* (London: Acumen, 2005), especially chapters 3 and 6.

6. See James Gilbert-Walsh, "Broken Imperatives: The Ethical Dimension of Nancy's Thought," *Philosophy and Social Criticism* 26:2 (2000), pp. 29–50. Gilbert Walsh's paper does not directly grapple with the specific questions I have posed in this chapter. Yet there can be no doubt that his confrontation of the discourse of interruption with the notion of a motivational imperative is one that may prove to be at the core of Nancy's thought.

7. Jean-Luc Nancy, *Being Singular Plural*, trans. Robert Richardson and Anne O'Byrne (Stanford: Stanford University Press, 2000), p. 63. Henceforth cited as *BSP*.

8. Jean-Luc Nancy, *A Finite Thinking*, ed. Simon Sparks (Stanford: Stanford University Press, 2003), pp. 78–81. Henceforth cited as *FT*.

9. See Jean-Luc Nancy, *The Gravity of Thought*, trans. François Raffoul and Gregory Recco (New York: Humanities Press, 1997), pp. 19–25.

10. Philippe Lacoue-Labarthe and Jean-Luc Nancy, *Retreating the Political*, ed. Simon Sparks (New York: Routledge, 1997), pp. 32–35, 41. Henceforth cited as *RP*.

11. Jean-Luc Nancy, "Of Being-in-Common," in *Community at Loose Ends*, ed. The Miami Theory Collective (Minneapolis: University of Minnesota Press, 1991), p. 12.

12. Nancy makes it very clear that singularity neither proceeds from anything nor has anything "behind" it (such as an ontological ground or rational foundation). Singularity is precisely what it (each one, this one, someone, etc.) is and is shared out in a multiplicity of ways (*IC*, 27).

13. For a detailed discussion of the significance of the "burst" or "surprise" of freedom, see *EF*, pp. 55–58.

14. In *The Experience of Freedom*, Nancy goes to great lengths to demonstrate that the notion of a self-legislating self, whose freedom is a Kantian "fact of reason," does not account for the singularity of freedom as its "bursts." Even to presume the existence of such a self embedded in a world of social relations is already to presuppose the very freedom that is established as a "fact of reason" through self-legislation. Alternatively, Nancy, influenced by Heidegger, proposes that freedom could not be an originary "fact of reason" if it were not always already a pre-originary "fact of existence." The reason that facilitates self-legislation is not the single origin of freedom. Rather, freedom's own "surprise," "bursts," and capacity to call itself into question are the singular creations or affirmations of its own groundlessness (*EF*, 23–30).

15. Nancy notes in *The Sense of the World* that politics, which does not arise from any idea, is the "seizure of speech," the "emergence or passage of some one and every one into the enchainment of sense effects," as well as into all signifying aspects of language, including even gesture and silence. The seizure of speech is not a competition among wills striving to define sense, but of each will that, tied to all its own existential conditions and through all social relations, "makes sense" merely by virtue of being tied (*SW*, 115–120).

NINE

JEAN-LUC NANCY ON THE POLITICAL AFTER HEIDEGGER AND SCHMITT

Andrew Norris

Jean-Luc Nancy's contribution to political thought is largely structured by his critical fidelity to Heidegger, that is, his attempt to read Heidegger against himself. Both alone and in conjunction with his longtime collaborator, Philippe Lacoue-Labarthe, Nancy seeks to decisively separate the Heidegger who joined the Nazi party (and who after the war was silent if not unrepentant about doing so) from another Heidegger who, Nancy argues, gives us the best resources to critique the first and everything for which he stands.[1] In contrast to Hannah Arendt, who obviously influences many aspects of his political thinking, Nancy maintains that Heidegger's political commitments in the 1930s were not "mistakes" analogous to Thales falling down a well while contemplating the heavens.[2] The contemplation and the fall were fully of a piece—as Heidegger himself acknowledged in 1936, when he agreed with Karl Löwith that "his partisanship for National Socialism lay in the essence of his philosophy," in particular in "his concept of 'historicity'" or *Geschichtlichkeit*.[3] That philosophy, however, was one that had not yet completely broken with the nihilistic history of the metaphysics of subjectivity and its will to power.[4] The concept of historicity, according to which "[t]*he historizing of history is the historizing of Being-in-the-world*," was tied to Heidegger's celebration of the German *Volk* as the most metaphysical people whose "historical *Da-sein*" and whose encounter with technology would be of decisive importance to the fate of Europe and hence for the fate of the earth.[5] The shift in Heidegger's thinking after his brief involvement with the Nazis is obvious enough if one compares the Rectoral Address of

1933 or the *Introduction to Metaphysics* of 1935 with, say, the *Gelassenheit* essay of 1955 or the interview with *Der Spiegel* from 1966. Twenty years after attempting to lead the *Führer* in a national confrontation with technology, Heidegger preaches a mode of meditative thinking or *besinnlichen Nachdenkens* that allows for a releasement toward things in which the thinker at once affirms and denies technology.[6] Although such thinking loses its association with the assertion of the essence of the German *Volksgemeinschaft*, in so doing it also loses all distinctively *political* force. Where the German people might once have at least participated in their own salvation through *Arbeitsdienst*, *Wehrdienst*, or *Wissensdienst*, now "only a god can save us," a god whose coming is readied solely by solitary thinking and poeticizing.[7] If Heidegger no longer calls on us to "Follow the Führer!," neither does he recommend a political alternative. He goes no further than to say, "A decisive question for me today is: how can a political system accommodate itself to the technological age, and which political system would this be? I have no answer to this question. I am not convinced that it is democracy."[8] Nancy's work will attempt to reconceive the relation of Heideggerian thinking to politics in a manner that avoids both Heidegger's later quietism and his earlier excesses. Although Nancy no more recommends a particular set of political institutions and norms than does Heidegger, he goes considerably further in thinking through the framework within which such norms and institutions must be understood and appraised, and suggests strongly that these will incline toward the democratic.[9]

Nancy does not, however, limit himself to drawing on the later Heidegger. Indeed, his central political claims draw directly on the critique of subjectivity that is already fully formed in *Being and Time*.[10] Heidegger argues that both subjectivity and objectivity are derivative, fallen modes of *In-der-Welt-sein* (Being-in-the-world). *Da-sein* is not a subject, a self-contained intellect or will that confronts a world of objects to be manipulated and investigated. Instead it is *ecstatic*: literally, beside itself, temporally and spatially dispersed. Nancy's writings articulate the implications of Heidegger's ontology for a thinking of community, and argue that our dispersal is first and foremost an experience of what he calls *sharing*. On his account, our being—that is, what it is to be a human being—is *being-in-common*. A community is not formed when a set of previously independent and self-sufficient beings unite and form a collective enterprise, as, say, social contract theorists would have it. Our relations are instead constitutive of who we are. But this does not imply that the *we* is ontologically prior to and somehow more real than the *I*. For Nancy, the community is no more a subject than is the individual member of it.[11] Conceiving of the community or the state as a *subject* entails that we understand the community to have an identity that is *immanent* to it, which simply needs to be brought out and put to work.

Who people are as a group is never simply an accomplished fact that could in principle be recorded in a census, but is rather a precarious achievement of collective self-assertion in the face of contingent circumstances and individual proclivities. Community identity is thus manifest in what the group *does*, in its *work*.[12] In Nancy's terminology, the community as subject necessarily implies the community as *subject-work*.[13] If one's "true" or "higher" or "more universal" self is found in a shared communal identity, it becomes the work of politics to acknowledge and bring forth that immanent communal identity. This will entail the assertion and purification of the community, and hence involve conflict with other communities. To realize their political identity, Germans must unite so as to become more "truly" German, and slough off what is *not* truly German by cleansing their community of the sick and the foreign while removing any limitations placed upon the community from without (such as limitations on *Lebensraum*). Demagogues like Hitler seek to put their communities "to work," articulating and drawing out the community's immanent identity and allowing it to express itself in functional activity. What is immanent must be made real, and that takes place in the work of politics. Because the immanent political subject (the *Volk*, the universal class, etc.) only makes itself known in this work of assertion/elimination, the work can never end. This is clearest in totalitarianism, the most extreme form of the politics of the subject-work. As Arendt argues in *The Origins of Totalitarianism*, totalitarian movements defy all utilitarian considerations precisely because the natural totality must be constantly reasserted, and this requires unceasing movement, the continual production and elimination of the unnatural—the Jew, the pervert, the class enemy. Terror as the free defiance of all laws can never settle into a way of life of a nation-state; instead it must endlessly purify itself and the outer world.[14] And what was then true of the rule of terror is in our own time true of the "war on terror," which we are told by leaders such as U.S. Vice President Dick Cheney is without end.[15] Here, too, the United States can show itself as the righteous nation it is—the defender of democracy, freedom, and so on—only in so far as it wages a war against the "enemy" of "terror." This is a process, obviously, that can never end or, to put the same point differently, can end only in failure.

On Nancy's account, these are extreme examples of a conception of political identity shared by much less obviously pathological communities. This is not to say that all forms of political life are equal, but that many of them share a common logic. As Nancy and Lacoue-Labarthe put it,

> Nazism does not sum up the West, nor represent its necessary finality. But neither is it possible to push it aside as an aberration, still less as a past aberration. A comfortable security in the certitudes

> of morality and of democracy not only guarantees nothing, but exposes one to the risk of not seeing the arrival, or the return, of that whose possibility is not due to any simple accident of history.[16]

Our victories against totalitarianism and "ethnic cleansing" will remain intermittent at best if we resist them only by supporting a rival community, one committed to norms and values that are, if nothing else, at least better than those of racists and Nazis. What is required is an understanding of how totalitarianism can erupt in the midst of what seems to be a civilized community or nation-state—an understanding that will allow us to resist totalitarianism in its genesis. To do this, we need to ask about the relation between the West and totalitarianism. There is a temptation to avoid this question, and to assume that totalitarian and racist movements such as Nazism are solely or essentially the result of evil, or pathology. But Nazism was not wholly devoid of sense. To all too many people it made all too much sense. To assume that all of those people were mad or evil or benighted will not allow us to understand what attracted them to totalitarianism. If our history is one of arbitrary eruptions of insanity, we would seem to be helpless in the face of an equally arbitrary future. If fascism and genocide are truly insane, they will lack all internal logic—which will make them all but impossible to resist in their genesis. Contesting this view, Nancy and Lacoue-Labarthe write, "There is a *logic of fascism*. This also means that *a certain logic is fascist*, and that this logic is not wholly foreign to the general logic of rationality inherent in the metaphysics of the Subject" (*NM*, 294). What we today count as politically rational has something in common with what counted for rational politics in Nazi Germany.

Nancy argues that our civilization has consistently misunderstood what community is, and has replaced the thinking of *being-in-common* with that of an essence of community. His central aim as a political philosopher is to attack those models of communion that would deny our ecstatic loss of ourselves by positing an essence that is immanent within us, an essence we must set to work.

> Such a thinking—the thinking of community as essence—is in effect the closure of the political . . . because it assigns to community a *common being*, whereas community is a matter of something quite different, namely of existence inasmuch as it is *in* common, but without letting itself be absorbed into a common substance. . . . Being *in* common means . . . *no longer having, in any form, in any empirical or ideal place, such a substantial identity, and sharing this . . . "lack of identity."* This is what philosophy calls "finitude." (*IC*, xxxviii)

Our finitude is our inability to contain either the world or ourselves. It is our inability to be absolutely self-sufficient. As being-in-common we are cast into a condition of plurality. And such a condition is by definition one characterized by difference.

> Finitude does not mean that we are noninfinite—like small, insignificant beings within a grand, universal, and continuous being—but it means that we are *infinitely* finite, infinitely exposed to . . . the otherness of our own "being" (or that being in us is exposed to its own otherness).[17]

Because being-in-common is itself differential, it is not self-identical. On Nancy's account, the ontology of the individual is always already that of what he terms "compearance." This is the mutually constitutive transitivity that paradoxically traverses interiority and exteriority. Ecstatically outside ourselves, we are exposed to one another, and in this mutual exposure, we share an infinite lack of infinite identity. To put it as baldly as possible, what we have in common is precisely not a shared identity, but rather the "fact" that we are different from one another. Because we share this difference, we are in relation to one another. "Being" is thus properly understood as *Mit-da-sein*, "as relational, as non-absoluteness, and, if you will . . . *as community*" (*IC*, 6).

Our basic ontological condition is to be open to what Nancy calls "communication" with one another. Communication here is not to be understood in instrumental terms as the transfer of information from one subject to another, but rather as the openness to and difference from one another that makes such transfer possible: "Speech—including silence—is not a *means* of communication but communication itself, an exposure" (*IC*, 30–31). Consider the phrase "being-in-common." On Nancy's account, existence is found in neither the "being" nor the "common," but in the preposition, "in." "As it becomes necessary to deconstruct all philosophical wordings of 'community' . . . all that is left to start thinking afresh is the *in* (which I had also called the 'inoperative')."[18] Or again: "The '*mit*' [in *Mit-da-sein*] does not even qualify the 'Dasein,' but . . . constitutes it essentially."[19] Or yet again: "*freedom withdraws being and gives relation*" (*EF*, 68). The phrase "being-in-common" thus refers us to the "in" as the community that provides the actual ontology of the individual. The basis of individuation is community: to be there with others. And the essence of community is plurality, not identity: "We" are different from one another. (Indeed, on this account the identity of either the individual or the group is a deceptive abstraction.) This difference is something we share, something that makes possible our sharing. Hence, the true community is the *communauté désœuvrée*: the idle or empty community. This community is empty because it contains no subjects; idle, because it lacks an essence that can be produced and put to work. But if this ontology of alterity cannot be put to work, it can be embraced. Indeed, doing so is for Nancy the crucial ethical and political move:

> [*J*]*ustice* can only reside in the renewed decision to challenge the validity of an established or prevailing "just measure" *in the name of the incommensurable*. The political space, or the political as spacing, is given from the outset in the form—always paradoxical and crucial for what is neither the political nor the community, but the management of society—of the common (absence of) measure of the incommensurable. Such is, we could say, the first thrust of freedom. (*EF*, 75)[20]

The first thrust of freedom toward justice is thus one of *resistance* against misunderstandings of community, politics, and justice. As we have emphasized thus far, for Nancy such resistance must be directed first and foremost at Heidegger, as Heidegger's embrace of National Socialism (and his rejection of the implications of his own ontology) threatens thinking as such. If we cannot distinguish between what is proper to thought in Heidegger's work and life and what is not, we shall be left with the unhappy conclusion that thinking is either unrelated to politics or is aligned with its most destructive and horrific forms. For many, however, we should not place too much emphasis on Heidegger's politics given the brevity of his political involvement while addressing politics, justice, and freedom, as well as their relation to philosophy. It is important to note, then, that Nancy's resistance is also aimed at a figure of much more obviously political significance, Carl Schmitt. In the works for which he is best known today, *Political Theology* (1922) and *The Concept of the Political* (1927), Schmitt advances theories of sovereignty, political authority, and political community that are, if anything, more relevant today than they were in the interval between the first and second world wars. Contemporary U.S. policy in particular participates in an intensification of the features of the political world most closely associated with Schmitt's name, such as the legal exception, the unregulated sovereign decision, and the hierarchically structured mortal conflict between friends and enemies that for Schmitt defines "the political." The Bush–Cheney administration's dismissal of international institutions that might compromise its sovereignty, its demand for unity in the face of "the enemy," its insistence that executive power be unchecked by the other branches of government or by robust doctrines of human rights, its blurring of the distinction between war and peace, and its use of states of exception such as Guantánamo Bay all recall Schmitt's work of the 1920s.

That Nancy would address Schmitt is not altogether surprising, given the fact that the account of political movements that Nancy appropriates from Arendt is itself likely indebted to Schmitt's *Staat, Bewegung, Volk: Dreigliederung der politischen Einheit* (1933).[21] Moreover, Nancy's claim that the politics of community as it is ordinarily (mis)understood entails the autogenesis or *autopoeisis* of identity through the elimination of what it is not (Jews, gypsies, terrorists) directly recalls central themes of Schmitt's *Concept of the Political.* As is well known, Schmitt commits himself to the idea that politics as such points towards the assertion of the community's "way of life" or "form of existence" in conflict with "the other, the stranger."[22] This conflict need not, as is often assumed, take the form of war or extermination—indeed, Schmitt explicitly cautions that the latter is a perversion more closely associated with the attempt to suppress the political than it is with its political itself (*CP*, 34, 54). Nonetheless, the assertion of the common identity will require the subordination and possible destruction of forms of life that it cannot incorporate. In "[t]he high points of politics," conflict with the existential enemy becomes a mortal matter, and the sovereign authority that utters the voice of the unified political entity or *Einheit* "demand[s] the sacrifice of life," a demand that "is in no way justifiable by the individualism of liberal thought" (*CP*, 67, 71).[23] In this process, the citizen him or herself becomes an object of purification in the sense that the private, embodied self is sacrificed in favor of the identification with the community. The Schmittian citizen recognizes his or her *true* identity as a citizen, as opposed to a private individual associated with *this* particular living body. The purification of the community thus takes place in part at least upon the scene of the citizen's own body.[24] The closeness of this position to the one that is Nancy's central concern in his work on the political is clear enough; that Schmitt in *Political Theology* emphasizes the *metaphysical* status of the sovereign decision driving the whole process only serves to highlight this fact.[25]

In their "Opening Address to the Centre for Philosophical Research on the Political" Nancy and Lacoue-Labarthe make their concern with Schmitt fairly explicit:

> If there exists . . . a *concept* of the political [*un* concept *du politique*] (which, moreover, we would distinguish rigorously from the *essence* of the political [*l'essence du politique*]), if a new concept of the political or something that one could present as such could become clear, then any such concept would, in our opinion, necessarily derive

> from the philosophical field and, for reasons . . . which are . . . well known, from a philosophical field itself determined, that is to say, ancient, past, closed.[26]

Schmitt himself makes no distinction between the essence and the concept of the political, and in fact begins *The Concept of the Political* by announcing that what concerns him in his conceptual determinations is the *Wesen* or essence of the political (*CP*, 19). That Nancy and Lacoue-Labarthe insist on this distinction is a function of the fact that they seek to place Schmitt's analysis of the concept of the political within a broader philosophical context. Politics on this account is always caught up in and determined by the essence of the political.

> This reciprocal involvement of the philosophical and the political . . . is, in reality, our situation or our state: by which we mean, in the mimetic or memorial aftereffect or *après-coup* of the Greek "sending" which defines the modern age, the actualization or installation of the philosophical *as* the political, the generalization (the globalization) of the philosophical *as* the political—and, by the same token, the absolute reign or "total domination" of the political. Such . . . is the reason for which, in speaking of *the political* [du *politique*], we fully intend not to designate *politics* [*la politique*]. (*RP*, 109–110)

The *essence* of the political as laid out by Nancy and Lacoue-Labarthe corresponds to the *essence* of metaphysics in Heidegger's account of technology. Indeed, their distinction is derived from his. According to Heidegger, technology is not the application of scientific theory. Rather, scientific theory itself arises in response to the philosophical demand that nature be reduced to "a calculable coherence of forces" that can be represented and used for the representation and application of force.[27] Physics and Cartesian philosophy serve Baconian ends: Knowledge is power in so far as a knowable world is one laid out on a grid that allows for the subject's control and manipulation of Being as beings. Although the technological mode of revealing is a nihilistic one in which instrumental reason reigns supreme, reason is not itself an instrument, least of all one wielded by humanity as some sort of super-subject. "Modern physics is the herald of Enframing, a herald whose origin is still unknown" (*QT*, 22).[28] As a mode of revelation, it is "the destining of revealing" or Being in our time. Hence Heidegger's famous dictum, "the essence of technology is by no means anything technological" (*QT*, 4). Lacoue-Labarthe echoes this phrase when he writes that "the essence of the political . . . is by itself nothing political."[29] The political, like the technological, is always brought to us by the destining of Being.

This raises the question of whether a philosophical confrontation with the political (*le politique*) will have any implications for *politics* (*la politique*). Given how closely Nancy and Lacoue-Labarthe follow Heidegger here, to what extent can they really break with his later quietism? In this context, it is crucial to see that for Schmitt the concept of the political in modernity is an object of *political struggle* as well as philosophical debate. As Schmitt emphasizes, in the final analysis, "all political concepts, images, and terms have a polemical meaning" (*CP*, 30). Schmitt fights to defend the political from the "depoliticization" of liberalism, a depoliticization he sees as the culmination of a centuries-long "striving for a neutral domain" that transcends potentially violent political conflict (*CP*, 89). In liberalism, one seeks to evade the demanding decision and hierarchical authority characteristic of politics as such. Schmitt argues that the attempt to purge the world of politics as he understands it leads to a dehumanization of all forces that might oppose this movement—a dehumanization that in turn encourages the extermination of the opponent. At the same time, the search for a "neutral sphere" in which the kinds of conflict that tore apart early Modern Europe might be set aside leads, in the end, to a celebration of technology. Here Schmitt's argument bears striking resemblances to Heidegger's analysis of the nihilism of technological modernity—with the important difference being that the rise of technology is the result of human, political demands and conflicts as opposed to the history of Being.

On Schmitt's account, Hobbes thought he could rise above theological debate by essentially removing God from politics. As an early empiricist, Hobbes argues (a) we can know only what we experience; (b) what we experience is always finite; and (c) an omnipotent, omniscient God is by definition infinite.[30] This implies that there is and can be no true knowledge of God. It follows that any theological debate about His qualities or the specifics of His revelation is essentially senseless. One can have no strong grounds for opposing a Catholic or Protestant sovereign, and hence no grounds for engaging in anything like the St. Bartholomew's Day Massacre. But if this secures a neutral domain by removing contentious religious debate from the public realm, Hobbes' discourse itself is based upon a metaphysical account of the nature of knowledge and being that not all could accept, and which thus could not itself achieve the desired neutral status. The same proves true of the attempt to ground (a)political neutrality on economic rationality, which collapses in the emergence of Marxist class war. In the end, only technology is truly neutral. But, paradoxically, this neutrality is not what we had hoped it would be: "the neutrality of technology is something other than the neutrality of all former domains. Technology is always only an instrument and weapon; precisely because it serves all, it is not neutral" (*CP*, 91). Technology is neutral because it is *instrumental*. If that is to be the defining characteristic of the neutral domain around which the community is to be organized, that community will be one that celebrates instrumentality, or power as such. Schmitt terms this "the spirit of technicity": "The spirit of technicity . . . is the belief in an activist metaphysics—the belief in unlimited power and the domination of man over nature, even over human nature; the belief in the unlimited 'receding of natural boundaries,' in the unlimited possibilities for change and prosperity" (*CP*, 94).[31] This nihilistic technicity is something that Schmitt *opposes* in asserting the concept of the political.

Schmitt is thus a more ambiguous figure than he is commonly seen to be, one who is closer to Nancy than Nancy's comments about him might suggest. The central point, however, is not whether Schmitt and Nancy agree or not, but that Schmitt *does* take a political position, whereas it is unclear if Nancy can bring himself to. On Nancy's account, the question of the political is an essentially philosophical one, and the question of the philosophical is an essentially political one. But there is no simple equivalence here. No pragmatic political engagement (e.g., to challenge the hierarchies that make possible authoritarian Schmittian decisions) can ever hope to address the essence of the political. However, the deconstruction of metaphysics does address political matters. Nancy's texts are not like texts on epistemology, for example. They are meant to show us something essential about the political, about sovereignty, and its inevitable demand for the sacrifice of the distinct individualities and lives of the "parts" of the sovereign whole. Hence, Nancy is committed to doing two very different things at the same time: first, developing a deconstructive reading of Heidegger that, as a critique of metaphysics, will take in those aspects of Schmitt that seem most disturbing (such as the celebration of sovereign authority in the realm of mortal conflict); and, second, clarifying the realities of political life in the terms of that reading in a matter that allows for the embrace of our finitude and, with it, justice and freedom. But, by insisting that the concept of the political is derivative from the essence of the political, Nancy would seem to undermine, if not deny, the latter possibility.

Consider in this regard a passage in which Nancy approaches and then retreats from the problems of the sovereign decision raised by Schmitt. In *The Sense of the World*, Nancy suggests that "the combination of four terms—*subject*, *citizen*, *sovereignty*, *community*—organizes, saturates, and exhausts the political space closing itself today."[32] In this space, which we never quite manage to leave, these four terms map out the coordinates of two ideal-types of political community: the politics of the subject and the politics of the citizen. The first names the metaphysics of the sovereign subject-work according to which "the community at work creates and works itself, so to speak, thereby accomplishing the subjective process of self-formation and self-production."[33] The second names the space of being-in-common of Nancy's "inoperative community," where there is no common essence to the community of ecstatic singularities other than their existent lack of essence and identity. But where *The Inoperative Community* celebrates the first option—essentially a more public and *gelassen* version of Heideggerian *Gelassenheit*—here Nancy suggests "one has good reason to ask oneself if these two options are not in an intimate solidarity or connivance" (*SW*, 107). To the extent that they are, it is hard to see what alternative there could be to Schmittian sovereignty, metaphysics, and all that Nancy attacks. Every community will require some instantiation, and that will only come at the cost of making citizens subjects, making the inoperative community operative, and, finally, sovereign: "subjectivity and citizenship turn out to be two interpretations or configurations of a single scheme of self-sufficiency. This scheme itself would correspond, on the side of the concept, to sovereignty, and on the side of the intuition, to community" (*SW*, 110). Nancy's version of Kant's famous dictum thus reads, "sovereignty without community is empty, community without sovereignty is blind."[34] Nancy accordingly does not sound a hopeful note here: "There is no possibility of choosing between the two poles of self-sufficiency, *nor is there any possibility of choosing the hypothetical happy medium*" (*SW*, 110; my emphasis). If he does still hold out hope, it is for nothing more than a thought: "Can one think a politics of nonselfsufficiency?" he asks (*SW*, 111). And later he writes, "*The whole question* is whether we can finally manage to *think* the 'contract'—the tying of the (k)not—according to a model other than the juridicocommercial model" (*SW*, 111; my emphasis).

If "the whole question" is a matter of *thinking*, mere politics would seem to be wholly beside the point. Nancy sometimes denies that this is the case. In introducing this approach to the political in the "Opening Address," he and Lacoue-Labarthe strike a very humble note, and say that they make "no pretension to *political theory*," in part because "we are in no way 'specialists' in the field of politics or in the sciences which deal with politics, and nothing—beyond the work of a (philosophical) teaching carried out in common for some years . . .—authorizes us to venture into this realm." However, it is not simply "a question of competence" that determines their interests here; it is also "a deliberate choice": "the direct approach to the political (which, even if this description is a little quick, might just as well be called the empirical approach) does not interest us—and for the very simple reason that, basically, we no longer believe such an approach still to be possible (or even less that it can still be decisive)" (*RP*, 108–109).[35] The second and bolder of these claims obviously undermines the first and more modest one. If they are right that a direct approach to the political is no longer possible, then anyone who *does* claim to be doing political theory or to be engaged in an empirical study of the political is simply wrong about what they are doing: their object of study has disappeared or is in the process of disappearing, and their "work" is simply an idle dream or a willful delusion. No doubt, Nancy and Lacoue-Labarthe refer to "other, assuredly always possible and in some cases even desirable, approaches to the political." But nothing is said of what these other approaches to the political might be. Because the two most obvious candidates are expressly rejected, this implies that Nancy and Lacoue-Labarthe's considered view does not allow for a division of labor between philosophical deconstruction on the one side and any less philosophical or more "practical" approach on the other. At the very least, we can conclude that, if they are indeed open to other approaches to the political, these other approaches must wait on Nancy and Lacoue-Labarthe's work, which defines the political and "renders . . . possible" the questioning of its essence in a way that the intuitions, received opinions, and empirical data of would-be political theorists and scientists simply cannot. And as that work of definition and delimitation is one that is not only not yet completed but scarcely begun, it is difficult to imagine these other approaches to the political might do anything more than stumble over their object of inquiry.[36] The challenge Nancy and Lacoue-Labarthe propose to the way we think about politics is a fundamental one that no one can avoid on the grounds of competence or interest or taste. If they are right in their main claims, they have to be wrong that they have "deliberately chosen" to approach the question of the political in the way they do. Unless that deliberate choice is to face decisively a reality that others—political theorists—are too meek or benighted to face.

In the end, *the political* here all but abandons politics. In a discussion of the need to move away from the subject's foundation in essence towards existence's transcendence in freedom in *The Experience of Freedom*, Nancy writes, "In all movements of liberation, as in all vested institutions of freedom, it is precisely this transcendence which still has to be freed. *In and through* [*À travers*] ethical, juridical, material and civil liberties, one must free that through which alone these liberties are, on the one hand, ultimately possible and thinkable, and on the other, capable of receiving a destination other than that of their imminent self-consumption." A footnote attached to the end of the first clause ("liberties"), however, cautions us, "We are not saying 'political' ['*politique*'] here. Either what is understood by 'political freedoms' more or less covers the series of epithets we have used, or we would have to consider in the political as such [*le politique comme tel*] the specific putting at stake of the transcendence of existence. It is uncertain whether one could do this today" (*EF*, 13, 183 n. 1; my emphasis). The note contradicts the sentence to which it is attached, as it distinguishes *the political* from these banal epithets, "political freedoms," so as to suggest that only the former opens up any possibility at all of politics being part of the "putting at stake of the transcendence of existence." But the original passage proposes that it is *through* these banal freedoms that we have to free "that through which alone these liberties are," namely, "the freedom of being." Nancy's distinction between these political freedoms and *the political* thus has the force of robbing practical, enforceable freedoms of philosophical significance, precisely what is promised in the main body of the text.

One would not want to suggest that Nancy fails to see how necessary these compromised practical matters are. As we have seen, he explicitly advocates forms of justice and freedom incompatible with all forms of totalitarianism. And he is explicit in discussing freedom as "a collection of rights and exemptions," which in their "suppression or even suspension . . . opens directly onto the intolerable itself" (*EF*, 2). But he does not engage his own *thinking* with the defense of these freedoms, or with the attempt to keep a *practice* of citizenship and respect for plurality from being sacrificed to the necessity of sovereignty. Indeed, his account of the practical is one in which all cows are pretty much black. Either one is caught up in the metaphysics of the subject-work, or one is in the process of twisting free of it by means of a deconstructive analysis. No doubt, Nancy argues that Being has left us in a more promising position than Schmitt thought. In reference to Schmitt's secularization thesis, Nancy writes that Schmitt "was right to affirm that 'The metaphysical image that a definite epoch forges of the world has the same structure as what the world immediately understands to be appropriate as a form of political organization.'" He adds only that Schmitt was "not in a position to appreciate the extent to which *the metaphysics of our age*, that is, the beginning of the twenty-first century—at least if we actually deal with it rather than replaying 'the thirties'—is what one can call *the metaphysics of the deconstruction of the essence, and of existence qua sense*" (*SW*, 92). But even if one grants that, appearances notwithstanding, our time is open to deconstruction in a way that Schmitt's was not, it is still hard to see how deconstruction alone can play the *political* role Nancy at times promises it will.[37] In his "Letter on Humanism," Heidegger argues that the highest form of action, *das Wesen des Handelns*, lies in thinking.[38] For all of his attempts to turn Heidegger against himself, Nancy at the end of the day would seem to agree. Whether thought alone shall suffice, however, remains to be seen.

NOTES

1. At a number of points, I refer to "Nancy's ideas and claims" when one might more accurately but more awkwardly speak of "Nancy and Lacoue-Labarthe's ideas and claims." The relationship between Lacoue-Labarthe and Nancy is complex. They are frequent collaborators, not only in their work on the political but on

topics from German Romanticism to Lacan. The basic premises of their approach to the political is found in their joint work of the 1970s and 1980s, an approach Lacoue-Labarthe has taken in his own direction in a number of essays and, most significantly, in his *Heidegger, Art, and Politics: The Fiction of the Political*, trans. C. Turner (Oxford: Blackwell, 1990).

2. Compare Hannah Arendt, "Heidegger at Eighty," in *Heidegger and Modern Philosophy: Critical Essays*, ed. M. Murray (London: Yale University Press, 1978), p. 301.

3. Karl Löwith, *My Life in Germany Before and After 1933*, trans. E. King (London: The Athlone Press, 1994), p. 60.

4. "[M]etaphysics as the history of the truth of what is as such, is, in its essence, nihilism." Martin Heidegger, "The Age of the World Picture," in *The Question Concerning Technology and Other Essays*, trans. William Lovitt (New York: Harper and Row, 1977), p. 109. Henceforth cited as *QT*.

5. Martin Heidegger, *Being and Time*, trans. J. Macquarrie & E. Robinson (Oxford: Blackwell, 1978), H. 388, p. 440; and Martin Heidegger, *Introduction to Metaphysics*, trans. Gregory Fried and Richard Polt (New Haven: Yale University Press, 2000), pp. 41, 44, 213. For an outstanding discussion of the relation between historicity in *Being and Time* and in Heidegger's political writings (one indebted to Nancy), see Miguel de Beistegui, *Heidegger and the Political: Dystopias* (London: Routledge, 1998).

6. Martin Heidegger, *Gelassenheit* (Tübingen: Günther Neske Pfullingen, 1992), pp. 13, 23.

7. Martin Heidegger, "The Self-Assertion of the German University," in *Martin Heidegger and National Socialism: Questions and Answers*, ed. Günter Neske and Emil Kettering (New York: Paragon, 1990), p. 10.

8. "*Der Spiegel*'s Interview with Martin Heidegger," in *The Heidegger Controversy*, ed. Richard Wolin (Cambridge: MIT Press, 1993), pp. 107, 104.

9. See, e.g., Jean-Luc Nancy, *The Experience of Freedom*, trans. B. McDonald (Stanford: Stanford University Press, 1993), p. 79. Henceforth cited as *EF*.

10. In the next few paragraphs I draw on my earlier discussion of these matters in Andrew Norris, "Jean-Luc Nancy and the Myth of the Common," *Constellations* 7:2 (June 2000), pp. 272–295.

11. Compare Heidegger: "Man as a rational being of the Enlightenment is no less subject than is man who grasps himself as a nation, wills himself as a people, fosters himself as a race, and, finally, empowers himself as lord of the earth." Heidegger, "The Age of the World Picture," in *QT*, 152.

12. Conversely, "Community understood as work or through its works would presuppose that the common being, as such, be objectifiable and producible." Jean-Luc Nancy, *The Inoperative Community*, ed. Peter Connor (Minneapolis: University of Minnesota Press, 1991), p. 31. Henceforth cited as *IC*.

13. The notion of the subject-work as "the possibility of a presentation of the infinite as the auto-production of the subject" is taken by Nancy and Lacoue-Labarthe from the German Romantics, who inherited from Kant "the problematic of the subject unpresentable to itself." Kant's transcendental and moral subjects present themselves only with their own activity; they can never make *themselves* present to themselves. The Romantics attempt to bridge this gap by identifying subject and work. Hence the subject-work is also defined as "the becoming-artist of the work or

absolute auto-production itself: man as the work of art creating itself, art henceforth identified with the being-artist." "A Poietics [*sic*] in which the subject confounds itself with its own production, and a Literature enclosed in and enclosing the law of its own engendering, romanticism (ourselves, in sum) is the moment of the *literary absolute*." Jean-Luc Nancy and Philippe Lacoue-Labarthe, *The Literary Absolute*, trans. Philip Barnard and Cheryl Lester (Albany: State University of New York Press, 1988), pp. 77, 30, 77, xxii.

14. Hannah Arendt, *The Origins of Totalitarianism* (New York: Harcourt Brace Jovanovich, 1973), pp. 389, 391, 444, 450, and 464.

15. "CIA Told to Do 'Whatever Necessary' to Kill Bin Laden,'" *Washington Post*, Sunday, October 21, 2001; Page A01; http://www.washingtonpost.com/ac2/wp-dyn/A27452-2001Oct20?language=printer.

16. They continue: "An analysis of Nazism should never be conceived as a dossier of simple accusation, but as one element in a general deconstruction of the history in which our own provenance lies." Jean-Luc Nancy and Philippe Lacoue-Labarthe, "The Nazi Myth," trans. Brian Holmes, *Critical Inquiry* 16:2 (Winter 1990), pp. 291–312, here 312. Henceforth cited as *NM*.

17. Jean-Luc Nancy, *The Birth to Presence*, trans. Brian Holmes (Stanford: Stanford University Press, 1993), p. 155. Henceforth cited as *BP*.

18. Jean-Luc Nancy, "*La Comparution*/The Compearance: From the Existence of 'Communism' to the Community of 'Existence'" *Political Theory* 20:3 (August 1992), pp. 371–398, here 393 n. 2.

19. Jean-Luc Nancy, "Of Being-in-Common," in *Community at Loose Ends*, ed. The Miami Theory Collective (Minneapolis: University of Minnesota Press, 1991), p. 2.

20. As Nancy puts it in his short book on Hegel, "Freedom . . . is indeed autonomy, but the law it gives itself is . . . the law to have no law." Nancy, *Hegel: The Restlessness of the Negative* (Minneapolis: Minnesota University Press, 2002), p. 68. Nancy argues that this is the true teaching of Hegel as well. This is an argument that is, at the least, hard to accept, given Hegel's spirited attack on "the hatred of law," the feeling that "does not recognize itself in the law and thereby recognize its own freedom in it." Hegel, *Philosophy of Right* (Cambridge: Cambridge University Press, 1991), Preface, p. 17. See also § 149. I discuss this further in Norris, "Beyond the Fury of Destruction: Hegel on Freedom" *Political Theory* 32:3 (June 2004), pp. 409–418.

21. I owe this observation to Hans Sluga's forthcoming book, *The Care of the Common: The Concept of the Political in an Age of Uncertainty*.

22. Carl Schmitt, *The Concept of the Political*, expanded edition, trans. George Schwab (Chicago: The University of Chicago Press, 2007), p. 37. Henceforth cited as *CP*. I silently modify the translation throughout when accuracy demands. German references are from *Der Begriff des Politischen* (München: Dunker & Humblot, 1932).

23. Compare *CP*, 33: "The friend, enemy, and combat concepts receive their real meaning precisely because they refer to the real possibility of physical killing."

24. I initially defended this reading of *The Concept of the Political* in Norris, "Carl Schmitt on Friends, Enemies, and the Political," *Telos* 112 (Summer 1998), pp. 68–88. Although I argue there that Schmitt is incorrectly read when he is seen (as he often is) as a warmonger, it is striking in the present circumstance that he

cites E. Lederer's comment, "We can say that on the day of mobilization the hitherto existing society was transformed into a community" (*CP*, 45).

25. I discuss Schmitt's own emphasis on the metaphysical status of his analysis of sovereignty in his 1922 *Political Theology* in A. Norris, "Sovereignty, Exception, and Norm," in *Democracy's Empire: Sovereignty, Law and Violence*, ed. Stewart Motha (Oxford: Blackwell, 2007).

26. Philippe Lacoue-Labarthe and Jean-Luc Nancy, "Opening Address to the Center for the Philosophical Research on the Political," in *Retreating the Political*, ed. Simon Sparks (New York: Routledge, 1997), p. 109. Henceforth cited as *RP*.

27. "There is nothing wrong if the 'man in the street' believes that there is a 'diesel engine' because Herr Diesel invented it. Not everyone needs to know that the whole business of invention would not have been able to advance one step if philosophy, at the historical moment at which it entered the realm of the its nonessence, had not thought the categories of nature and so opened up this realm for the research and experiments of inventors. Of course, this does not mean that one who knows the true provenance of modern power machinery is thereby in a position to build better motors. But he is perhaps uniquely situated to ask what machine technology *is* within the history of man's relationship to Being." Martin Heidegger, *Nietzsche*, Volume Four, trans. Frank Capuzzi (San Francisco: Harper & Row, 1982), p. 39.

28. See also *QT*, 116.

29. Philippe Lacoue-Labarthe, "In the Name of . . . ," in *RP*, pp. 55–86, here 71.

30. Hobbes, *Leviathan*, ed. C. B. Macpherson (New York: Penguin, 1968), p. 99.

31. This is the source for Arendt's argument that totalitarianism is devoted to the notion that "everything is possible." Arendt, op. cit., p. 440.

32. Jean-Luc Nancy, *The Sense of the World*, trans. Jeffery Librett (Minneapolis: University of Minnesota, 1997), p. 103. Henceforth cited as *SW*.

33. *Heidegger, Art, and Politics*, p. 70. Lacoue-Labarthe is summarizing Nancy here.

34. Compare Kant: "Thoughts without content are empty, intuitions without concepts are blind." Kant, *Critique of Pure Reason*, trans. Norman Kemp Smith (London: Macmillan, 1964), A51/B75.

35. Lacoue-Labarthe and Nancy repeatedly emphasize the *decisive* nature of the urgent task they claim to take up. See for instance, *RP*, 108 where they sum up their plans for the Centre: "to pose, today, the question of the essence of the political seems to us to be a task finally—and decidedly [*et décidement*]—necessary. And our aim here would be finally—and decidedly [*et décidement*]—to render it possible."

36. Compare Heidegger's discussion of the inability of the sciences (presumably including whatever political science we might have) to *think* in *Was Heißt Denken?* (Stuttgart: Reclam, 1992), p. 25.

37. I write "appearances notwithstanding" because of the manner in which politics today, as I have already emphasized, seems to repeat many of the most disturbing aspects of political life in the 1930s.

38. Martin Heidegger, "Letter on Humanism," in *Martin Heidegger: Basic Writings*, revised & augmented, ed. David F. Krell (San Francisco: Harper, 1993), pp. 217, 262.

TEN

THE TASK OF JUSTICE

David Pettigrew

Contemporary discourse about human rights makes particular use of the 1948 UN Universal Declaration of Human Rights, as the Declaration presents a set of guidelines that are based on assumptions about the nature of human beings: their thoughts, ideas, freedom of expression and freedom of association.[1] Article 1 of the Declaration states, for example, "All human beings are born free and equal in dignity and rights. They are endowed with reason and conscience and should act towards one another in a spirit of brotherhood." The document engages the idea of the human being as having rights, regardless of ethnicity or gender. Such rights include life, protection from harm, and access to the latest advances in scientific technology.[2]

The Declaration, then, is based on the idea of the inalienable moral worth and sovereignty of every human being as such. The philosophical basis for such a principle can be found in the ethical theory of Immanuel Kant, who asserts that every rational being is an end in itself: "Now I say that man, and in general every rational being, *exists* as an end in himself, *not merely as a means* for arbitrary use by this or that will: he must in all his actions, whether they are directed to himself or to other rational human beings, always be viewed *at the same time as an end*."[3] The ethical significance of this formulation for Kant is that one should, "*Act in such a way that you always treat humanity, whether in your own person or in the person of any other, never simply as a means, but always at the same time as an end*."[4] Thus it would be my assumption that a document such as the Declaration depends on the Kantian postulation of the absolute and inalienable moral worth and sovereignty of the human being solely on the basis of its rational existence.

Yet, given the increased incidence of dehumanization, human rights violations, and catastrophic violence in the past century, including the all-too-familiar names of Auschwitz, Hiroshima, Vukovar, and Srebrenica, one wonders about the ultimate efficacy of the theoretical framework provided by the Declaration as well as by Kant's ethics. Perhaps Kant's presentation of the idea of the intrinsic worth of each human being, which I uphold, and the ideas contained in the Declaration are overly ideal and abstract and, hence, do not allow for the consideration of the visceral suffering and death of the victims of dehumanization and catastrophic violence. Perhaps we need an ethics that could respond to the vulnerability of the singularity of human existences, one that could give thought to the fragility of a community made up of those very singularities. Furthermore, one could speculate that the Declaration, along with Kant's moral theory, is overly static, even a limitation on freedom, rather than its reliable guarantor. Kant speaks, for example, of a principle that is "the supreme limiting condition of every man's freedom of action."[5]

In this respect, in relation to the possible limitations of Kant's moral project, I address the work of Jean-Luc Nancy, who offers a framework for giving thought to the singularity of human existence in the contemporary world. For Nancy, beings are "singular" in their finite being, in the finitude of their existence that is theirs alone. Nancy's thinking of singularity is grounded in Heidegger's thinking of Being and involves a strategic appropriation of Heidegger's notion of the human beings' "ownmost" being-towards-death or finitude.[6] Nancy appropriates this theme and emphasizes that one's being-towards-death cannot be taken over, taken on, or shared by the other.[7] For Nancy, such singularity insures the consequent impossibility of cohering in an absolute community with others. Nancy indeed insists on the danger of the absolute immanence or absolute coherence of community because he associates any such immanence with totalitarianism.[8] The finitude of singularity interrupts any such absolute immanence of community that would stifle freedom or difference.

But, for Nancy, the finite singularity of our "ownmost" being-towards-death is shared with others in the following paradoxical sense. One shares, precisely, the impossibility of sharing in any traditional sense. We share that which we cannot share: our singular being-towards-death. Nancy expresses this paradoxical sense of sharing with the French term *partager*, which can mean both to share and to divide, and has been rendered in English as a "sharing-out" in an effort to capture each of these nuances. To be singular is always already to be-with other singular beings, or, according to Nancy's well-known formulation, it is "being singular plural." Nancy writes, "Being cannot *be* anything but being-with-one-another, circulating in the *with* and as the *with* of this singularly plural coexistence."[9]

In his text *The Inoperative Community*, Nancy cautions that such a "being-with" "is not a communion . . . nor even a communication as this is understood to exist between subjects. But these singular beings are themselves constituted by sharing, they are distributed and placed, or rather spaced, by the sharing that makes them others" (*IC*, 25). These singular others communicate by "not communing." The communication of sharing takes place in this "very dislocation" (*IC*, 25). Any community would be composed of singular existences that "share" the exposure of their singularity in their being-towards-death. What is "communicated" is nothing other than the exposition of singularity (*IC*, 29). Community means that there is "no singular being without another singular being" (*IC*, 28).

However, it is crucial to recognize that, for Nancy, singularity is not the same as individuality.[10] Singularity, he writes, "is not individuality; it is, each time, the punctuality of a 'with' that establishes a certain origin of meaning and connects it to an infinity of other possible origins" (*BSP*, 85).[11] Each singular existence, then, in its ex-position, is a source from which the world can be created and recreated. He proposes that, as part of this being singular plural, we are exposed with language through an "originarily singular sharing of voices" that exposes not the voice or a meaning but "the world and its proper being-with-all-beings in the world" (*BSP*, 85). This exposure "makes the world 'hold' or 'consist' in its proper singular plurality" (*BSP*, 85). Nancy asserts, "*The speaker speaks for the world, which means the speaker speaks to it, on behalf of it, and in order to make it a 'world'*" (*BSP*, 3). This struggle for making or creating a world in its singularity and infinitely finite enactment of possible beginnings is, for Nancy, nothing less than the condition and definition of justice. We read in *The Creation of the World* or *Globalization*:

> *To create the world* means: immediately, without delay, reopening each possible struggle for a world, that is, for what must form the contrary of a global injustice against the background of general equivalence. But this means to conduct this struggle precisely in the name of the fact that this *world* is coming out of nothing, that there is nothing before it and that it is without models, without principle and without given end, and that it is precisely *what* forms the justice and the meaning of a world.[12]

Each "singularity" makes sense or creates a world in a finite way, in a sense that this making sense happens as a singular event. The finite event of sense making, which leaves room for other events of sense making, is infinite.[13] Nancy thematizes a world that is always already under formation, and he concludes from this that justice would entail a world that is constituted by this inexhaustible creation of meaning.[14] The prevention of such a creation of meaning would be injustice. The work of "*mondialisation*" or "world-forming" is itself then, the work of justice.[15] The inexhaustible nature of this work does not mean that justice cannot be achieved but that each time it is achieved or enacted as a fact, it still remains to be created, or re-created. Perhaps Nancy's emphasis on beginnings, on the fact that each singular existence can inaugurate a world, is an advance on Kant's thinking of autonomy in the sense that the concept of a sovereign autonomy is rendered more dynamic, particular, and more fragile. The "undecidability," the singularity of each act and its openness to the next, is what preserves "incompletion," ensures the "inoperativity" of any given community and thus resists totalitarian closure.

Moreover, Nancy's treatment of the finite singularity of the human being, a singularity that is at the same time constitutively ex-posed to and with others, opens onto a nuanced thinking of sovereignty. The sovereignty articulated in Nancy's thought is a "*shared sovereignty* shared *between* Daseins," that is, "between singular existences that are not subjects" (*IC*, 25). With such a paradoxical treatment of sovereignty, Nancy seeks to approach the possibility of a nonsubstantial place from which another beginning, another creation, or another world, could ensue.

In *The Creation of the World* or *Globalization*, Nancy advances on his proposition in *The Sense of the World* that such a "being-in-common" can make itself "sovereign in a new way" (*SW*, 91). This "new way" could be formulated as follows: A sovereignty is based on nothing, "no finality, no order of production or subjection, whether it concerns the agent or the patient or the cause or the effect. Dependent on nothing, it is entirely delivered over to itself, insofar as precisely, the 'itself' neither precedes nor founds it but is the *nothing*, the very thing from which it is suspended" (*CW*, 103). Such a sovereignty, which he contrasts with a sovereignty of autonomy, domination and mastery, calls for a thinking of an "anti-sovereignty," a kind of "negative sovereignty" or a "sovereignty without sovereignty," a negative sovereignty that marks the withdrawal of substantiality and subjectivity. Such a thinking of non-sovereign sovereignty casts his use of the term "ex-position" in a new light. The singular being is "sovereign" in its ex-positioning. For Nancy, this paradoxical sense of sovereignty plays or opens as the "origin of the world," an origin that occurs "at each moment of the world. It is the each time of Being and its realm is the Being-with. The origin is for and by way of the singular plural of every possible origin" (*BSP*, 83). Nancy's articulation of a being-with as a singular ex-position is significant, then, as a challenge to the sovereign autonomy of the Kantian ethical subject.[16]

I would like to speculate further about the ethical implications of such an exposure, or of an ex-positioning, and of such a paradoxical non-sovereign sovereignty, by drawing on the work of Emmanuel Levinas. This is not to assert that it is necessary or even possible to reduce the treatment of singularity and exposure in Nancy to that of Levinas. In fact, in the concluding section we show that Nancy develops a profoundly singular and suggestive notion of a bodily sense of exposure. The point rather is to develop their respective accounts of singularity and exposure as an alternative to the sovereign autonomy of the Kantian subject, and to thus open a space for giving thought to that alternative.

For Levinas, human beings are singular and irreducible to a whole or to a same. Each singular being that we face remains an irreducible alterity. More importantly, this irreducible alterity demands an ethical response. It is intrinsic to Levinas' thought that we respond to the Other; respond to the face (*le visage*), that is, to a singular face. In a 1981 interview with Richard Kearney, Levinas said that the approach to the face is the most basic mode of responsibility. The face is the other who asks me not to let him or her die alone.[17] This face, Levinas writes, speaks (*le visage parle*).[18] The notion of "speaking" bears particular mention in Levinas's work because he raises a distinction between "the saying" (*le dire*) and "the said" (*le dit*). "Saying" is an event that conveys something such that I respond. Levinas distinguishes this from the predicate content of the said, a statement. In the 1981 interview, Levinas stated, "Saying is ethical sincerity insofar as it is exposition."[19] One could speculate that the event-like exposition of the saying is free of the linguistic content of any particular statement and as such it allows for a plurality of voices, each one containing a demand for a response. The "saying" entails an excess that exceeds the semantic or linguistic content of the statement. The excess lies in the very fact of the address of the saying; an address that raises the necessity of response and recognition. For Levinas, the saying means speaking to the Other and for the Other, and brings about an ethical proximity.

For Levinas, this responsibility for the address of the other is the fundamental structure of subjectivity. In his 1968 essay "On Substitution," he writes, "To be a 'self' is to be responsible without having done anything."[20] I am responsible for responsibility itself. We must substitute ourselves for the other and expiate for their transgressions. Our response to the face of the other, however, can never be completely satisfied. The call is infinite. This is a constitutive insufficiency that must be understood in a positive sense. Levinas' ethical thought offers, in this respect, a resource for the interruption of the dehumanization and violence of our age. For Levinas the responsibility to the other, the response to the face of the other, is a significantly nonreciprocal relation. This nonreciprocity begins to intimate the counter-intuitive and seemingly impossible nature of his thought. Levinas is conscious of the radical nature of his thought: "I employ this extreme formulation. The face orders and ordains me (to serve it)."[21]

What sort of ethical framework could be woven from the work of Nancy and Levinas? With Nancy, we give thought to an inoperative community that entails the exposure of each to all, an inoperative community that recognizes a fundamentally constitutional limit at the heart of its composition. Furthermore, with Nancy, we encounter a world of singular plural beginnings, each beginning a fact, each beginning a creation of a world. This process is impossible in the sense that it is never complete but always justice in act. With Levinas, the face of the other makes an impossible demand. We substitute for the other in a self-effacing expiation. Would such an ethics drawing on singularity and alterity be an impossible ethics? Perhaps, however, after Kant and after the Universal Declaration, an impossible ethics—not abstract and ideal, but grounded in singularity and alterity—is precisely what is needed for our time, which in some respects, with "ethnic cleansing" and genocide, is an impossible time. Is an impossible ethics needed for impossible times?

But how would one participate, with Nancy, in such an inoperative community comprised of the exposition of each singularity? How, with Levinas, would one respond to the impossible demand of the other? Is such a framework just as theoretical and inaccessible as that of Kant's notion of sovereign self-worth? It is in this context that I identify a genre of literature that has emerged from recent catastrophic events. The texts I address provide a possible model for thinking of the exposition and exposure of singularity, for responding to the suffering of the other, and for the creation of the world. Some of the most important texts about the war in Bosnia and Herzegovina, for example, were already published in 1994 and are now either out of print or difficult to obtain. It may be unique to our time that so many accounts of dehumanization and catastrophic violence, from different perspectives and in different styles, have been published and disseminated so quickly. Of course the violence and suffering outpaces the reports, as in the case of Rwanda, where as many as 800,000 were slaughtered in one hundred days, roughly 8,000 per day. It is said that this was at a faster rate than was achieved at Auschwitz.[22] In other words, as quickly as it comes, the literature always comes too late. The publications are not immediately capable of stopping the violence but, insofar as they expose the suffering of the other, they might slow the violence. However, it was too late when Michael Sells wrote in 1998 that the Yugoslav Army had captured Vukovar and handed over the inhabitants in the hospital to the Chetnik irregulars for interrogation. A mass grave had already been found in 1992 at the nearby village of Ovčara.[23]

Although the literature is generally "too late," in many other crucial respects, the work continues to be indispensable. Comprehensive texts by

Michael Sells and Ed Vulliamy, for example, provide important historical, geographical, cultural, linguistic, and other forms of information.[24] The texts weave a historical context in which the people of the region lived. In the face of ignorance and dehumanization, the lives of the inhabitants, along with their historical experiences, are rehumanized. There are details about specific events and the human beings who suffered, endured, or perished. There are reports about the destruction of buildings, the shelling of markets and playgrounds, the murder of intellectuals, and the effacement of cultural memories and traditions.

Sells asserts that the Serb artillery systematically targeted major libraries, manuscript collections, museums, and other cultural institutions for destruction. When armies were able to get closer, the buildings were dynamited. "In many cases," Sells writes, "the mosques have been ploughed over and turned into parking lots or parks; every evidence of their existence has been effaced. Graveyards, birth records, work records and other traces of the Bosnian Muslim people have been eradicated."[25]

Vulliamy was one of the first journalists to discover the concentration camps at Omarska and Trnopolje. Following the first rumors of mass killings and the conditions in such camps, he managed to convince Serbian authorities to allow him to visit the sites. Despite restricted access and close supervision at Omarska, Vulliamy was able to see and report on groups of men:

> [T]heir heads newly shaven, their clothes baggy over their skeletal bodies. Some are barely able to move. . . . The men are at various stages of human decay and affliction; the bones of their elbows and wrists protrude like pieces of jagged stone from the pencil thin stalks to which their arms have been reduced. The skin is putrified, the complexions of their faces have been corroded. These humans are alive but decomposed, debased, degraded, and utterly subservient.[26]

Later that day at Trnopolje, Vulliamy encountered another startling sight: thousands of men, women, and children surrounded by barbed wire fencing. He writes, "The men were stripped to the waist, and among them was the young man with the famished torso and xylophone rib-cage who that day became the symbol of the war: Fikret Alić. . . . Fikret had literally been starved into a dismal, malnourished condition in which we found him, after fifty-two days in Kereterm."[27] Vulliamy's text provides remarkably personal detail about both the Serbian guards and the Bosnian Muslim prisoners behind the barbed wire. The reports from Omarska and Trnopolje brought international outrage and led to further investigations that revealed Omarska, for example, to have been a place of "savage killing, torture, humiliation, and barbarous cruelty."[28]

Chuck Sudetic's book, *Blood and Vengeance: One Family's Story of the War in Bosnia,* is a text that follows a particular family, the Čeliks, who endured the Srebrenica siege and massacre that took the lives of more than 8,000 Bosnian Muslims. The book provides remarkably personal details of the Čelik family and the community, including the marriage and marriage feast of Huso and Hiba Čelik.[29] We partake of family travels and travails against the backdrop of the gathering storm. We accompany them on their perilous arrival in Srebrenica on September 19, 1992. We are given an intimate glimpse of the Čelik family taking shelter in a cramped basement on a night when the shells were falling every two minutes; little Edin, born in 1994, had a stuffy nose and was romping around and getting on everyone's nerves, Mirza, born in 1990, was running a fever and refusing to eat. The adults were trying to console them while dreading the days ahead.[30]

As the Bosnian Serb Army closed in on Srebrenica the residents tried to flee. Men made their way through the woods through shelling and gunfire. In *Srebrenica: Record of a War Crime*, Jan Willem Honig and Norbert Both tell of the fate of one thousand of the men captured and herded to a soccer field in Nova Kasaba:

> Many more of the men from Srebrenica never even made it beyond Nova Kasaba. The Serbs had captured them in the hundreds. . . . They were assembled on the football ground just north of Nova Kasaba. On Thursday, Dutch soldiers spotted an estimated 1,000 squatting on the football pitch.[31]

A few days later an American U-2 spy plane detected that the field was empty "but that a nearby field had changed in appearance: it showed signs of recent digging and experts identified what they believed to be three mass graves."[32]

In addition to the accounts of the systematic murder of men and boys, there are unbearable accounts of the violence against women during the war in Bosnia, violence that Sells refers to as "Gynocide," "a deliberate attack on women as child-bearers," a strategy of dehumanization and brutalization through organized "rape centers."[33] Vulliamy provides further accounts of this violence against women with names and extensive testimony reporting that 20,000 women had suffered sexual violation.[34] He details organized camps such as Kod Sonje, a motel at Vogošća outside of Sarajevo.[35]

The range of books that have been published are too numerous to discuss in the context of this chapter. However, one other book bears mention in order to clarify the diversity and value of the genre: Clea Koff's *The Bone Woman: A Forensic Anthropologist's Search for Truth in the Mass Graves of Rwanda, Bosnia, Croatia and Kosovo*. Koff is a forensic anthropologist who worked for Physicians for Human Rights, a Boston-based nongovernmental organization that assembled a team of forensic experts to investigate mass graves for the International Criminal Tribunal on Rwanda and the International Criminal Tribunal for the former Yugoslavia. Koff's goal was to end human rights abuses by making the "bones talk" in order to bring the murderers to justice.[36] Koff's book provides us with a voice that is exemplary of this genre. It is not that of the reporter or analyst, but a very personal voice. The book offers a journal-like account of the exhumation and identification of bones in Rwanda, Bosnia, Croatia, and Kosovo. Koff speaks of the "power of human remains."[37] We learn intimate details about the land, the roads, and the mines. We gain a sense of what it is like to arrive in a field, on a hillside that is a mass grave before the exhumation and markings of graves, identification of bullet holes, and the sound of shovels.[38] We learn something about the victims. Additionally, we learn something of the catastrophe. The majority of the dead at Srebrenica were men, unlike the victims in Rwanda, which meant that the surviving women could help with the identification.[39] We learn of the details of the remains at Ovčara, Croatia. Allegedly marched to their death from the hospital, some are in hospital garb and their medical records assist in the identification of the bodies (some with casts on their limbs). One man is found buried with x-rays that he tucked in his bathrobe.[40] Finally, we read of her work in Kosovo:

> Then I picked it up and realised it wasn't a bone fragment loose from the trauma; in fact, it was an intact distal epiphyseal cap of the tibia. It had not even begun to fuse with the rest of the tibia, and the superior surface of the epiphysis was billowy with youth. The skeleton was that of a young person.[41]

Koff had found a child: "The boy in my grave had a pocket full of marbles, and that told me more about his life than almost anything else could."[42]

Perhaps such books respond to singularity as they give voice to the suffering of the other. To some extent they take responsibility for the other and they give the other a voice to which we must respond. By offering this responsibility for the other, perhaps the writers, journalists, and intellectuals, engage in what Levinas called "the authentic relation."[43] The fact that the representation of the loss and the suffering can restore the voice and the humanity to those who have suffered and died recalls Levinas' comment that the other "asks me not to let him or her die alone."[44]

Both Nancy, with the notion of singularity and ex-position, and Levinas, with his rearticulation of a self that substitutes itself for the other, problematize the ego-based conception of the self as an autonomous, isolated, or discrete phenomenon. For Levinas, for example, the responsibility for the other occurs in a passion of obsession and passivity, a passion that exceeds consciousness and the identity of the self.[45] He writes that the obsession "strips the Ego of its self conceit."[46] To be a self is to be responsible for the other and to be delivered over to this responsibility, to be hostage to this responsibility.

The texts cited here, which bear witness to the singularity of suffering of the other, would also seem to problematize the position of the self. In many cases, the act of bearing witness carried a traumatic personal cost for the authors. Engaged in this "authentic relation" of bearing witness, the authors were ex-posed from and decentered from their personal egos or selves. They write openly of the psychological and physical traumas they endured. This trauma becomes part of "the authentic relation," part of what renders it ethical. Their egos are undone by the act of bearing witness. We are reminded of Levinas' statement in *Otherwise than Being*, "One is exposed to the other as a skin is exposed to what wounds it, as a cheek offered to one who strikes it."[47] Anthony Loyd, a photojournalist and reporter in Bosnia, reported some of the worst atrocities of the war and his stories later guided the war crimes investigations. Loyd maintained his composure when on assignment but on return to England he lapsed into alcohol and drug abuse and was unable to sleep. He reports that his own face was ravaged from bearing witness to the suffering. Looking in the mirror he writes, "The face that looked back at me was haunted and furtive."[48] Bill Carter, an aid worker in Sarajevo during the siege, writes of dodging sniper bullets and mortar shells and of severe weight loss, due to the scarcity of food and water, as well as to the stress. He writes of the way the stress, fear, and adrenalin began to rot the flesh and transform the features: "premature wrinkles show up and the hair begins to fall out. Teeth rot, skin turns grey and sullen."[49] Koff, for example, after hours at exhumation sites and hours in the morgue, writes of nervous exhaustion, nightmares, and loss of a sense of self in letters to her family, reporting that she felt "out of touch, homesick, and cynical about too many things."[50] Koff wrote in her journal of having "lost track of who I used to be, because I could barely remember the things I used to like."[51] A sign of her fragile state, a state that she would normally deny or repress, was that she would burst into tears at the sound of her brother's voice on the phone.

Nancy addresses the bodily dimension of such a witnessing and writing that would expose the suffering of the other, a writing that "in its essence touches upon the body."[52] For Nancy, such writing is an "*exscription* [excription]," a "being placed outside the text" as the most proper movement of the text. He writes, "we have to write from a body that we neither have nor are, but where being is exscribed" (C, 19). In the process of writing we are undone and we "lose our footing" (C, 13). It is as though the authors of the witness literature are touched and traumatized by the suffering of the other, experiencing weight loss and memory loss, and then exscribed in their writing.[53] Nancy writes that he knows "of no writing that doesn't touch" (C, 11), and in this touching there is a "breakthrough" [*effraction*] as the body "exposes a breakthrough of sense . . ." (C, 25). Nancy addresses this breakthrough proper to the body with the neologism "*expeausition*," a term that replaces the phoneme "*po*" (in ex*po*sition) with the homonymically equivalent French word for skin, "*peau*" (ex*peau*sition) (C, 33). For Nancy, writing is a breakthrough from body to body that is always already underway. The witness literature we have described embodies such a visceral exposure.

Indeed, both in their singularity of style and content as well as in the cost of bearing witness that wears on their authors' flesh, the texts enact an ethos that would be prior to any ethics of norms. The authors have attempted to respond to the suffering of the other, to expiate for their pain. They and their texts speak the names and places of those who suffered the violence and who were unable to speak for themselves. In the context of Nancy's *The Creation of the World* or *Globalization*, the acts of literature discussed here rehumanize those who have been dehumanized and restore, in some sense, worlds that war criminals attempted to erase. In this respect, we recall Nancy's assertion that "*the speaker speaks for the world, which means the speaker speaks to it, on behalf of it, and in order to make it a 'world'*" (*BSP*, 3). I suggest that as these texts respond to the singularity of the suffering of the other, they undertake the task of justice. As multiple restorations and beginnings of worlds, each of the texts is each time an act of justice, a fact of justice.

NOTES

1. An earlier version of "The Task of Justice," appeared in *Pathways to Reconciliation: Between Theory and Practice*, ed. Philipa Rothfield, Cleo Fleming, and Paul A. Komesaroff (England: Ashgate Publishing Ltd, Hampshire, 2008). The present version has been extensively revised and expanded for inclusion in this volume. The author would like to thank John P. Dudley, of the Philosophy Department of Southern Connecticut State University, for his editorial assistance in the preparation of this chapter.

2. See the Universal Declaration, Articles 3, 4, 5, and 27.

3. Immanuel Kant, *Groundwork of the Metaphysic of Morals*, trans. H. J. Paton (New York: Harper and Row, 1964), p. 95.

4. Ibid., p. 96.

5. Ibid., p. 98.

6. I refer to this as a strategic appropriation because, in a number of texts, Nancy suggests that Heidegger either did not recognize or did not fully develop the implications of the finitude of Dasein and its being with other Dasein for an ethics. See, for example, Jean-Luc Nancy, "The Being-With of the Being-There,"

in *Rethinking Facticity*, ed. François Raffoul and Eric Sean Nelson (Albany: State University of New York Press, 2008).

7. See, for example, Martin Heidegger, *Being and Time*, trans. J. Macquarrie and E. Robinson (New York: Harper and Row, 1962), § 47.

8. Nancy writes: "Yet it is precisely the immanence of man to man, or it *is* man, taken absolutely, considered as the immanent being par excellence, that constitutes the stumbling block to a thinking of community. . . . Consequently economic ties, technological operations, and political fusion (into a *body* or under a leader) represent or rather present, expose and realize this essence necessarily in themselves. Essence is set to work in them; through them, it becomes its own work. This is what we have called 'totalitarianism.' But it might better be called 'immanentism.'" Jean-Luc Nancy, *The Inoperative Community*, ed. Peter Connor (Minneapolis: University of Minnesota Press, 1991), p. 3. Henceforth cited as *IC*. Furthermore, "if [immanence] were to come about [it] would instantly suppress community, or communication, as such . . . immanence, communal fusion, contains no other logic than that of the suicide of the community that is governed by it" (*IC*, 12). Nancy equates such immanence with the totalitarian political culture of Nazi Germany.

9. Jean-Luc Nancy, *Being Singular Plural*, trans. Robert Richardson and Anne O'Byrne (Stanford: Stanford University Press, 2000), p. 3. Henceforth cited as *BSP*.

10. Nancy equates the concept of the individual with immanence; an abstract form of atomism: "it is another, and symmetrical figure of immanence" (*IC*, 3). It is such an immanence that he contrasts with singularity.

11. For Nancy, the term "punctuality" refers to the discontinuity of the moment, the "each time" of a "being-with" that is a singular and unique event of encounter, but as "being-with" it is always already plural. He writes, "'Each time' implies *at one and the same time* the discreteness of 'one by one' *and* the simultaneity of 'each one'" (*BSP*, 65).

12. Jean-Luc Nancy, *The Creation of the World* or *Globalization*, trans. François Raffoul and David Pettigrew (Albany: The State University of New York Press, 2007), pp. 54–55. Henceforth cited as *CW*.

13. Nancy writes, "To sense oneself making sense, and even more, to sense *oneself as the engenderment of sense*—this is without a doubt the ultimate stake of philosophy." Jean-Luc Nancy, *The Sense of the World*, trans. Jeffery Librett (Minneapolis: University of Minnesota, 1997), p. 162. Henceforth cited as *SW*.

14. Nancy writes, "What we call a world is nothing more than this dispersal of origins, their dissipation, and their prodigality. Neither an absence of origin . . . nor an origin compacted in on itself . . . but the violent irruption of possible origins and of the equally multiple sense of sense. Sense: nothing but sculpted shards of sense" Jean-Luc Nancy, *Multiple Arts: The Muses II*, ed. Simon Sparks (Stanford: Stanford University Press, 2006), p. 177.

15. This justice is a justice that is appropriate, a justice that is due. What is appropriate to sovereign singularities in their being? The ultimate measure of appropriateness is the exposure of singularities to one another. Nancy writes, "But existence is nothing other than being exposed: expulsed from its simple self-identity and from its pure position, exposed to the event, to creation, thus to the outside, to

exteriority, to multiplicity, to alterity and to alteration. (In a sense, certainly, this is nothing other than being exposed to being itself, to its own 'being' and also consequently, being exposed as being: exposition as the essence of being)" (CW, 110).

16. In its displacing ex-position, singularity is neither sovereign in the Kantian sense of autonomy nor sovereign in the sense formulated by Carl Schmitt, who claimed that the sovereign "is he who decides on the exception" Carl Schmitt, *Political Theology: Four Chapters on the Concept of Sovereignty*, trans. George Schwab (Cambridge: MIT Press, 1985), p. 1. In Schmitt's state of exception the sovereign is above the law. But for Nancy, the non-sovereign sovereignty, conceived in terms of singularity, is exposed both in the sense of being desubstantified and exposed in the sense of "being with" or being plural.

17. Richard Kearney, ed., *States of Mind: Dialogues with Contemporary Thinkers* (New York: University Press, 1995), p. 189.

18. Emmanuel Levinas, *Ethics and Infinity*, trans. R. Cohen (Pittsburgh: Duquesne University Press, 1985), p. 87.

19. Kearney, op. cit., p. 193.

20. Emmanuel Levinas, "On Substitution," in *Emmanuel Levinas: Basic Philosophical Writing*, ed. Adriaan T. Peperzak, Simon Critchley, Robert Bernasconi, (Bloomington & Indianapolis: Indiana University Press, 1996), p. 94.

21. *Ethics and Infinity*, p. 97.

22. Philip Gourevitch, *We Wish To Inform You That Tomorrow We Will Be Killed With Our Families: Stories from Rwanda* (New York: Picador, 1998), p. 3.

23. Michael Sells, *The Bridge Betrayed: Religion and Genocide in Bosnia* (Berkeley: University of California Press, 1998), p 185 n.4.

24. Ed Vulliamy, *Seasons in Hell: Understanding Bosnia's War* (New York: St. Martin's Press, 1994).

25. Sells, op. cit., p. 3.

26. Vulliamy, op. cit., p. 102.

27. Ibid., pp. 104–105.

28. Ibid., p. 108.

29. Chuck Sudetic, *Blood and Vengeance: One Family's Story of the War in Bosnia* (New York: Penguin Books, 1999), pp. 50–51.

30. Ibid., p. 270. In addition to the story of the Čeliks, we read of the beating of Muslim men in Bratunac, including the humiliation, beating, and murder of Mustafa Mujkanovic (ibid., pp. 152–153).

31. Norbert Both and Jan Willem Honig, *Srebrenica: Record of a War Crime* (New York: Penguin Books, 1997), p. 59.

32. Ibid.

33. Sells, op. cit., p. 21.

34. Vulliamy, op. cit., pp. 195–196.

35. Ibid., p. 199.

36. Clea Koff, *The Bone Woman: A Forensic Anthropologist's Search for Truth in the Mass Graves of Rwanda, Bosnia, Croatia and Kosovo* (New York: Random House, 2004), p. 7.

37. Ibid., p. 177.

38. Ibid., pp. 127–128.
39. Ibid., p. 120.
40. Ibid., p. 180.
41. Ibid., p. 226.
42. Ibid., p. 227.
43. *Ethics and Infinity*, p. 88; trans. modified.
44. Kearney, op. cit., p. 189.
45. *Basic Philosophical Writings*, p. 82.
46. *Basic Philosophical Writings*, p. 88.
47. Emmanuel Levinas, *Otherwise Than Being: Or Beyond Essence* (Pittsburgh: Duquesne University Press, 1998), p. 83.
48. Anthony Loyd, *My War Gone By, I Miss It So* (New York: Penguin Books, 1999), p. 262.
49. Bill Carter, *Fools Rush In* (New York: Wenner Books, 2003), p. 199.
50. Koff, op. cit., pp. 149–150.
51. Ibid.
52. Jean-Luc Nancy *Corpus*, trans. Richard A. Rand (New York: Fordham University Press, 2008), p. 11. Henceforth cited as C.
53. Nancy writes that there is "only exscription through writing." As the breakthrough or swerve of being, the exscription signifies an edge or limit of sense. Nancy writes that "In all writing *a body is the letter*, yet never the letter, or else, more remotely, more deconstructed than any literality, it's a 'letricity' [*lettricité*] no longer meant to be read" (C, 87; my emphasis). For Nancy this exscription of the letter is what could be referred to as a bodying-with. For it entails "the exposition of bodies . . . their being laid bare, their manifold population, their multiplied swerves" and "the rule and the milieu of a proximity" (C, 91).

PART FOUR

EXPOSITIONS OF SENSE

Art and the Limits of Representation

ELEVEN

DE-MONSTRATION AND THE *SENS* OF ART

Stephen Barker

> I can hear the piercing cry
> Echoing in the music, I know in myself
> The poverty of sense.
>
> —*Yves Bonnefoy*[1]

> The sense that is the world right at or right next to itself, this immanent sense of being there and nothing else, comes to show its transcendence there, which is to have no sense, to neither engage nor permit its own assumption into any kind of Idea or End, but to present itself always as its own estrangement. (To be there inasmuch as the there is there, monstrously there, is to be the there itself . . .)
>
> —*Jean-Luc Nancy*[2]

Nancy has focused on *sens* in and on art with increasing strategic specificity and force. It is within this context that the complex sense in which *sens* as "poor" transcends any echo of Heidegger's "poor in world" (*Weltarm*), characteristic of animals, and Bonnefoy's powerfully different idea of its "poverty," springing from a deep, all-too-human sensuality coupled with a longing for a chimerical "other place." While carefully distinguishing among art, art*works*, and work*ing* on and in art, Nancy, more than anywhere else in his orchestration of what might be called a world of *sens*, plays on the multiple meanings of *sens* in in French, gliding among the senses of *sens* as "(the) sense(s)," as "meaning," and as "direction." Each contributes a particular field of shadings and dynamics to his perspective. This is just as true of his works on particular works of art, from sculpture to the portrait to cinema to the text, and on artists, ranging from Caravaggio and Pontormo to On Kawara, as it is of his theoretical writings on art. While Nancy continuously takes advantage of the in-built ambiguities proliferating in *sens*, in disparate contexts requiring more solid definitions for it than its multilayered *senses* offer in French, this strategy itself allows him to manifest and traverse or even transgress thresholds joining and separating the various slipping laminations of *sens* as well as of art. A passage such as the following demonstrates what occurs throughout Nancy's references to *sens* (across the "senses") on art:

> Art disengages the senses from signification, or rather, it disengages the world from signification, and this is what we call "the senses" when we ascribe to the (sensible, sensuous) senses the sense of being external to signification. But it is what one might just as correctly name the "sense of the world" ["*le sens du monde*"]. The sense of the world as suspension of signification—but we now understand that such a "suspension" is touch itself. Here, being-in-the-world touches on its sense, is touched by it, touches itself as sense. (M, 22)

For Nancy, touch, as both the central sense and the metonymy for *all sense*, leaps to the foreground here: Artfully employing *les sens* and *le sens* eight times in this short passage—at least once in each of its guises and in several of its [physical] senses), Nancy manages both to define and consistently reopen the sense of *sens*, giving the reader an initiatory *sensory* experience of art-as-conundrum, on which he will build consistently—to the point of disorientation.

The major tactical deployments of *sens* Nancy undertakes in his more theoretical treatments of art provide a focus for the first part of this chapter. The goal is to separate (and link) the central ways in which *sens* applies to art, working from the relatively consistent plural, *les sens*, "the senses" (this ascription is reliable in the plural), to *sens* as "meaning," and finally as "direction" (as in *le sens du voyage*, the direction in which one is or will be moving, e.g., in a train). This last usage of *sens* as direction provides a threshold across which to move in order to engage what for Nancy is, specifically in the context of art and contrary to its sense in other contexts, the *dynamics* of *sens*. As direction or vector, *sens* "looks" both forward and backward across the trajectory of our sense of the experience of the world, forming a constellation of forces both with Derrida's sense of *à venir*[3] and with Bernard Stiegler's sense of a para-human *technics*.[4] One might say that in his deployment of this dynamic sense of *sens* Nancy is *on the other side* of *sens* as he uses it elsewhere, in a political or sociological sense, outside the context of art and its work(s). For Nancy, art (the instrumentalization of art-ing *in* art) *is* meaning, as *sens*.

The *sens* of art, Nancy claims, is its immanence, the plenitude of its self-sameness. For Nancy, prior to art's being emphatically *there*, as a "work," it is already dynamic thereness, as plenitude. Art *as such* (art before art-ing) precedes matter and materiality: "art itself is in essence *nonapparent* and/or disappearing. It even disappears twice: its unity syncopates itself in material plurality *and* its essence is dissolved beyond itself (The moment of the Kantian sublime or that of the Hegelian dissolution is always present, at work *in* aesthetic 'immanence' itself)" (M, 36; trans. modified). As an introduction to Nancy's slipping senses of *sens*,[5] this multiply laminated para-definition[6] of art requires some explanation. Art's essence is *inapparent* because "art itself" (*l'art elle-même*) is vectoral and dynamic. Nancy claims that art-work, in both senses of the term (as both the artwork and the work involved in art), "appears" out of *le gouffre*, the abyss; "art itself," as inapparent, never emerges and could not do so: art-work, in its effortful emergence, is the effect of an invisible sense of art.[7] Art's *double* dis-appearance ("it even disappears twice"), as a result of a result, re-doubles art's nonappearance. Art's "unity," that is, its *être-là*, which can only occur in advance of any appearance, is, Nancy says, "syncopated in material plurality and its essence is dissolved beyond itself." Art's being syncopated—and here Nancy is being very precise in his choice of words—consists not only in its reversal of predictable rhythms and accents (manifest art-work creating in its manifestation the conditions for its own constitution), but in the sense in which *syncope* is a lapse of consciousness, that is, an egoistic inappearance. Art's material plurality, its existence *there*, is its occlusion. *And* with the constitution (i.e., the emergence) of the art*work*, art's essential inappearance is "dissolved" in(to) the artwork's super-saturated materiality, as both form and structure; that is, art's very inappearance dissolves in the appearance of the art*work*. These multiple vectoral reversals and shifts, within the context of exactitude, provide a key to Nancy's coming to terms with—making sense of—the *sens* of art.

This amounts to Nancy's claim that "it is impossible to touch (through the discourse of *sens*) on a work of art" (M, 63). In approaching the threshold of the "art/sense" conundrum he is signaling something quite different from what such a nontouching seems to say: it is not concerned with the impossibility of touching—far from it—but rather with the *discourse* of *sens* that interrupts and truncates touching. Because it is the sensorium that "interrupts the direction of the discourse,"

> it is only possible to bring [the artwork] into the medium of sense, first of all into the medium of an eventual "sense of art" as such

> (and of a "sense" of the word "art"), by interrupting the hold of the discourse (in conformity with the law of touch) through this "hermeticism" whereby the work only touches itself, or is itself its own transimmanence. And this not valid only . . . for a style, for a genre, for each of the arts and for the new "arts" to come: that is, it is valid for the *singular plural* of the essence of the arts. (M, 35; my emphasis)

Thus, the singular plural, Nancy's framework for difference-at-the-origin, reveals itself as a figure for "trans-immanence" as the decentered (sensuous) essence (es-*sens*) of art. This decentering is a release, according to Nancy, from signification, for art and indeed for the world. The senses as receptors, saturated with images but simultaneously free of signs, "suspend" the image beyond the threshold of signification. *Sens*, as "the senses," is precisely this singular plural suspension of meaning-making; however, free of signification, this suspension is Nancy's notion of touch: impactful being-in-the-world touched as (the) sense(s). But the sensorium can operate impactfully only if it is oriented by—touching on—an object or form providing an "operational context." On the perceptual plane, the sensorium becomes restricted, limited by the structured forms catalyzing perceptual (insignificant) images.

Perception as embodied sense isolates a sense or, as Nancy points out, "one part or feature" of a sense (M, 21). In forcing a sense "to be what it is," however, "to touch itself," perception catalyzes and thus includes a *sens intelligible* that alters the nature of sensory receptivity. Following this line of thought, near the conclusion of *Les Muses*, Nancy makes this remarkable claim:

> Art is sensible visibility of this intelligible, that is, invisible, visibility. The invisible form—Plato's *eidos*—returns to itself and appropriates itself as visible. Thus, it brings into the light and manifests the being of its Form, and its form of Being. All the great theories of "imitation" have never been anything but theories of imitation, or the image, of the Idea (which is itself, you understand, but the *self-imitation* of being, its transcendent or transcendental miming)—and reciprocally, all thinking about the Idea is thinking about the image or imitation. (M, 89)

Properly understood, Nancy's reference to the *eidos*, surprising as it may at first seem, helps us see further into a new sense of touch*ing*, one that is at once immanent, transcendent, and invisible, but in no sense metaphysical. Art is beyond the senses in that although the various senses register various senses of artworks, Nancy claims that the plurality of the senses, as opposed to "sensibility as such," is in fact a result of art: Art is not mimetic; art catalyzes *thoughts* of *mimēsis* (M, 30). The initial forms of art, as art-works, present us, in their exposure but prior to their signification, with an absence of *sens* (as "meaning"), that is, with an "existant"[8] as such. Yet given the singular plural nature of the senses, the image-as-existent manifests itself as outside of the world, separated from the world and dis-oriented from it. The image is *sens sans sens*, form without meaning, suspended outside of discourse, thought, and (thus) sign-value. Nancy refers to this suspended state as "the art of the residual Idea [*l'Idée résiduelle*]" (M, 91), yet again finding precisely the word required: the art of the residual gestures not only to a remnant but to evaluative measure, the difference between measured value and "true value." "The art of the residual Idea" renders not only the artwork but the Idea as residual, as remnant, revenant, and differant. Absolutely incorporeal, the suspended residual Idea "descends" on forms through what Nancy calls "discourse" in order to give those forms (residual) meaning. This is why the "first" sense of *sens*, *les sens*, is so vital to the constitution of existants: In their singular plurality they produce a texture, a weaving together. Nancy shows that only through the slippage of *sens* from the sensuous to what he calls the "productive" can we begin to touch on a more exact sense of art's impact. "Production," he says, "is nothing other than the production of *sense*," and now Nancy has slipped to its second sense, meaning. But production thus "shows itself to be pro-duction," as an untenable tension toward "a before-ness (or a behind-ness) of sense" (M, 28). The tensions implicit in the suspension of the residual Idea *in* the image are extraordinarily powerful catalysts[9] in the production of *sens* as meaning.

Beyond this notion of the residual Idea, the pro-duction of *sens* is also an in-duction, a vectoral force tapping into the third sense of *sens*. As directional, carrying pre-, pro-, and in-duction across sliding temporal thresholds of "world experience," *sens* reveals itself as dynamism, the trajectory of *mimēsis* and *methexis* along and among the forms and pre-forms, existant and existent, which constitute its weave.[10] This directional sense of *sens* is vital to Nancy's metaphor of art as perpetually emergent and in metamorphosis, precisely because of the strength and complexity of its cross-vectors. Such production is a process that can be denied, ignored, degraded, (perpetually) critiqued, but is never and could never be finished. Among their anguished interdictions, art and *sens* count that of finishing or completing the experience of art, seeing a/the work of art as a bracketed entity. This is a central reason why On Kawara's work so fascinates Nancy: It consists of nothing but the direct reference to that obscure object of desire that arrests fleeting temporal experience.[11] The evocation of a single date (or of a million years) slides into the *hic et nunc* of both the sensuous and memory, both the narrative of history and the interdiction of language (in numbers). The backward and forward of directional *sens* evokes Ovid's Janus-face, evokes proximity *and* exclusion, attraction *and* repulsion, in the manner of the vectoral doubling to which Nietzsche refers in *Zarathustra*'s "Gate of Moment." The latter is perhaps the quintessential image/metaphor for the double relationship of time and value Nancy touches on not in an image, as Nietzsche does, but in a word, *sens*. Nancy's *sens*, however, like the Janus-face and the Gate of Moment, is radically *open*, a process without progress, and also a revaluation of all values. *Sens* moves without advancing; it passes without being past. The one who is capable of responding to this dynamic—who is responsible to and for it—is the artist, Nancy's anonymous "weaver,"[12] the passer-by, always in motion in a pure dynamism. Indeed, for Nancy the artist is a conduit, *is* passage, "coming, departure, succession, passing the limits, moving away, rhythm, and syncopated blackout of being. Thus not the demand for sense, but the passage as the whole *taking place* of sense, as its whole presence" (M, 99). The "demand for meaning,"[13] which is radically open in the field of art, points not toward an *être-là*, but an *être-à*, being-toward, that is, it indicates the momentum of the anonymity of the artistic "impulse," derived from the multiple senses of *sens*, which is neither sensuous nor meaning-ful nor vector-al, but a lamination of the entire weave of *sens*; this is how Nancy defines the openness of *sens*, its *être-à*, as being-toward, at once the artist's being-*as* and being-*to*.

Both of these senses of being are estrangements, and "estrangement" is at the core of Nancy's "vestige," one of his central referential terms for art,[14] as a copula for the varieties of *sens* by which art reveals itself as *plural singular/plural*. In *Les Muses* this discussion focuses on vestige as "*presque rien*," nearly nothing, that is, the trace—but with a *différance*[15]: in the third, dynamic sense of *sens*, the art-image is endemically "in retreat," perpetually redrawn [*retrait*], in either case passing into memory or displaced by other, subsequent images (which one might say is the same thing). Doubtless, "*retrait*" means "retreat" here, in the sense of fading or receding (dynamically becoming "almost nothing")—but "*re-trait*" echoes a secondary (perhaps primary) *sens*: "re-marking" or "re-drawing." In its "re-trait" or "retreat," the vestige reinscribes itself, not regressing to a *nothing* but only to a (singular/plural) *nearly nothing*. In subtle but powerful ways, Nancy "draws" our attention to this linked cross-current as *différance*: "what remains withdrawn from the image, or what remains in its withdrawal, as that withdrawal itself, is the *vestige*" (M, 94).[16] Nancy points out that the strategic history of this word, "vestige," comes to us through the doubled cultural hegemony of theology *and* mysticism, initially through Thomas Aquinas, through whom "the vestige" is an effect representing "solely the causality of its cause, but not its form" (M, 95), it "shows that someone has passed by but *not who it is*" (M, 95; my emphasis).[17] But *différance* at the origin persists: *Vestigium*, as Nancy enigmatically informs us, is "to follow the trace"; but as a word, "vestige," it derives from a lost etymological history: Its trace has been lost. And this loss is *tactically* vital to Nancy in terms of the estrangement of art's *sens* as "vestige." As for art, it makes no sense (according to Nancy) to search for the lost origins of *vestigium* or *vestigare*, but only to put "one's steps into the traces of steps [*mettre ses pas dans des traces de pas*]" (M, 95)—to follow up on the residue (vestige) of the trace, *without* its "origin"; in Nancy's words, "art is smoke without fire, vestige without God, and not [the] presentation of the Idea. End of image-art, birth of the vestige-art" (M, 96). The vestige is not rational but sensuous; it points to *la plante du pied* itself, the foot's imprint, its trace; vestige indicates a *previous step*, a passage through which the "foot" has passed: it bears witness to a stepping, walking, leaping—a succession, an energy, a *transire*. Vestige is not ruin, the ravished remainder of presence but, like a painter's brushstroke, "a touch right at the ground" (M, 97). Art is the *remainder* of a step (*un pas*); it cannot be its own image because the step itself consists in nothing but its vestige.

Nancy's sense of art (both art*work* and art-*désœuvrement*, unwork), vestige-as-step is, finally, *event*, and thus excessive. The event for Nancy, as border-violence, is always in excess of signification, of signs, even transgressive: The image reveals nothing but its excess. As what comes to the world through art, the image-event has no "place" in the world (certainly not "its" location as image): its event is singular plural. The artwork (and thus art in its antecedence) is not and cannot be *mimetic*; it does not *represent* an absent "thing," but "draws the form of presence out of absence," as *retrait* that, given the double vector of *prae-sentia*, is a dynamic structure of excess (GI, 22). Here is where Nancy's art of the grotto and Georges Bataille's sense of Lascaux's images as the dawn of "the human" come into alignment.[18] The "artist" is the mark-maker, an animal in the company of other animals. But Nancy takes this a step further than Bataille: For Nancy, the *vestige* of the beast, through the anterior and exterior nature of the mark itself and the *making* of the mark, remains in the maker—the beast in the human. Thus, the mark-making animal remains laminated across the Idea-conceiving (human) animal:

> Man began in the calmly violent silence of a gesture: here, on the wall, the continuity of being was interrupted by the birth of a form, and this form, detached from everything, even detaching the wall from its opaque thickness, gave one to see the strangeness of the being, substance, or animal that traced it, and the strangeness of all being in him. (M, 74)

The strangeness, as es-strangement, becomes for Nancy the mark of *différance* as the singular plural. The excessive event, a discontinuity "detached from everything," resembles Deleuze's as an intensity. "Self," the mark of the human, is both gained and lost in it, through the intensification and revaluation of values and the dynamic convergence of gesture and mark.

In this regard, the initiatory gestures on cave walls bring Nancy's central question into focus: What is being demonstrated *there*, at the site of the artwork, the working-out of art, and its *désœuvrement*? Nancy's response to this question forces us to look again at the very nature of mimesis, as imitation and representation. Because, as Nancy says, art's gesture differs each time, and because the trace, as event, is never *one* but a constellation of intensities, art is sensed and valued each time anew, by doer and viewer. In demonstrating multiple senses, artwork demonstrates "nothing other than its manner—its *tekhnē mimētikē*—of de-monstrating itself, of configuring its absence of figure. It never resembles itself, being the monster and the monstrance [*la monstre*] of resemblance that itself resembles nothing" (M, 132). Through the configuring gesture and its absence of figure, the mark-maker is caught in the play of pre-sentation, not representation: *Homo monstrans* does not install a figure in or on a ground, but rather dis-figures the ground or support. The spat charcoal on the stone raises away from the ground and is no longer "supported" by anything. Nancy's sense of this dis-figuring has become endemic to contemporary art, far beyond the specific instances in which Nancy has examined it.

The mark, as free of or estranged from any ground, is anticipated in Antonin Artaud's experimental demonstrations of anti-technique in the 1940s, in his wildly dynamic drawings combining text, image, design, and "disaster." Artaud, who was actually a fine technical artist, *strategically* and violently rejected technical proficiency, making "bad" drawings exhibiting a wide variety of "sigla" that might be surrounded by scrawled text or by Artaud's name.[19] By 1947, Artaud was also burning holes in his drawings, inflicting physical damage on the support medium in order to "blast" any art that might attempt to appear there. In this border-transgressing, violent gesture, Artaud demonstrated the double vector of what Nancy calls "monstration" or (even more appropriately for Artaud, "monstruation"). Artaud referred to this gestural violation, the actual destruction of the very substance of the artwork, making an opening (*ouvre*) in the work (*œuvre*) as a "living sign" of absence, but a living sign that could not be seen as in any way mimetic. Artaud called this "process" and its result the *subjectile*,[20] a collapsing together of "subject" and "projectile": Artaud demonstrates the "monster of resemblance" in its most dynamic form, bringing every sense of *sens* into play, into question, and into erasure. As the "subject-figure" who makes and destroys marks, Artaud accomplishes in his *subjectile* what he could not accomplish in or through language. Indeed the very nature of language as sign-system prevents it from functioning as a purely *gestural* mark. Neologisms such as Artaud's *subjectile* and Derrida's *différance* attempt to transcend this in-built limitation of language (as does Nancy's laminated sense of *sens*), but as Nancy points out it is only in the *de*-monstration of art-work that monstration becomes possible.

Monstration, becoming-monstrous or other, is at the core of Nancy's sense of vestige and of art's being-toward (the) art-work. The event of art must be made strange in order for it to retreat—to be redrawn—into experience. Monstration is the *sens* of art. But monstration cannot come into being without the *pas*, the step-ping, that makes it an event. Thus de-monstration, the artwork as such, marks the being-toward of art as *sens*. In its existential manifestation as artwork, art is both demonstrated and de-monstrated, shown forth and domesticated, while never touching on nor excavating—think of Lascaux—but only being-toward art-as-such.

Willem de Kooning's work runs parallel to Nancy's sense of de-monstration. De Kooning's tellingly titled "Excavation" of 1950 is a direct echo of grotto artwork and the grotto event, its sandy-yellow, stonelike "ground" ornamented with fragmentary elements that float somewhere between "primitive" art and abstraction. Like Artaud's dynamic non-figures, de Kooning's excavations show both the emergence and the decay of "homination," indeed, of figuration. De Kooning's later, more famous "Woman" canvasses show de-monstration even more clearly, through their violent layering and their grotesque exaggerations of the body arrested at the moment of explosion. De Kooning's "process" involved repeatedly, roughly scraping away paint he had applied to the canvas and starting over again (although never eradicating traces of previous marks—a literal tactic of *prae-sens*). In his "Woman and Bicycle" (1950–1952), de Kooning plays with the mark of the present–absent as Nancy lays it out: The title's "bicycle" is (perhaps) gestured toward by a rough, obscured oval of dashed-on paint in the lower left-hand corner of the canvas; the "woman" is vaguely indicated through several gestures suggesting, obscuring, and denying figuration (e.g., cursorily drawn lines in the general position of lower legs, abstract circular shapes suggesting an enormous bosom), but any "figure" slips between appearance and disappearance in a thick, layered primal sea of color and gestural energy. Perhaps most tellingly, the marks where the face of the "woman" might be expected to be found consist of enormous "eyes" echoing ancient Sumerian god-figures, which are so enlarged as to cover the entire upper half of the hidden "face." Additionally, the "woman" has what appears to be two mouths, an upper and a lower—unless the viewer chooses not to accept the work's title as literal and sees the painting as an interrogation of Nancy's monstration, a portrayal of *dis*-figurement.

Nancy's sense of de-monstration is clearly visible in Andy Warhol's silk screens, pitting form, figure, and resemblance against the Other, making use of what seems at first to be straight-forward figuration to demonstrate a technical/mechanical process (literally mechanical as silk screens) diametrically opposite to cave-painting. Yet in some specific respects Warhol's "technique" (which is in fact all about technique and its dis-figuration) is identical to the monstration Nancy evokes from the grotto. Silk screening involves the building up of various layers of abstract color and form "above" an obscured ground, and Warhol's images defy any simple manifestation of representation, focusing rather on absence either through the employment of the multiple—an interrogation of the singular plural—as a loss of connection to "the image," through the adoption of radically "unnatural" color schemes and through the treatment of the image not as figure but as a *vestige* of technical procedure, not as functions and effects of reproduction but of a reproducibility pro-ducing nothing but "original copies." In his "Skulls" series (1976), for example, Warhol uses all these techniques, partially obscuring the monochrome image of a human skull with geometric shapes and swaths of color to produce, once again, something between garish morbidity and abstraction. Warhol's employment of image both emphasizes and challenges its sign-nature, evoking enigmatic or ambiguous gestures toward *sens*. Warhol in fact carries Nancy's notion of demonstration *beyond* its logical conclusion, displacing "art" with "process" and "originality" with "celebrity," just as Nancy's sense of slippage and denial of conventional ideas of *mimēsis* ineluctably monstrate both "art" and "originality."

The supreme examples of Nancy's monstration/de-monstration can be seen in Francis Bacon's (dis-) figurements, the very notion of figure having slipped into another (non-)form, within the doubled framework of the work's outer frame as well as the geometric and architectural backgrounds with which Bacon frames his swirling, monstrous non-faces on the canvas itself. From his early "animal" images, which echo grotto imagery and Bataille's transitional homination, through his later self-portraits and triptychs, Bacon explores the monstration—the making-monstrous—of the vestige of the beast in the human. His project, as Deleuze points out, is "to produce resemblance with nonresembling means"[21]; in Bacon's *œuvre*, "man becomes animal," Deleuze says, "but not without the animal becoming spirit at the same time, the spirit of man . . . the common fact of man and animal. Bacon pushes this to the point where even his most isolated Figure is already a coupled Figure, man is coupled with his animal."[22] Bacon's disfigurements of figure, and his violent treatment of painting technique itself, pro-duces portraits that *manifest* Nancy's multiple sense of *sens*, slipping (literally on Bacon's canvas, in his sliding images) between sensing, signifying, and the dynamically directional. Bacon's "monsters," once again, clearly depict in gestural, vestigial images what Nancy lays out in *Les Muses* but which can only be pro-duced *outside of language*. As for Artaud, de Kooning, and Warhol, for Bacon the figure is also non- or anti-figure, a monstrous scream emanating from a non-body, "out of" the grounding medium, somewhere between presence and absence. Bacon's figurations manifest the dynamic slippage of *sens*, as animal, human, and spirit.[23]

In all of these works, it would be possible to say, as Nancy does in *Les Muses*, that

> at the advanced tip of the first tracing, the first painter sees coming toward him a monster who holds out to him the unsuspected reverse side of presence, its displacement, its detachment, or its folding into pure manifestation, and the manifestation itself as the coming of the stranger, as the brith into the world of what has no place in the world, like the birth of the origin itself. (M, 76)

For Nancy, such a vestigial gesture is a spacing-out by which world becomes world *as other*; the event of the world is neither mimetic nor representational but absolute and perpetual *étrangeté*: "*homo sapiens* is only what it is by virtue of *Homo monstrans*" (M, 70). The mark on the grotto wall, and each subsequent mark through the ensuing history of art-work, is what Nancy calls the manifestation and simultaneous monstration (emergence and estrangement) of the human. In making the mark and thus initiating the human, *homo monstrans* shows itself as human and stranger. Presentation distances; reproduction produces *différance*:

> What men subsequently will name with a word that means knowledge and know-how, *tekhnē* or *ars*, is at man's beginning the total of his science and his consciousness. . . . Science and consciousness of fascination with the monster of presence exited from presence. *Tekhnē* or *ars* of a fascination that does not paralyze, but that turns the light or serious abandon over to non-knowledge. This fascination does not fix on the image, except to let bottomless appearance—aperity, resemblance without original, or yet again, the origin itself as monster and endless monstration—come forward. Art's quick turn of the hand is the turning of this gesture. . . . Art . . . traverses . . . the twenty-five thousand years of the *animal monstrans*, of the *animal monstrum*. . . . to be *there* inasmuch as the *there* is *there*, monstrously there, is to be *the there* itself, to incise or excise the intimate with its immanence, to carve or paint the wall, its appar(t)ition [*apparoitre*]; the *there* is always a grotto. (M, 70–71)

Nancy's notion of humanity, of which artwork is the initiatory gesture, is engulfed in its strangeness as it emerges. Art is "colossal and labyrinthine" and our encounter or confrontation with it is "invasive and evasive in the same moment" (*GI*, 107). The world in which monstration occurs is not one of place or subject, but one whose demonstration is "tracing the contours of the apparition that nothing either supports or delimits" (M, 71). Nancy's case is that what the Plato/Aristotle axis, at least through Hegel, establishes as a fundamental *mimēsis* is actually something radically different—a monstrosity; what emanates from "art" is not imitation nor representation but estrangement, representing, if anything, what Nancy calls "the apparition." The image (the work of art), in whatever form and whatever medium, is violent. The gesture of demonstrating or displaying is one in which the dynamics of *sens* surge forth, as force, strange and "monstrously similar" (M, 121): resemblance without resembling anything. Nancy concludes that the artist does not portray form(s) but force(s); indeed, the work of art is evidence—demonstration—of working *through* forms with forces that in fact deform.

The deformation immanent in *sens* and in art is fragmentary; as Benjamin reminds us, "the ideal of art's pure content is only manifested through the plurality of the Muses."[24] The forces of the arts clash and vie with one another within the context of a perpetual synaesthesia: artworks are *sensed*, which means that for Nancy they ubiquitously *touch*, and as such manifest a dissociation that provides a frame for seeing, sensing, and being in the world. The plurality of the Muses, for Nancy, is a trope for the way in which *sens* functions and, through the course of *Les Muses*, increasingly what Nancy's language itself attempts to manifest:

> Once more the body—and that it senses: that it is a plural unity of senses. (. . . but it is impossible to distinguish the plural and the singular of the word *sens*.) "A body" means that the same one sees, hears, smells, tastes, experiences motion, warmth, contraction, expansion, emptiness, exasperation, vertigo, tension, scansion, disequilibrium, speed, variety, confusion, waiting, transport, vitality, abatement, retreat, nausea, etc.—without going further in the multiplication of these rough categories (as we would have to do by breaking down or "cutting up" [*(dé)taillant*] sight into sight of colours, of shades, of lines, of forms, of volumes, of depths, of movements, of compactnesses, of lights, of transparencies, of brightnesses, of grains, of invisibilities . . .). (*ARE*, 162)

This remarkable tumble of language, fragments broken into subfragments and potentially into "ever-increasing categories," strikes at the laminated senses of *sens* in an exploding barrage of words that, like all artworks (as resemblance that doesn't resemble anything) in any conceivable medium, de-monstrates the impossibility of any sense of a *body of art*. Nancy casts us, late in *Les Muses*, increasingly before the plurality of the Muses as forces of disruption in a kind of writing that, like Blanchot's *L'attente l'oubli*, demonstrates linguistic or literary *sens* as "a heterogeneity and a heterotopia of sense," whose base state is fragmentation, dispersion, disorientation. Such an encounter with an artwork in any medium is, Nancy says, "shock, disruption, disappearance, transport, contamination, osmosis" (*ARE*, 162). Once the straightforwardness of *sens* is revealed as multiple at the origin, ranging across the meanings and usages of *sens* as a framework for art and world, any chance of a singularity of sense, in any one of its senses, is shown to be—and to have been—impossible; without this non-totalization of sense experience, as Nancy tells us, experience "itself" would not be possible.

Yves Bonnefoy's haiku-like poem, with which I began, has slipped into different territories of sense now:

> I can hear the piercing cry
> Echoing in the music, I know in myself
> The poverty of sense.

The poverty of sense is only poor from the vantage point of "echoing" and "knowing"—and from a chimerical "in myself" that Nancy insists is the one thing *sens* does not and cannot give. Nancy's disorienting musical prose flows with the force, if not the music, of a *sens* poor only in relation to that *other* aesthetic, or even bodily, singularity. Two pages from the conclusion of *Les Muses*, this astonishing *single sentence* operates as a correlative for Nancy's de-monstrative force. Let it be the last word:

> Between all bodies—sensible or insensible, if it is possible to delineate with precision what these adjective seem to separate—circulate an abundance of contacts, reflections, pressures, affinities, displacements, erosions, vibrations: a sensibility that might be called *panic*—spreading everywhere, in all directions—and everywhere agitated, stretched according to various rhythms and modulations, always referring from everything to everything, to what is close (contiguity of colors, use of shades, brightnesses, iridescences, of their proximity with grains, surfaces, folds, etc.) and to what is far (separation between color and sound, between distance and scent, between line and tint, etc.), referring from the immediate world, available to eye, nose, ear, all the way to the universe whose communication one begins to sense (starlight, tectonic shifts, butterfly wings in the Sunda Islands . . .), yet whose exchange, sharing, and division thus plays from one sense to another, forming a new sense in excess of signification, without any subsumptions or resolutions other than those operated

> by a form, provisional and suspended, composed of one of these fragments (or one of these states) [*éclats (ou états)*], or for one of them, or as one of them (*mimesis*? *methexis*? *expression*? *impression*? *creation*? *extraction*? how does the painter "produce" this color, the musician that sound?). (*ARE*, 163–164)

NOTES

1. Cited in Jean-Luc Nancy, "The Necessity of Sense," in *Multiple Arts: The Muses* II, ed. Simon Sparks (Stanford: Stanford University Press, 2006), p. 109.

2. Jean-Luc Nancy, *The Muses* (Standford: Stanford University Press, 1997), p. 71. Henceforth cited as M. Because it is in *The Muses* that Nancy makes his most concerted (i.e., kaleidoscopic) presentation of art and *sens*, much of the following focuses on the progress of *sens* through that text, keeping in mind that the Muses "themselves" are "singular singular/plural" and thus both imagistically and conceptually exact analogues for both the *sens* and monstrosity of art as they are explored here.

3. Derrida's *à venir*, to come, and *devenir*, to become, contrast with *futur*: The future is determinate, the *to come* radically open to contingency.

4. Bernard Stiegler employs the ancient notion of "technics" to define the "technical condition" underlying techniques, technology—and the human; Stiegler's thesis in his multi-volume *Technics and Time* is that technics creates the human through an accruing evolution and devolution of technical "prostheses," which range from tools to language.

5. Typically, Nancy employs both slippage and "exactitude" in his use of *sens*. That is to say, the slippage of *sens* within a single paragraph, as we have already seen, is slippage significantly because of the exact way in which Nancy locates each "point" of the slippage.

6. A para-definition, as opposed to a quasi- or pseudo-definition, is one that, like the *para-modern*, parallels the general idea of a definition. Nancy's "definitions" are generally para-definitions.

7. Nancy's sense of art's "disappearance" could more accurately be called "inappearance," because its "dis" works in the same way as Blanchot's "*dés*/dis" in *désœuvrement*. This is potentially confusing: *désœuvrement* is not a word in French, but its *sens* is "un-work" or "un-work-ness"; not refusal of work but (a) work that is not (a) work.

8. In its "raw" state, the sensory image manifests itself as already a "vestige" (Nancy's word), a remnant of a previous, infinite desire for meaning and for the production of meaning. Thus, the image in Nancy's sense is a function of différance, and is therefore not "existent" but an "existant."

9. Nancy refers to this as itself a, perhaps *the crise du sens*: "to refuse the anguished prohibition on images without necessarily bringing back the man of humanism, that is, of self-imitation of the Idea" (M, 100). Implicit in this "anguish" lurks Nancy's central concern with regard to *sens*: the problematics of (and the prohibition again) *naming*. Nomination in its most elementary forms insists on the presence of

language and its own exactitude, which runs parallel to *sens* and, in a Kantian sense, leads to a sense of language that rapidly becomes disastrous for meaning. As Nancy writes, "I say 'a flower,' and now the flower, *as such*, that is, as nothing presentable, absent from every bouquet, from every garden or botanical book, begins to link 'such' to 'such,' relating endlessly to itself as its own *sens* or idea, which never finishes linking itself to itself, all the better to let loose and unwind its parcel of silky fibres while also spinning out its *sens* or its indefinite metaphor." Jean-Luc Nancy, *The Ground of the Image* (New York: Fordham University Press, 2005), p. 67. Henceforth cited as *GI*. In the *gouffre* between (the refusal of) the image and its "anguished interdiction" Nancy accentuates the fact that *sens* is not image nor significance but a weaving together of all senses of *sens*, in which the separate "strands" maintain their autonomy and force—and only through so doing produce art's impactful essence.

10. Bataille, in a context that in some respects is radically different and in some respects quite similar, says that *sens* as meaning *and* direction is "*excrit*," ex-truded, ex-creted, and ex-scribed. Nancy's notion that meaning, in art and culture in general, comes from elsewhere and goes elsewhere, it is "written out" and "written out *of*."

11. On Kawara's work—the work that fascinates Nancy, consists of a simple rectangular "support," black, on which a date, for example, "Mar. 5, 2000," is printed in white. The date is both illusion and allusion, crossing between text and imagination ("how is this a work of art?") and alluding to what may (or may not) be a "date to remember": Does 5 May, 2000 matter to On Kawara uniquely, to us all, to *no one*? The "work" has no convenient "point of exit," and is therefore un-finishable.

12. It is important to Nancy that the weaver/artist be anonymous ("name-less") because the artist's *vestige* is not an identity: Vestige is not identity (it is, in fact, its *other*) but *n'importe qui*. In fact, the artist is even more radical than *n'importe qui*—the artist is *le passant*, the passer-by. Each time the artist pro-duces or in-duces an artwork, the artist passes by it. And yet it is in this *passage* that the artist *has-place*, enters into *prae-sence*. This is further discussed below.

13. Here it is important to keep in mind that the French "*demander*" translates as "request" or "ask," as in "*je me demande*," "I wonder (I ask myself)."

14. Art as "vestige" is explored near the end of "The Vestige of Art"; Nancy is interested in its Latin root, *vestigium*, "footprint"; hence the connection to both the trace and the dynamics of becoming—of *sens* as directional movement.

15. Nancy's sense of *différance*, diverging from Derrida's, has to do with space and time just as differing and deferring but as the double sense of "*retrait*," as both the retreating of the chimerical image as being-toward and as the re-drawn, the image as infinite regression.

16. This "withdrawing" contains within itself the notion of "drawing-with," "*traiter*," so that a withdrawal is also a re-drawing, a fading of the drawing, of the *trait*.

17. Here, Aquinas cites the example of a statue of Mercury, which *represents* Mercury and is his/its image. Aquinas and Nancy remind us that for Aristotle the "model" is a "formal" cause of the image. The notion of causality itself, in an Aristotelian sense, echoes *sens* as dynamism.

18. Georges Bataille, *Lascaux ou la naissance de l'art* (Geneva: Albert Skira, 1980). Bataille claims that the Lascaux drawings of animals—and the "Lascaux Man" with his erection—mark the transition from animal to human: the animal images

on the cave walls are, for Bataille, *vestiges* of that transitional leap, *retraits* of the step to the human. As genealogical referents, they are at once erotic and "archival."

19. Further anticipating Nancy's notion of the "presence of absence," Artaud frequently signed his notebook "Art-0" (Art-zero), a homonym for his name itself and, simultaneously, a rejection of art and artwork as aesthetic.

20. See Jacques Derrida and Paule Thévenin, *Antonin Artaud: Dessins et portraits* (Paris: Gallimard, 1986); Margit Rowell, *Antonin Artaud: Works on Paper* (New York: The Museum of Modern Art, 1996); and Jacques Derrida and Paule Thévenin, *The Secret Art of Antonin Artaud*, trans. Mary Ann Caws (Cambridge, MA: MIT Press, 1998).

21. Gilles Deleuze, *Francis Bacon: The Logic of Sensation*, trans. Daniel W. Smith (Minneapolis: University of Minnesota Press, 2003), p. 127. Though Deleuze entitles the book "The Logic of Sensation," throughout the text he addresses "the logic of sense" or "of the senses."

22. Ibid., p. 20.

23. On a different but related note, that of literature, it would be possible to make a similarly convincing case regarding much of Blanchot's work, particularly his late prose such as *L'attente l'oubli*, in which the writing of the disaster takes the form of a radical break between seeing and saying, and in which all saying and reading is detached from both figuration and narrative solidity, suspended outside of genre and between syntax (as form) and abstraction. The book is a triptych, its three parts fragmentary and cross-referential; it is impossible to know whether the book's opening is its beginning or its ending.

24. Walter Benjmain, *Theorie der Kunstkritik*, *Gesammelte Schriften* (Frankfurt a.M.: Suhrkamp, 1980), Band I, 3, p. 834. Cited in Jean-Luc Nancy, "Les arts se font les uns contre les autres," in *Art, regard, écoute: La perception à l'œuvre* (St-Denis: Les Presses Universitaires de Vincennes, 2000), pp. 157–166. This text was reprinted in the augmented edition of *Les muses* (Galilée, 2001) but does not appear in the English translation of *Les muses*. Translation is mine. Henceforth cited as *ARE*.

TWELVE

POETRY'S PROMISCUOUS PLURALITY

On a Part of Jean-Luc Nancy's The Muses

William Watkin

WHY ARE THERE SEVERAL ARTS AND NOT JUST ONE?

Jean-Luc Nancy's *The Muses* (1994) begins with a rather odd question: "Why are there several arts and not just one?"[1] That said, the ancient discord between the one and the many remains at the very forefront of contemporary continental thought and its three leading voices: Alain Badiou, Giorgio Agamben, and Nancy himself. In this sense then, any questioning after ontology, here the being of art, to remain credible in a contemporary setting, must tackle directly several-ness and oneness. It is even more so as regards art due to the historical peculiarity of our tendency to speak of art as always already plural (i.e., the arts). And more so because Nancy pins so much on the severalness of art in relation to his overall ontology.

Yet the question is not so easily resolved as that. For example, Nancy does not ask why there are multiple or infinite arts, and not just one. Severalness is not multiplicity but an indefinite numerical essence that is more than one but less than the many as proliferation toward dreaded Hegelian bad infinity. In asking after art's ontological severalness, therefore, Nancy is referring directly to his first major interlocutor within his theory of the arts, Hegel, and his subdivision of the species art into several named subcategorical genera in his two-volume *Aesthetics*. Still in conversation with Hegel, the one-ness of art also is given in Hegel's work under the name poetry. This complex resolution of the severalness of the arts as species into a unity under the name of one of arts' genera, poetry, is the essence of the issue of the aesthetic in Nancy's work. Yet the title also refers to Heidegger who, one suspects, would profoundly disagree with its premise. For Heidegger and all those thinkers of aesthetic singularity that proceed from his intellectual dwelling place, Gadamer, Derrida, Badiou, Lacoue-Labarthe, Agamben, and Nancy himself to a degree, it is simply not the case that there are several arts. There is just one, *Dichtung*, *poiēsis*, poetry. Thus, the question of the essay and of all of Nancy's work in the arts is, after Hegel and Heidegger, why do we still speak of the arts in the plural and not accede to ontological unity through the designation of art as *Dichtung* (poetry)? Nancy makes it clear that, as is the case in Heidegger, art provides unique and thus singular access to being as such,[2] but that it does so precisely because of the unresolved issue within art of the one and the many and the ontological condition of belonging.

I have chosen the pairing of poetry and plurality precisely because until the publication of *The Muses* in 1994, the question had been for so many decades that of poetry and its singularity and for many remains so today. I believe we are now more than adequately appraised of the quality of poetic singularity,[3] but have not even begun to touch on poetic plurality. For Nancy the presupposition of singularity cannot be divested from already existing multiplicity,[4] so that, if poetry has come to stand in for singularity, as I believe to be primarily the case, then poetry must always be considered thus: poetry (singularity) and plurality. If one were for a moment to take multiplicity as the world in Nancy's thought, or the infinite totality of intentional consciousness within an immanent sphere of universal and endless extendibility,[5] then the singularity of sense, the "meaning" of that world, only *makes* sense by creating this world, each time as if for the first time, radically finite, absolutely singular, over and over into an infinite set of reticulated and related multiplicities.[6] Put as succinctly as possible, being singular plural implicates all finite singularity into an infinite, relational, yet separated and distinct multiplicity by the same gesture, event, or process of creation that interrupts the infinite world of multiples via the radical intrinsic exteriority of finite, singular sense.[7] Plurality in the world is the shared finitude of related singularities that Nancy calls transimmanence (*SW*, 18–19; 55–56), by which he is insisting that the world is always interrupted by that which precedes it, sense (*SW*, 78), and yet in such a way that sense as such does not form an outside to the world but the coming to presence of world as radically finite and hence other to its immanent multiple universality (*FT*, 8).[8] This is the essence of Nancy's brilliant reconfiguration of ontology based around the standard phenomenological insistence on the presupposition of being in the world.[9]

Being singular plural amid the creative transimmanence of the sense of the world somewhat radicalizes the question that opens *The Muses*: "Why are there several arts and not just one?" The issue of why there is a multiple of entities rather than a being as such is the very basis of Nancy's ontology, wherein he is able to declare that the ontico-ontological difference so central to Heidegger's thought is now null (*CW*, 71). It is nullified precisely because there is no difference between several beings and being as such. There is only difference as the spacing relational dynamic between world and sense (*SW*, 34–35). So at the very least for Nancy, the question as to why there is a multiplicity of any singularity is the very basis of his entire conception of singular plural ontology, which he also terms the sense of the world (the singularity of plurality) (*BSP*, 185–186). If we therefore read poetry in light of these complex observations, we are required to think again about the presupposition of singularity and concede that the being of poetry is not so much its singularity as its singular plurality (*MA*, 7–8). This observation not only contests the very powerful arguments in favor of poetic singularity that have come into print of late, but also the long history in twentieth century thought of taking poetry to be univocal as opposed to prose's assumed heterogeneous worldliness.[10]

Yet Nancy is not interested in poetry per se. Of all his contemporaries and forebears, he commits the least amount of time to reading actual poems. In the many essays that make up the two volumes of the *Muses*, only a handful address poetry and these are rather brief. This negligence in terms of reading specific instances of poetry seems to suggest hat one must not simply read poetry in terms of singular plurality, but in fact read the access to the singular plural in ontology as somehow the result of poetry. This is poetry's irrepressibility and, as we will see, promiscuous plurality. Poetry is never poetry as such, but always lending its dark powers to something else.[11] The very essence of poetry is its inability to occupy one place of being, singular or plural.

THE PRINCIPLE OF MONOGAMY, FOR THE MOST PART

The Muses begins, monogamously, with a discourse on the essence of the Muses: their ability to excite, their multiplicity, and the means by which they consistently lend their name to another entity, here the arts. Already from these general observations, however, three central elements of art within Nancy's ontology are made apparent. First is what one might name, after Lyotard and Kant, the "tautegorical" element of the sensuous presence of sense or its ability to sense itself sensing.[12] This affective sense of sensing is found in art because historically art has been ascribed with affect and exteriority (*SW*, 128–134). These two, indeed, comprise the meaning of the term *aesthetics* within metaphysics: a material exteriority that gives pleasure, with exteriority as such always implicated in the act of pleasure (giving and taking). Second is artistic multiple finiteness. Elsewhere, Nancy names art "a fragment" and explains that it is art's ability to present an infinite number of finite, fragmented, and radically exterior worlds that provides access to the world's factual sense. Not *what* the world is but *that it is* (*CW*, 52). Placed together, these qualities provide a compound summary of the qualities of art in relation to ontology as I see them in Nancy's work. Art gives access to being singular plural and the sense of the world due to its qualities of sensuousness, exteriority, and multiple finiteness. Art provides the sense of sense, as Nancy argues, because it presents a sensuous material exteriority that is both multiply finite and self-sensing.[13] The final quality mentioned in *The Muses*, however, is less easy to ascribe directly to Nancy because it names perhaps a disturbance in his own thought: how art is able to borrow and lend its name, its self-identity, to other things; in other words, art's promiscuity.

The three qualities of the Muses are different—sensuous affect, plurality, and nominal promiscuousness—and yet Nancy first reticulates and then collapses the three into a self-founding and self-destabilizing one.[14] Placing the tripartite qualities of art under one principle of plurality he then asks two further questions: "What one might mean by a principle (or a reason or an essence) that would not be a principle *of* plurality, but the plural itself as principle? And in what way must this properly belong to the essence of art?" (*M*, 1–2). This is a profound observation in terms of ontology allowing for the subsumption of principality beneath plurality and the collapse of their oppositional distinction, what one might call classic Nancyean deconstruction. However, in asking this question, Nancyean reticulation appears to momentarily give way to a much more troubling receptacularization or involution. In English, although "principle" means the highest or leading element, such that one could take the plurality of principle to mean singular plurality, it also means the largest part of something. This shift in Nancy from the collapsing of identity into a singular composite entity, generality, and particularity becoming singular plurality, into a part being taken for the whole, plurality being the largest part of singularity but not its entirety, necessitates the following admission. If the principle is mostly plural then singular plurality is mostly art.

Yet within the transimmanent world of singular plural sense, how can there ever be "for the most part" if there is instead a perpetual state of *partes extra partes* or parts outside of parts?[15] As Nancy insists, the world coincides with its own inherent exteriority because the finitude of sense's singularity is absolutely without remainder.[16] Defining the sensible as "nontotalizable totality and still without remainder," Nancy clarifies by explaining, "or at least without remainder that would not be in turn traced out along the surface of this world here" (*SW*, 129–130). He then goes on to stipulate that this law even puts at risk the conception of *partes extra partes* if such a designation results in "the impression that it is a matter of parts of a unity" (*SW*, 130). The law that dictates that there can be no excessive remainder out there also stipulates of course that there can be no incompletion interior to the sensible world either. If *partes extra partes* suggests parts of a unity located in an impossible place outside of the world of sense, "for the most part" insists of the same thing inside the world of sense. Just as the world cannot be seen as incomplete without an exterior remainder, it is as impossible to conceive of it as completable through the aggregation of interior elements.[17] In the world, there is always an exterior excess that is not a remainder. This being the case, the transcendent part of transimmanence cannot be onto-theological through a gesture of locating it beyond or outside world of sense, but rather must be endlessly, internally involuted and reticulated. Sense is constituted by the world's total and absolute exteriority to itself resulting in a conception of excess as absolute excess or better excess without excess (an excess that is not a remainder, akin to art's status as a fragment without a presupposed whole). In the singular plural sense of the world there is no "for the most part." One cannot opt into some elements of Nancy's world and opt out of others, pocketing the singular while letting the plural pass. Rather one must opt entirely in and entirely out or nothing at all. It is typical, perhaps, of art's promiscuousness, sensuousness, and finitude that it will not readily submit to this law that it is in part, or for the most part, exemplifies.

In *The Muses*, Nancy notes first how the plurality of the arts cannot be contained purely within its subdivisions (painting, sculpture, music, poetry, etc.), but rather extends into art's status as technology. The classification is really nothing other than a symptom of art's impossible to contain, sensuous, and technical proliferation. If technics is the opposite of nature, as Nancy argues, in that it lacks both ground and end, then certainly art's technicity is infinite or, more accurately, multiply finite (M, 25–26). In contrast, time and again, art in its multiple specificity is reduced to a profound augmentation: Art as the disclosure of being. Between art as radical discreteness and as totalizing unity, Nancy contends, "In one way or another, art would thus be in default or excess of its own concept. One could also say: 'art' never appears except in a tension between two concepts of art, one technical and the other sublime. . . . Art and the arts inter-belong to each other [*s'entr'appatiennent*] in a tense, extended mode in exteriority, without any resolution in interiority" (M, 4).

This is the crux of the matter.[18] Art is typified in Western metaphysics, if one can name such a category, as simultaneously a principle of discreet illimitable particularity *and* totalizing unity. Is this not the unnamed dark interior of the singular in fact: the irresolvable collapsing of oneness into particularity and vice-versa? Art's simultaneity then reduces art to being a sensuous *mimēsis* or an exteriority that mimes or gives a strong localized example of the unity of the world at large. Nancy's reading of art as fragment also succumbs to art as exteriorized *mimēsis*,[19] but here what art presents first of all is a double impossibility within presentation. Art does not come to presence as simple exteriority, for as such art would be merely *technē* or endless, proliferating, and senseless exteriority (M, 24–27). Yet, if one tries instead to make art into a unity or principle, one denies the very quality, impenetrable exteriority, that makes it so essential for the disclosure of being in the first place. As Nancy correctly asserts, discreteness as generic categorization without a conception of discreetness as such, art as *technē*, or unity of presence as such at the expense of the very basis of artistic presence, namely exteriority, *poiēsis*, both name what art is only by denying its essence. Worse than this, it is not just that arts or art do not name the being of art but that the being of art is based on the relation between the two. This is the third denial of art at the very heart of its metaphysical definition, but it is not the last. Not only has Western thought misconstrued art in its plurality, in its unity, and in the relation between the two qualities under the designation singularity, but it has failed to realize that the relation of plurality to unity is the definition of art as such as the singular plural. This is Nancy's great observation.

GESTALT—*PAR PRO TOTO*

Nancy describes how over time the term *art* became divided from itself so to speak, with art naming a certain conception of aesthetic unity away from technics or material difference. Thus, he argues, although art and technics mean essentially the same thing by virtue of their Greek etymology, tautologically a debate rages regarding art and technics.[20] Art is at odds with itself for the very thing, material sensuousness, that allows art to come to being as disclosure of being is then divided from art at the moment of its apparent access to its own self-identity:

> Why did art divide itself? And why did it divide itself in such a way that on one side, the side of "art," the unity of the presumed genus seems at least indifferent to and at most rebellious against the plurality of the presumed species, while on the other side, that of

> "technics," the unity of the genus . . . is immediately understood as effectuated in a plurality of species that are multiplied indefinitely? (M, 5–6)

Nancy wonders if one could trace historically the moment of art's division from itself, or whether, perhaps more likely, it is not rather the case that division as such is "congenital to art" (M, 6), and that art was never in possession of the unity we ascribe to it. For example, he notes, Plato already speaks of *poiēsis egasiai teckhnais* or "creations produced by techniques or by arts" (M, 6). Plato not only divides *poiēsis* from *technē* via the *entelechy* of the variety and process-nature of works. He then also further divides within *technē* certain arts that *pars pro toto* not only become raised above *technē*, but are then delivered across the divide of "work" or *entelechy* back to *poiēsis* as such. These arts, metrics, and music, archetypally represent *technē* by being excised from it and placed under the heading *poiēsis*, which is already opposed to *technē* as being one remove less from *aletheia*.

This appropriation, breaching, and subordination of *technē* is, I believe, hypostatized by Heidegger when he repeats the same procedure in his division of poetry from itself in the word "*Dichtung*." Heidegger differentiates *Dichtung* from *poesy* and then locates all art under the heading of poetry not as *poesy* (metrics) but as *Dichtung* (saying as such). In doing so, he seems to repeat an ancient and impossible-to-avoid gesture. Heidegger divides poetry from the very element that allows poetry to function as the disclosure of being, its metrical technicity, and then takes all of art and places poetry, whose essence it is to be divested of its essence, above it. One could describe this complex, and common, procedure as follows. One operates simultaneously a *gestalt–par pro toto*, or places in operation the dual elements of synecdoche within the same conceptual figuration. In one act of synecdoche, one takes the whole of poetry, its non-natural material technicity as merely an excessive part, and then one takes a part of art, poetry, a severely degraded part at that, and places that as the categorical being of the whole of art as such.

In a dense but essential reading of Heidegger's re-enactment of Plato's original division of art from itself, Nancy describes the fate of art within Western thought between the *Republic* and the Reich as follows:

> The division separates, then, the name of the product, *poiēsis*, from the name of the process of the mode of production, *technē*. What is thus divided at the origin is the producing action, *ergasia* or *ergazomai*, the act whose subject is *demiourgos*, the one who works, who puts to work. The work has been divided, not according to the multiplicity of the ways in which it is put to work, but according to two poles, each of which tends toward unity: the product and the

> production, or in other terms, the finite operation and the infinite operation. Between the two, uninterrogated, is the diversity of the works and the modes of work. (M, 6)

We have, simply put, divided singularity from plurality creating two false senses of art, as Being or as beings, and in so doing ignored not merely the very presence of art, but of art's central role in coming to presence: its being singular plural.

POETRY AND THE SENSIBLE PRESENTATION OF THE IDEA

The Muses is one of Nancy's several skirmishes with Hegelian thought.[21] He argues Hegel's fundamental demand is that art be the sensuous presentation of the idea, which in turn reveals the basic logic of art's distinctive singular plurality. Hegel's formula defines art's self-sufficient unity only in terms of its multiple exteriority. Certainly, this tension dominates his two-volume *Aesthetics* where he strives for the essence of art by subdividing and categorizing this essence in terms of the variety of arts that are not art as such. Nancy distils from this immense effort the following formula: "The plurality of the arts is essentially irreducible as the unity of art is absolute" (M, 9). Hegel contends that, on the one hand, art is a sensuous presentation, and yet, at the same time, art as such is the dissolution and sublation "of its own end in the element of thought" (M, 9). In this way, Hegel develops art as a tension between the two poles of unity and multiple singularity.

Nancy's critical conclusion is essential not merely for his revision of aesthetics for our own age, but also his whole philosophical method: "We will retain merely that the self-overcoming of art has as its absolute corollary and symmetry what one might call the induration of the arts in an irreducible material difference" (M, 9). If we pause on this reading/deconstruction of Hegel for a moment we can draw the following conclusions. First, Hegel's definition of art is the precise tension between the self-overcoming of artistic specificity into unified generality and the dependence of this sublation on the fact that in so doing art confirms and enshrines the opposite, namely its irreducible materiality. Art 'becomes' itself through a double negation: first through self-overcoming, and second due to the collapse of this self-negation into generality by the irreducible presence of its material singularity. That Nancy names this materiality "difference," reveals of course the fundamental law of all sensuousness: material and thus exterior difference. Second, the definition of art as the sensuous presentation of the idea remains in play. Hegel's contribution to the field is immense and all but impossible to overcome, but the definitions of the terms at issue extend far beyond anything

Hegel could have intended. Aesthetic presentation is not a representation of a concept using material means, nor even the necessity that every idea be presented materially in the world to benefit from the prophylactic and transmissive qualities of language. Rather it marks the idea as the very process of exterior, singular, material presentation of presentation as such. As Nancy insists the presentation of presentation as such is the groundless basis for all sense: Not what it is but that it is. All of which forms our third conclusion. The condition of artistic tension between interior unity and exterior multiplicity is the very condition of sense as such. Art's tension is ontology's coming to presence.

Yet before we hasten to this formulation we must take account of the role of poetry within art's ability to bring to presence a new form of ontology. Although Hegel argues for art as the sensible presentation of the idea, categorical differentiation and its relation to identity is also a central feature of the arts. This is why, for him, there are several arts and not just one, and yet at the same time why all forms of artistic self-overcoming are subsumed under the single category poetry. In his categorization of the arts in his chapter on poetry, Hegel first attests to the principality of poetry among the arts due to its power of self-dissolution into thought. Poetry, like all the arts, is sensuous at base but, poetry is able to render exteriority intimately.[22] This is the case for the materiality of poetry as such, graphematic, phonetic, in translation, and the like, is so irrelevant to the "matter of poetry"' that poetry can, he argues, become prose and still remain poetic.

So-called poetic "self-overcoming" allows Hegel to locate poetry at the center and apex of the arts. On one side he places those arts that are pure semiotics, namely music, and on the other those that tend toward sonorous interiority and progressively move toward absolute exterior symbolism: painting, sculpture, and architecture. In music, for example, the individual items of materiality, the notes, carry no meaning as such away from an integrated and totally self-absorptive melodic whole. By comparison, poetry's elements of materiality, words, do carry meaning aside from rhythm. Thus Hegel argues that the material elements of the poem, the tempo of words and syllables, rhythm, euphony, and the like constitute not the proper element "for conveying subject-matter but as a rather accidental externality which assumes an artistic form only because art cannot allow any external aspect to have free play purely by chance."[23]

Poetry's accidental externality explains initially why poetry "can harbor the entire content of art and all the forms of art," yet paradoxically, it is also the source of poetry's undoing in favor of painting as the essay progresses.[24] Comparing poetry to architecture, Hegel notes that these two constitute the real "polar opposites" of the arts. The linear hierarchy is suddenly reconstituted with poetry at one extreme where its materiality is entirely vestigial to spiritual inwardness only present accidently and so as to avoid free play, and architecture at the other. "The beautiful mean between these extremes of architecture and poetry is occupied by sculpture, painting, and music."[25]

Hegel even goes one step further by suggesting that poetry, when it has need of exteriorization, has no material sufficient to itself and has to borrow from the other arts, leaving poetry "free in the main" from the restrictions of material exteriorization enforced on the other arts by the nature of their specific medium.[26] Nancy's reading of Hegel concerns itself with this second hierarchy but I believe one can only get a full sense of Hegel's impact on the arts if one reads the passage from the first model materiality (music–poetry–visual arts/architecture) to the second one (poetry–visual arts/music–architecture). While Hegel goes on to contend that poetic sonorous materiality is intrinsic to its relation to self-overcoming in thought—in other words that poetry's ideas are only possible through sonorousness and its subsequent sublation marking them out as different from thought as such or materiality as such (music say)—one cannot help but see that just as Hegel has inherited the Muses' qualities of sensuousness and plurality, it is the promiscuity of poetry that allows for its powerful self-dissolution. Poetry can overcome itself and become the arts, and become thought, precisely because its essence is in a state of flux. Its power of self-overcoming relies on an intrinsic materiality that, however, does not belong to it, an example of Nancy's intimate exteriority. Its ability to stand in for the arts depends on its place among the arts in terms of this loose relationship with its materiality.

TOUCH, TAUTEGORY, AND THE FOURTH SENSE OF *SENS*

In its ability both to reticulate the arts with thought and yet to remain separate from both, poetry shares central qualities with what Nancy calls "touch," a long consideration of which precedes and sets up his reading of Hegel.[27] Nancy first defines touch as "nothing other than the touch or stroke of sense altogether and of all the senses" (M, 17). Like poetry for Hegel, therefore, touch is the very sense of sense and also the sense that exists above all other senses. He then explains that touch exists only by also touching itself as touch, meaning that "touched by what it touches *and* because it touches—touch presents the proper moment of sensuous exteriority; it presents it *as such and as sensuous*" (M, 17). The double action of touch as such and as sensuous is the basis of Nancy's revision of the Hegelian sensible presentation of the idea and his ideas on poetry's negation of sensuousness in favor of as-suchness. Overreliance on as-suchness at the expense of sensuousness undermines the power and force of art as the touching of touch, for touch is the interruption of itself at every point that it favors immanence over transcendence (or indeed transcendence over immanence). Thus, Nancy avers, "touch *is* the interval and heterogeneity of touch. Touch is proximate distance" (M, 17). The four qualities of touch—singular plurality, self-sensing, spacing, and proximate distance—are essential to Nancy's overall ontological conception of the sense of the world.

Artistic sensuousness obviously relates directly to sense in all of its manifestations. Traditionally, critics have taken Nancy's central conception of *sens* to consist of a tripartite definition in his work suggesting meaning, the sensuous, and orientation.[28] Sensuous as-suchness is an orientation toward the unity of a meaning as perpetually interrupted due to the exterior excess of the sensuous. There is also, however, beyond the sensuous affect, plurality, and nominal promiscuity discussed in the last section, a fourth meaning in contention here, that of sensing, or the sensation that meaning in this instance is not an expressible and provable universal truth but a sensation of unity. This combination allows Nancy to say of art that it is "the sensuous presentation of truth," due to its quality as sensuous presence (*SW*, 134). If this can be taken to be the case, art "is merely that which takes as its theme and place the opening [*frayage*] of sense as such along sensuous surfaces, a 'presentation of presentation,' the motion and emotion of a coming" (*SW*, 135). Yet art does not create sense. Rather, like sense, art creates a world, if only a world in fragment. This second ability, which it shares with sense or perhaps better which augments an element of sense,[29] depends not merely on exteriority but on multiplicity. World comes to being from sense. Sense preexists a world or worlds that it presupposes. The world here is, as in phenomenology, the totality of one's existence in a world although not, as in Husserl, the totality of consciousness or, as in Heidegger, world as gathering or appropriation. Sense is that part of world without which it could not come into being but which coming to being also fixes into a single instance of sense called truth from which it composes a universal meaning, which Nancy first terms the symbolic and then later myth.[30] What stops a world from becoming a grounded unity, however, is its dependence on that which it cannot contain within itself, namely sense or excessive sense singularity.

One can see here the parallels therefore between world and sense and sensuous as-suchness in that in each case what constitutes their presence is an exteriority which is, however, not "out there" but rather an inaccessible intimate exteriority that one senses. The world fixes a sense of sense, but because this sense of sense is always in excess to the world, it precedes the world and cannot be captured by any one example of the world. Each world is but one singular unity amid a multiple infinitude of such unities. As Nancy says, "the multiplicity of the world does not remain even the multiplicity of *a* world: it qualifies the world as heterogeneity of worlds *in which consists the unity of the world*" (M, 27). To which he adds, "In other words the sensuous and technical plurality of the arts is bound up with intelligible sense."

POETIC SENSUOUS ESSENCE

Nancy warns against assuming, however central sensuousness is, that the sense of the world resides simply in sensuous presence as exteriority, an *aporia* he terms the "hyletic circle" (M, 14). Sense must form into some order of unity if it is to become world and sensory perception and pleasure become art. Art is to the sensuous what world is to sense. This necessity, he believes, explains the predominance of poetry as the art of all arts, because it is in *Dichtung* that "we witness simultaneously the renewal of the arts beneath the unity of a pure production of sense *and* the sensuous dislocation of sense" (M, 27). At this juncture, we are cast back to Nancy's explanation of the "contradictory double determination" of poetry in Hegel, wherein it is both "the extenuation of the sensuous" while at the same time the "end in itself" of poetry (M, 27). Nancy is quoting in this case the third and final contradiction of Hegel's treatment of poetry to be found in his consideration of versification. Here, Hegel concedes of the sensuous element of poetry, "that a poetic idea is not only clothed in words but is actually *uttered* and therefore passes over into the perceptible element of sound."[31] Thus, although sensuous sonority as such is not poetic, versified prose remains just that, poetic ideas are ideas that occur through sound. This leads Hegel to admit that in poetry the sonorous element does not merely assist or augment the supersensuous, but more than this "the poet is also given what without this impetus would never have occurred to him, namely *new* ideas."[32] Sensuousness is not supplemental to poetic *Aufhebung*.

Going even further, Hegel then makes the point that Nancy highlights, namely that "sensuous existence is essential to art from the very beginning," that it must be a form of speech augmented by sonorousness, so that "even if it chimes in as an external medium, it still must be treated as an end in itself."[33] Hegel's comments confirm Nancy's point that for the German the centrality of poetry is its combinatory contradiction of the negation of the sensuous on the one hand, and the dependence of poetry on sonorous particularities on the other. For Hegel, he argues, poetry "names a division, a dissension of technical production, *and* the paradoxical (or unlocatable) production of this very dissension as essence, but 'sensuous essence,' if one may put it that way, of production" (M, 27–28).

The conception of a "sensuous essence," is itself, for Nancy, a type of contradiction in terms for the sensuous as intimate exteriority can neither be entirely self-present essence (immanence) or essence conferred on something from beyond (transcendence). Sensuous essence is a form of production but as the pro-duction or presentation of sense as such or presentation itself. All that sensuous essence is able to produce, to bring to presence, is the sense of sense or sensing of sense. One could say: Sense senses itself, and the truth, the *touch* or *stroke* of truth, is the interruption of the "sensing itself." This construction is, Nancy rightly stipulates, almost impossible to sustain due to the "untenable tension towards a before-ness of sense" (M, 28). Sense senses itself as previous to its coming to presence as a sense that can be identified as a truth. Sense, therefore, precedes its own coming to presence, whereas the truth that proceeds from sense is the only means by which sense can be named as such. In between these two impossibilities resides poetry (art), leading Nancy to exclaim "that is why there is not poetry that does not bear upon the extremity of its own interruption" (M, 28). If poetry is meaningful in relation to thinking sense, or thinking the truth of the world as sense, meaning can only be gifted to poetry by the interruption of its sensuous essence. Indeed, as I have already explained, the essence of poetry is not merely the interruption of sonorousness but its dereliction and neglect. A negation or destruction that, however, always leaves a remnant or vestige, the so-called "Vestige of Art" (M, 81–100).

The tension that exists between sense as the subsequent sensing of itself as precondition, and truth as the subsequent interruption of self-sensing by this very observation, is the tension of poetry. Poetic sensuous essence can only come to presence through its interruption by supersensuousness, not because the supersensuous explains or names the sensuous, as has traditionally been assumed to be the case, but because self-sensing sensuousness is defined as exteriority and excess only by its being interrupted (otherwise it would succumb to the hyletic circle). Nancy goes on to define this need for sensuous interruption by considering the part–whole conundrum that has occupied much of our considerations here. Poetry is both, he believes, "the *pars pro toto* of art" and the "*totum pro parte* of technique" (M, 28). He describes a chiasmus between intelligible sense and sensuous sense or *poiēsis* (production into material, finite exteriority). Here poetry stands in for all art in terms of its intelligibility, and yet regarding its materiality its completion can only ever be incomplete. Poetry is able intellectually to possess, as species, the entirety of the genus art, but in so doing it is unable to coincide materially with itself in perfect unity or harmony.

The chiasmus between intelligible sense and sensuous sense is to be found in any production of technics, is heightened in the arts, and most powerfully and paradoxically prevalent in poetry. Thus, sensuous sense must be orientated toward an object that it "valorizes . . . in a meaningful, informative, or operational context" (M, 28). At the same time "reciprocally, (intelligible) sense makes sense only if it is, as one says, 'perceived'" (M, 28). This being the case, Nancy is able to make the following statement that depends on first there being a plurality of arts, and, from there being an art of arts, poetry. It is a statement that emerges, therefore, out of poetry, but it is not a statement about poetry. Instead it is a foundational dictum of Nancyean being: "(Sensuous) sense makes (intelligible) sense; it is indeed nothing but that, the intellection of its receptivity as such. (Intelligible) sense is sensed/senses itself; it is indeed nothing but that, the receptivity of its intelligibility" (M, 28).

Again we have on display here the four senses of sense as sensuousness, sensibility, orientation, and self-sensation. Of these four, however, it is the final tautegorical sense of sense sensing itself that is central in this respect. Nancy goes on to argue this when he states that the double "subsumption" of poetry, that of the subsumption of the arts into poetry and then poetry into philosophy, entirely depends on sensational tautegory. Thus, poetry's sacrifice of its self-presence on behalf of all the arts is not a waste but in fact "indicates clearly the unique and unitary place of 'art'" (M, 29). The means by which it does so, by overcoming its own sensuous sonorousness in favor of philosophical truth and thought, seems to suggest that poetry represents "a reunion *without exteriority* of the intelligible and the sensuous" (M, 29). Yet, as we know, poetry can only make a sacrifice of its sensuousness in favor or intelligibility by virtue of its being in excess of itself. Previous to its subsumption, poetic sonorousness does not exhaust the "being" of poetry, which naturally moves towards communication, intelligibility, and self-negation. Yet at the moment of poetic *Aufhebung* it is precisely the fact that poetry is gifted with sonorous excessive exteriority, however vestigial, that allows for its subsumption in the first instance. Sensuous presence, if it exists, is the interruption of the sensuous by the intelligible defined as the interruption of intelligibility by the exteriority of sense. This is, after all, what Nancy means by a finite thinking (*FT*, 3–30).

Speaking now of poetic rather than intelligible exteriority, although accepting such a division is no longer so easy to impose, Nancy explains that the Hegelian reconciliation between poetry and philosophy takes place "in an irreconcilable mode, according to exteriority and to an exteriority that is doubly qualified, since it is at once the exteriority of the phenomenon as such or of the sensuous as being-outside-itself, *and* the exteriority of the poetic reconciliation in relation to the thought reconciliation" (M, 29). This second precondition is precisely because thought can only think itself within thinking, that is exterior to exteriority,

> or as *finite* thinking whose finitude separates it from the thing, its most proper thing, *and* precisely renders thereby sensuous the

> stakes of thinking. For that very reason, thinking senses itself (feels its weight, its gravity) two times outside itself: once in the thing "itself" (that is, the thing that is the same as thinking *insofar* as the thing makes itself felt as "thing outside," impenetrable, touchable and impenetrable), and a second time in poetry (as sensuous assumption of sense itself that thinking only thinks or in some way "pre-senses. (M, 29–30)

Nancy draws three conclusions from his remarkable reading of Hegel and, by implication, Heidegger. The first is that the exposition of thought is composed of a thing plus poetry, which between them constitute the opening up of the *poiēsis* of the thing. This constitutes a powerful model for a type of creation *ex nihilo*, which partakes both of the interim unity of art, and its irreducible plurality. If creation, therefore, exists always as singular plural, the influential Romantic end of art narrative that Hegel is in part responsible for, is impossible unless one denies the very thing that constitutes the being of art and its value as a thing overcome for philosophy: sensuous presence. Thus, there is an end of art every time philosophy sublates sensuousness, but this being the case, this end is destined to an infinite repetition. As Nancy says, modifying Hegel's famous declaration: "The end of art was always yesterday" (M, 30). Finally, although it is in poetry that the resistance to the dialectic is revealed in Hegel, this is only possible if one re-subsumes, as it were, poetry back under the heading of the arts: "The poetic or poeticizing subsumption turns out to be *in itself* heterogeneous. The place or the form in which art would come to touch on its essence can only be the *partes extra partes* of artistic worlds. Poetry names its proper outside, or the outside of the proper: the sense of sense. . . . So sense is multiply unique, and uniquely multiple" (M, 30–31). This conclusion on Hegelian sensuous presentation explains why there are several arts and not just one. It is also reveals why there is always also just one art, poetry. And finally it brings to presence the relation of poetic singularity to plurality.

CONCLUSION, POETRY, AND PLURALITY

Although Nancy names plurality as the principle quality of the Muses that one is forced to transcribed in the following fashion (the arts (art (poetry))), one might now actually come to a very different conclusion and suggest that it is nominal promiscuity that defines art. This would suggest, of course, that Nancy's reading of art as sensuous presence is perhaps a violence committed to the Muses to make them take on a more heroic and philosophical garb than perhaps they warrant. If we were to sum up the narrative of the category art "since the Muses" we might note that art as such is a shapeshifting, cross-dressing term whose self-definition through negation, the classic Hegelian inheritance, is due not entirely to the paradox of the sensuous presentation of the idea as much as in the effect of art itself on category, the belonging of part to whole and the subsumption of whole to part. It was originally the Muses who manifested the qualities we term art. The Muse, therefore, what Agamben terms the impersonal dictation of language as immediate and indifferent medium or support for thinking,[34] is that which combines the qualities of plurality, tautegory, and trans-nominality (if I can call their nominal promiscuity thus) and passes these on to art and, by default, poetry. Even the aporia of plurality as principle is not therefore an *aporia* as such on Nancy's part, but an unconscious or perhaps simply understated understanding that the Muse is that wherein the principle is never complete. This is its principle. The whole is only ever a part, a fragment, which is also, by definition within the arts, subsumed under the part (historically in the West poetry). Therefore, it may be the case that the combination of plurality and sensuous affect results in the very logic of principle as part that Nancy's designation of plurality as principle reveals.

Plato's inaugural gesture, division of art from itself, application of categorical named differentiation, application of whole as necessarily incomplete, then subsumption of fragmented whole to a part of the whole, is not brought into full effect until Hegel's central definition of art as sensuous presentation of the idea. As we should now be more than aware of, Nancy's conception of art, upon which his whole ontology resides "for the most part," is the result of his brilliant critical reading of Hegel on this point. The sensuous presentation of the idea names, not a unity, nor even part of the totality of dialectic *Aufhebung*, but the very aporetic process wherein that which defines the Muse/art/the arts/poetry is the quality which denies it full self-presence. Poetry's role in this definition is central not because, as the art most open to self-dissolution under the beguilement of thinking, it is the best example of the law of the sensuous presentation of the idea. Although this is true, but rather as I argued by the means in which poetry's place, its centrality, its definition, and its relation to sensuousness cannot be fixed either by Hegel or those who write after him. It is not because poetic materiality is most readily renounced in favor of thought that makes it the archetypal art, but the manner in which its very sensuous self-definition resists thinking within thinking itself that makes poetry the art of arts. After Hegel, poetry is the most true term for art because it is the most nominally promiscuous.

What gives poetry the ability to manifest being is that which robs poetry of its own being, namely the subsumption of materiality to ideality or sensuousness to supersensuousness. We may draw any one of several conclusions from this tendency before asking does Nancy behave any differently that his forbears. The direction Nancy seems to be orientating our thoughts toward in his reading of poetry presents the ontological violence of whole against part that results in the subsumption of whole to part. Thus, it is that the very being of being as handed over to the negation of being to be found in poetry when placed under the category of thought is the essence of being as such. That poetry's sensuous essence is the operation by which its essence, its sensuousness, must be negated in favor of the supersensuous, yet at the same time with the proviso that it is poetic sensuousness that the supersensuous needs to appropriate to manifest being as such, means that being as such must pass through excess and exterior non-being as such. Poetry manifests being precisely because of its nominal promiscuousness whose source resides in the impossible yet essential relationship in art as thought between sensuous essence and supersensuous negation of essence in pursuit of actual being.

The law of the Muse is as follows in Nancy's work. The totality must be divided from itself. Then a principle part must be named and founded. This principle part, however, to found itself as universal and unified, relies on a sensuous exteriority that is a *partes extra partes*. This reliance is dualistic and contradictory in that sensuousness must be excised as having no place in supersensuous thought, and yet also appropriated as a means by which sensuousness can be negated. Having taken a part as a whole, and then admitted that the principle whole is in fact incomplete, the part excised from the whole by which the whole can be said to come to presence, sensuous exteriority, is then given a special dispensation. The means by which part of the whole of this excised part subsumes the totality beneath its particularity, in other words how poetry which is only part of art comes to stand for the whole of art, first of all operates as a localized example of the operations of thought and being as such. Then, this mimetic exemplarity comes to stand for the process of being as such so that the part excised, art, from which another part is excised, poetry, under which the localized whole is subsumed, art beneath poetry, then returns to the whole from which it was excised, philosophy, and comes to stand for the very exemplarity of being as such. That Hegel names the exemplarity of poetry as based on its plurality of genres and its nondependence on a material particularity is not, however, the essence of poetry's plurality. Rather, poetic plurality is the inability of poetry to be immanent and yet its failure to transcend itself. Poetry cannot be itself, for it is always standing in for something else be it art, thought or being, yet neither can poetry be anything other than itself, by which one means its essence, poetic essence, is this very inability to fix poetry to essence or negation. The essence of poetry, its materiality, is its negation, its tendency toward self-dissolution in favor of thought. Yet the very status of poetry as negated essence, immaterialized presence, is the basis, Nancy believes, of the only option for being.

In "Art, a Fragment," Nancy makes a powerful case for the role of poetry in what I elsewhere call "logopoiesis" or poetic thinking. The localized problems of art/poetry give open access to the wider complexities of the sense of the world and being singular plural. The question remains however as to whether Nancy is in fact interested in poetic plurality at all or, like Hegel and Heidegger before him, presents poetry as a localized mimetic example of *sens* as a whole. What is poetry's relation to sense? Is it a part of the whole, a *mimēsis*, an example, a fragment?

That poetry takes on many forms, or even many names, or comes to name many different things, is not the key here. Rather it is the manner in which poetry as plurality becomes the singular instance of exterior multiplicity not through coming to self-identity (poetry equals the singular instance of plurality), but the means by which it cannot come to self-identity. In this manner it is not what poetry is that defines its essence in relation to sense, but how it comes to be through its sensuous inability to coincide intelligibly with its own exteriority and sense that this is the case. Poetry fails to be and senses it, and in so doing, it is born to presence. So that although Nancy prefers to speak of art and the arts in relation to sense, it is the problem he has with poetry as the art of arts through the work of Hegel and then Heidegger, that is the centrality of poetry to his work, the future of aesthetics, and ontology. Poetry names therefore the very aporetic process of *partes extra partes—gestalt—par pro toto* that may be the only future avenue for ontology and metaphysics. A radical intimate exteriority wherein the parts are both more than the whole, and yet wherein each part is in excess of the whole so as to be subsumed by the whole as the part in excess, which is the very sense of exterior particularity as the precondition of a unity perpetually in excess of itself and yet intrinsic. Poetry, in other words, poetry as process and medium, is the very sensuous essence of transimmanence as such, both as a solution, and as a highly problematic formulation. In this way I suggest that although Nancy comes on the essential relation of poetry to the sense of the world, like all those before him, he provides access to the essence of poetry through the self-same problematic logic of the part–whole subsumption. This is his great achievement but also potentially one of his most weighty oversights.

Yet who here can blame him? To see poetry in its entirety as plurality one must squint, approach it at dusk, through tears, smoke, or the kind of momentary, revelatory blindness that results from staring too long at the sun or at a light bulb suspended above one's head.

NOTES

1. J.-L. Nancy, *The Muses*, trans. Peggy Kamuf (Stanford: Stanford University Press, 1997). Henceforth cited as M.

2. It is the first essay of the second volume of *Muses*, *Multiple Arts*, that presents the case for a post-Heideggerian poetry as access to being as such: "If we understand or, in one way or another, accede to a dawning of sense, we do so poetically . . . poetry cannot be defined except by such access . . ." Jean-Luc Nancy, *Multiple Arts: The Muses II*, ed. Simon Sparks (Stanford: Stanford University Press, 2006), p. 3. Henceforth cited as MA.

3. See, for example, Timothy Clark, The Poetics of Singularity: The Counter-Culturalist Turn in Heidegger, Derrida, Blanchot and the later Gadamer (Edinburgh: Edinburgh University Press, 2005) and Derek Attridge, The Singularity of Literature. (London: Routledge, 2004).

4. Jean-Luc Nancy, *Being Singular Plural*, trans. Robert D. Richardson and Anne O'Byrne (Stanford: Stanford University Press, 2000), pp. 28–29. Henceforth cited as *BSP*.

5. What Nancy terms *areality* in *The Sense of the World*, trans. Jeffrey S. Librett (Minneapolis: University of Minnesota Press, 1997), p. 62. Henceforth cited as *SW*. I am indebted to two recent excellent introductions to Nancy's work in helping formulate my summaries of Nancy's ontology here. See B.C. Hutchens, *Jean-Luc Nancy and the Future of Philosophy* (Chesham: Acumen, 2005), and Ian James, *The Fragmentary Demand: An Introduction to the Philosophy of Jean-Luc Nancy* (Stanford: Stanford University Press, 2006). Their work informs much of the general background to this close reading.

6. See *SW*, 40 and *BSP*, 16–17 on reticulated space. See also its full development in the later essay "Of Creation" in *The Creation of the World* or *Globalization*, trans. François Raffoul and David Pettigrew (Albany, NY: The State University of New York Press, 2007), pp. 57–74. Henceforth cited as *CW*.

7. See *CW*, 67 on the relation of finitude and multiplicity in the act of making and Jean-Luc Nancy, *A Finite Thinking*, ed. Simon Sparks (Stanford: Stanford University Press, 2003), p. 27 for a summary statement as regards Nancy's complex conception of finitude. Henceforth cited as *FT*.

8. In the earlier essay "Myth Interrupted" (1986), Nancy explains the relation of literature to the interruption of unified meanings by revealing how the literary is defined as the interruption of any stable set of communally held meanings that he terms *myth* although he also uses the term *symbolic order* in his early work as well, and yet is that which precedes myth as the finitude that is the precondition of all unified meaning. See *Inoperative Community*, ed. Peter Conner (Minneapolis: University of Minnesota Press, 1991), pp. 43–70. This forms the outwork for the more sophisticated rendering of these issues in the work of the mid-1990s.

9. For the relation of Nancy's thought to phenomenology, see Ian James, op. cit., pp. 65–151.

10. See William Watkin, "The Materialization of Prose: *Poiesis* versus *Dianoia* in the work of Godzich & Kittay, Shklovsky, Silliman and Agamben," *Paragraph* 31.3 (2008): 344–364.

11. Again the second part of *The Birth to Presence*, titled "Poetry," has few direct comments on actual works of poetry and is made up of diverse readings of wit, laughter, painting, Joyce, Freud, Bataille (that poetry hater) and so on. See Jean-Luc Nancy, *The Birth to Presence*, trans. Brian Holmes et al. (Stanford: Stanford University Press, 1993). Henceforth cited as *BP*. In the preface to this work whilst

conceding that poetry can name the new "poverty of thought," which he calls for, he is just as willing to call it literature or art "in general" (*BP*, 4).

12. See my reading of this nexus in William Watkin, *The Literary Agamben: Adventures in Logopoiesis* (London: Continuum, 2010). The sense of sense is an essential component of sense as ontology and recurs, for example, in relation to thought in *FT*, 5.

13. See Ian James' excellent alternative reading of these issues, op. cit., pp. 202–230.

14. This is a methodological gesture that is typical of Nancy. Hutchens is particularly strong on detailing Nancy's methodology. See for example Hutchens, op. cit., pp. 4 and 7–15.

15. See *SW*, 130 and M, 30. As Ian James has revealed in his recent study, Nancy's use of this term is a modification of a central term in the work of Merleau-Ponty. For more see James, op. cit., pp. 143–151.

16. This is the basis of Nancy's early reading as to the relevance of art to a singular-plural ontology in "Art, a Fragment." In particular see *SW*, 128–130.

17. This is the crux of the problem of structure per se to be found in Derrida's foundational "Structure, Sign, and Play in the Discourse of the Human Sciences," in *Writing and Difference*, trans. Alan Bass (London: Routledge, 1978), pp. 278–294. In his own important reading/definition of structure Giorgio Agamben attributes this problem to Aristotle thus installing the question at the root of first philosophy, see Giorgio Agamben, *The Man Without Content*, trans. Georgia Albert (Stanford: Stanford University Press), pp. 94–103. Finally, it is obviously essential to Badiou's adoption of certain tenets of set theory in *Being and Event* to solve precisely this ancient problem interior–exterior completion in terms of set, subset, belonging, multiple, and excess. In other words, philosophy emanates from can only progress through the quagmire of this aporia.

18. I have no space to develop this idea but clearly Nancy's use of the awkward *s'entr'appatiennent* [interbelong] stylistically demonstrates how interbelonging combines both interruption and unity in equal measure forming indeed a tensile crux that, I argue elsewhere after Agamben, is the essential structural nature poetic tabularity. See my *Literary Agamben*, pp. 124–134.

19. In speaking of Art's ability to interrupt the signifying chain of the symbolic–mythical unity he concluded that is holds a "position similar to that of truth: the sensuous presentation of truth" (*SW*, 134). When he later adds that art takes as its theme "the opening of sense as such along sensuous surfaces" (*SW*, 135), the effect is complete I believe. Art stands in relation to sense as a fragment, it occupies a relation of spatial similarity, and takes as its totality a part of sense namely sensuousness as such. Art, therefore, still serves thought in Nancy's work, not through direct mimetic representation but through an appropriated or subordinate presentation of presentation. Art is a fragment of sense by definition, for if it were not art would be sense.

20. Here he is most certainly speaking of Heidegger's *The Question Concerning Technology*, trans. William Lovitt (London: Harper Perennial, 1977), pp. 3–35.

21. The second chapter of *The Muses*, "The Girl Who Succeeds the Muses," is a reading of the allegory of art as presentation to be found in Hegel's *The Phe-*

nomenology of Spirit (M, 41–55). See also Jean-Luc Nancy, *Hegel: The Restlessness of the Negative*, trans. Jason Smith and Steven Miller (Minneapolis: University of Minnesota Press, 2002) and *The Speculative Remark: One of Hegel's Bon Mots*, trans. Céline Suprenant (Stanford: Stanford University Press, 2002).

22. See G.W.F. Hegel, *Aesthetics: Lectures on Fine Art*, in two volumes, trans. T. M. Know (Oxford: Oxford University Press: 1998), p. 964.

23. Ibid.

24. Ibid., p. 968.

25. Ibid.

26. Ibid., p. 969.

27. Since the publication of Derrida's *On Touching* in 2000 and its translation into English in 2005 all eyes turn to Nancy's 1992 text *Corpus* when speaking of touch as indeed they should. However the complex of issues that now congregate around this conversation between arguably the two most important thinkers of our time necessitate an engagement with these issues that I cannot facilitate here.

28. See, for example, James, op. cit., p. 106.

29. Sense as such is not reducible to art as in the arts only the sensuous self-sensing element of sense is in operation not the full gamut of potential meanings of sense that must included meaning and orientation.

30. This marks a shift in terminology from "the symbolic" in Jean-Luc Nancy and Phillipe Lacoue-Labarthe, *The Title of the Letter: Reading of Lacan*, trans. François Raffoul and David Pettigrew (Albany, NY: SUNY Press, 1992), through "myth" in *The Inoperative Community* to "world" in *The Sense of the World.*

31. Hegel, *Aesthetics*, p. 1011.

32. Ibid., p. 1013.

33. Ibid.

34. See my reading of language as indifferent medium in *The Literary Agamben*, pp. 4–40.

THIRTEEN

FORBIDDING, KNOWING, CONTINUING

On Representing the Shoah

Andrew Benjamin

> L'éclosion du monde doit être pensée dans sa radicalité: non plus une éclosion sur fond de monde donné, ni même de création donnée, mais l'éclosion de l'éclosion elle-même et l'espacement de l'espace même.
>
> —*Jean-Luc Nancy*, La Déclosion[1]

1. There will always be poems whose sense of engagement is with the moment at which writing encounters the necessity to end, a moment that once it has been staged, in the production of an ensuing silence and thus in the cessation that will have been created, there is an opening. An opening is, of course, not inherently positive. That opening could be the space left by the impossibility of continuing: an opening therefore as the trace of continuity's impossibility. Such is the case with Dan Pagis' remarkable poem "Written in Pencil in the Sealed Freight Car."[2] The poem reads as follows:

> Here in the carload
> I, Eve, with my son Abel.
> If you see my older boy,
> Cain, the son of Adam
> Tell him that I

The obvious point of departure for any discussion of this poem is to begin with the reiterated presence of the biblical names. That reiteration would invoke the story of filial murder in Bereshit 4:1–15. The question of murder equally the question posed to G-d concerning the locus of human responsibility would all figure. And yet, what haunts the poem is the way it ends. It is not just that the full stop that should bring it to its proper end is absent; what matters—mattering both as content and as language's material presence—is announced by that absence. Although there is the questioning of responsibility that occurs in the biblical source—thus the need to incorporate its active dimension within an evocation of succession and continuity—here what figures emphatically, a figuring that repositions questions of human action, is absence itself. That absence, as the interruption of continuity and thus also of the realm of questioning, is the poem's proper end. An end improperly demanded because it had been improperly imposed.

The poem stages the impossibility of any straightforward sense of continuity. The staging, however, cannot be differentiated from the work of poetry. The impossibility of mere continuity that occurs here is a form that acknowledges that stricture while nevertheless continuing.[3] Although the interplay between continuity and discontinuity on the one hand and the repositioning of absence and presence on the other stand in need of genuine development, their provisional adumbration provides the frame of reference in which to develop a productive engagement with Jean-Luc Nancy's profound reflection on the relationship between the representation and the demands made for with regard to questions of memory, particularly as a consequence of the Shoah. The central text is his "*La représentation interdite*."[4]

Nancy's text continues a tradition of sustained philosophical, literary, and artistic reflections on the Shoah.[5] The text itself is demanding. Its argumentation begins with an examination of what is at work in claims that representing the Shoah is either impossible or should be forbidden. Rather than a simple affirmation of this position on ethical grounds or its counter in the name of history, Nancy's approach is to take up what such a claim means within a more generalized understanding of representation.[6] Indeed the overall argument is that the truth of representation as a dominating and structuring dimension within the Western philosophical tradition is revealed by the Shoah. In order to identify the force of this position, it is essential to follow the development of Nancy's argument.[7]

2. The argument begins with a continual repositioning and working through of what representation is taken to be. It is essential that representation be understood properly in order that the claim that the Shoah's representation is impossible, or should be forbidden, acquires greater precision. The intricacy of the argument involves recognizing that Nancy begins with the

position that what is fundamental to representation is that it is "the bringing to presence of an intelligible reality (or form) by the formal mediation of a sensory reality" (*GI*, 69/33). Consequently, the forbidding of representation needs to be linked to this conception of representation. Nancy's opening move is to reposition the interdiction. That move takes the following form:

> [T]o declare that the representation of the Shoah is impossible and/or forbidden can have no other meaning other than to declare that it is impossible and/or forbidden either to reduce the reality of the extermination to a massive block of signifying presence (to an "idol") as if there were still a meaning possible, or to offer a sensory reality, a form or figure that would refer to an intelligible form as if there has once been one. (*GI*, 69/33)

The reason why it is vital that Nancy open up what is at work within representation is that what is integral to his argument is the position that part of what made the Shoah possible is a potentiality within the structure of representation. The latter is at work as a mode of philosophical thought and provides the implicit ideational structure of political activity. The possibility occurs at the absolute limits of representation's enactment. Although he argues that what is important is "the condition that the Shoah creates for representation" (*GI*, 71/34), it is equally the case that representation as a mode of philosophical thought, a mode of thought enjoining activity, is deeply implicated in the Shoah's own actuality. (The Shoah is not a chance occurrence.)

Integral to the analysis of representation is its relation to absence. Representation presents what is "absent from pure presence" (*GI*, 74/36). Nancy doubles this relation by distinguishing between "absence" and "absense." The former is what is straightforwardly absent from presence. The latter, on the other hand, needs to be understood as that which only becomes present, or, more exactly, only is present through what he terms its "retreat" from presence (*GI*, 74/36). The importance of this distinction is twofold. In the first instance it indicates that the possibility of representation is necessarily marked by modes of nonpresence. In the second instance, it shows that what exists—coexists—does so in a way that is traversed by the continual possibility of an attempt to realize and thus to enact complete presence. If this is the case, then it demands that the question of the forbidden quality of representation be reposed. Nancy formulates this possibility thus:

> If, therefore, what is essential to representation is the relation to absence and absense upon which all presence sustains itself—that is upon which it exhausts itself, hollows itself out, radiates, and comes

> to presence—on what grounds could the representation of anything be at all subject to condemnation? By the same token, however, how is it that not all representation is forbidden (*interdite*), in the sense of surprised, taken back struck dumb (*medusée*) confounded, or disconcerted by the forbidding hollowness at the heart of presence? (*GI*, 76–77/38)

Indeed, the mode of argumentation within which the question of the image and its presentation is positioned in terms of a form of limitation is consistent with the definition of the image within Nancy's wider considerations of the topic. Of this more generalized sense of absence and its relation to the image, he writes:

> The absence of the imaged subject is nothing other than an intense presence receding into itself, gathering itself together in its intensity. Resemblance gathers together in force and gathers itself as a force of the same—the same differing in itself from itself. (*GI*, 24/9)

The image and representation are defined by the interplay of presenting and receding. In terms of what is proper to the image, and there is on Nancy's behalf an unequivocal commitment to the image as having a founding propriety, there cannot be an image that is co-terminus with itself such that an identity would be established in which the image would be a self-completing finality. (Any representation is always open to its own deconstruction.) This becomes a general claim about the image and thus about the nature of presence. Absence is a constitutive part of it. The maintenance of "absence/absense," as opposed to its attempted effacement, an effacing in the name of a possible full presence, defines the site of two importantly different philosophical and political projects.

3. The next stage of the argument's development takes this conception of representation and the interrelated conception of the image as its point of departure. If there is a counter to the positioning of representation in terms of the interplay of absence and "absense," then it is not a conception of the image defined by a possible, although futural, mode of self-completion. The counter would be found in what Nancy defines as a "super-representation." Again, the force of this term is grounded in the necessity that modes of absence be inherent to the nature of the image and thus the nature of representation—though this will become presentation—conceived as a practice (rather than as a posited given). The "super-representation" is a conception of representation's enactment, its staging, as full. Nancy will also make use the term "saturated" to describe this state of affairs. Representation as

"super-representation" is the represented's presence envisaged as complete and thus as an absolute enactment. This yields the self-conception of the Aryan within the ideology of Nazism. Hence, the Aryan in Nancy's terms is the "representative of a representation" (*GI*, 79/39). In this way, the "super-representation" operates within what he calls "the sharing/dividing of representation-exposition" ("*le partage de la representation-exposition*").[8] This is a position that draws on the division found in the French *partage*, which allows for a form of completion while also sanctioning a possible separation. The *partage* identifies the co-presence, as a possibility, of the shared (completed unity) and the shared out (divided and incomplete). The inscription of the "super-representation" into what could be described as the logic of the *partage* entails that, to the extent that representation is defined in these terms, there is both a taking part that "prevents a strict separation" of the elements, while at the time there is a demand that the constitutive components of the representation be separated.[9] This logic reveals therefore a tension within representation, a tension that is manifest as a foundational weakness.

Although Nancy does not pursue the logic of *partage* in a more detailed way in this text, the tension that it both identifies and names locates a fundamental aspect of his approach to representation and the image. In sum, it is the following. The logic indicates that there is a form of fragility within the image. (This needs to be understood as a claim about the ontology of the image.) Moreover, it is a fragility that could always undermine the attempt to secure the image within an asserted completion, that is, within the assertion of the "super-representation." What this entails is that the "super-representation" not be posited as though its assertion both established and secured its continuity. The ineliminable fragility of the image means that action is necessary in order to secure the continual re-enactment of the "super-representation." The logic of *partage*, therefore, exposes a weakness at the heart of the image, which supplant that weakness's realization activity as necessary. Thus, if the Aryan is positioned as the "representative of a representation" this, as a mode of representation, enjoins the activity necessity to sustain it. To the extent that the "super-representation" aspires to be "fully completed," there has to be the reciprocal move in which there are those actions—actions that will involve everything from personal attitudes to the actualization of State policy—that will secure this positioning. It is in these precise terms that the Jew is to be understood as the potential destroyer of the mode of representation identified as the "super-representation."[10] The Jew, in other words, is positioned to expose the impossibility of completing the "super-representation," which is an impossibility that gives rise to a form of possibility—possibility as actualization—through acts of violence. The attempt to secure the "super-representation," an attempt to shore up representation against its inherent fragility, entails violence against the Jew. The consequence of this positioning of the Jew—a positioning demanded by the logic of *partage* and thus the exposure of the possibility of an undoing of the "super-representation"—is that Auschwitz becomes,

> a space organized in such a way that presence itself—that which shows itself and also shows the world without remainder—lays out the spectacle of annihilating what, in principle, is forbidding to representation. This is what I am calling "forbidden representation." (*GI*, 82/40)

The Jew therefore cannot, within the frame of reference created by the "super-representation," have access to representation. For Nancy, this means that the face of the Jew becomes a non-face defined by the "anonymity" of the exterminated. And yet, there is a sense in which the face still endures as the face of the Jew. (It will be essential to return to this point.) Nonetheless, within the overall analysis, this positioning of the Jew in relation to the maintenance of the "super-representation" allows Nancy to draw an important distinction between the operations of the police within the Gulag and what occurred at Auschwitz. In the former, the police carried out "acts," while at Auschwitz "the West was exacting revenge upon itself and upon its own opening—the opening, precisely, of [re]presentation" (*GI*, 87/43). What Nancy identifies with his description of the exterminated as anonymous is their removal from the domain of representation and thus from the domain of meaning. The important element of the argument, however, is that this removal is a consequence of what representation allows. This position is announced in summary form in the claim that,

> Insofar as the West tirelessly beckoned sense to a presence that was complete and without remainder (whether as power or knowledge, as divine essence or human authority) . . . our history took the risk in which it has foundered. (*GI*, 98/49)

As part of the formulation of this position, Nancy maintains a description of the camps as the "execution of representation" (*GI*, 94/47). Precisely because this description locates the camps within the philosophical project of representation, it is important to take up elements that form an essential part of the argument's formulation.

The distinction between the "super-representation" and the retention of "absence/absense" is that the former is necessitated by a mode of representation that was complete unto itself. In Nancy's terms, it was saturated with itself" (*GI*, 94/47). There was as such the impossibility of an element that was external to the enactment. This impossibility can be understood in terms of a distinction between the finite and the infinite in which the former continues to open onto the latter. However, this is a possibility that necessitates the retention of absence. With "saturation" this possibility is closed off. (Hence, a setup of this nature, namely one holding to this possibility, one in which "absence/absense" is retained, becomes a form of production defined by its inherent endlessness.) What is described as the "remainder," which would have been there, has become exhausted. As such the "execution of representation" gives rise to a conception of exhaustion as completion. The subject is fixed—the paradigmatic instance of which is the Aryan as the "representative of the representation"—it becomes "a power that is exhausted in its own act" (*GI*, 95/47). This is, of course, consistent with the more general examination of the relationship between the image and violence undertaken by Nancy. In this regard, he writes in relation to Sorel's conception of the "general strike" that,

> the completed form of violence that is the "general strike" has all its power in the fact that it realizes what [Sorel] calls "a myth": a totality in which the entire image of the social project that violence would serve immediately presents itself. (*GI*, 45/21)

For Sorel, what mattered was a form of interruption that did not clear a space in which something other was to happen. The contrary is the case: The general strike becomes a form of interruption in which what is actualized already has an image. There would not be the space of work. A space given by the interruption and that projects without predetermined forms, be they specific or general undertakings, would come to be enacted. This would be a working out that brings an original sense of the incomplete into play. The image would be imposed and thus work would be already sanctioned in advance. The inherent danger here is that the imposition of myth will necessitate the enforced separation of those who do not form part of it.[11]

4. There are at least two different types of conclusion that can be drawn here. The first, which involves a reiteration of Nancy's specific concern in relation to the Shoah, could be grounded in the recognition that while it is possible—at times a possibility given with the necessity to document—to present images (indeed *all* images no matter how harrowing), the acknowledgment of this possibility is quite distinct from the position that asserts the impossibility of "recreating the gesture of the murderer" (*GI*, 95/47). That gesture is, of course, articulated within the acts that were themselves the destruction of possibilities. These were destroyed because the continuity of the "super-representation" demanded it. (Here, representation as

a philosophical position cannot be separated from attempts to enact it.) Furthermore, it should be noted that destruction in this context is always present as a means. A critical engagement with the destruction necessitated by "super-representation"—the necessity both to establish and to maintain the presence of the "super-representation"—must remain scrupulous in its identification of the reason for destruction's imposition and therefore of the nature of the destruction involved.

Although the second conclusion draws on the first, it opens up a wider problem that concerns the relationship between representation and continuity. Continuity remains a problem for at least two reasons. The first concerns Adorno's well-known, although nonetheless stark claim made in 1949. He wrote the following:

> Even the most extreme consciousness of doom threatens to degenerate into idle chatter. Cultural criticism finds itself faced with the final stage of the dialectic of culture and barbarism. To write poetry after Auschwitz is barbaric. And this corrodes even the knowledge of why it has become impossible to write poetry today.[12]

The second is that continuity opens up the question of what continues. Thus, how would the Shoah register within that which is taken to continue? Once posed in this way, what matters is the way in which philosophy, poetry, or even Judaism are transformed by the act of continuity, that is, transformed by having to continue.[13] Hence, Nancy's argument, which was that with the Shoah there was the "execution of representation," can be understood as an argument about continuity. The Shoah marked both the truth of representation—a truth within its actual structure—and as such ceases with the Shoah. (That cessation however defines a philosophical task rather than working out a simple assumption.) Indeed, it is possible to argue that Nancy's own project is an instance of the way that philosophy is able to continue after the Shoah. That continuity necessitates that what occurs within the philosophical, as the philosophical, is a transformation in which the Shoah is at the same time an event for philosophy, although it is equally an event whose possibility is inextricably bound up with philosophy's own history. It is in regard to the latter that Nancy writes, "the Shoah is . . . an ultimate crisis for representation" (*GI*, 71/34). What needs to be drawn together are these two conclusions.

What, then, of Adorno's judgment? Adorno's evocation of "barbarism" recalls the position advanced by Walter Benjamin in "On the Concept of History." Benjamin's formulation, however, complicates the attribution of barbarism in the singular.

> There has never been a document of culture, which is not simultaneously one of barbarism. And just as it is itself not free from barbarism, neither is it free from the process of transmission, in which it falls from one set of hands into another. The historical materialist thus moves as far away from this as measurably possible. He regards it as his task to brush history against the grain.[14]

If one accepts Benjamin's position, the response to Adorno would be to concede the inevitability of barbarism. Moreover, one would argue that the possibility of barbarism was already work within the history of representation (a history in which the concerns of the philosophical overlaps with those of the political). Yet what needs to be resisted is the automatic identification of every document of culture, poetry included, with the barbaric. Even then questions remain. After the Shoah, what would it mean "to brush history against the grain"? What is to continue? Part of the force of Nancy's argumentation, a position that he himself notes, is that precisely because the possibility of the "super-representation"—and thus the desire for full presence—was integral to the operation of that which culminates in the Shoah, the Shoah was not an imposition that came from a force that was external to history. Philosophy must continue by acknowledging that this is the case. Equally, poetry has to take this predicament as bound up with its continuity. What this means for both philosophy and poetry is the presence of a setting that has to be worked through—a process that must occur in the work of philosophy and poetry, not simply in their content. Not only will this delimit the plurality of possibilities that marks the philosophical and the poetic—a plurality arising with the effective abeyance of representation—it will also define their continuity. Indeed, it identifies what continuity actually entails: Continuity is opposed to the mere marking of time.

Philosophy after the Shoah need not be about the Shoah. It need not dwell on its detail. It need not link moral positions exclusively to the Shoah. Philosophy after the Shoah works with the recognition of philosophy's already present implication in that event. Because they are linked to the project of representation (a project to be rewritten now in terms of presentation, a sense of presence in which "absence/absense" figure), art, and literature bear the same burden. There is, after the Shoah, a radically different sense of the "process of transmission." This difference, however, cannot obviate the need for continuity.

5. Pagis' poem can be understood as the enactment of the recognition that continuity needs to be rethought, a task at hand as a burden. In the case of this poem, the necessity arises from the way the poem was itself present,

that is, presence as work. Continuity has as much to do with history as it does with the possibility of an utterance. Continuity's impossibility becomes its possibility. Hence, the question: What would come after the poem's final line "Tell him that I"? Here, there is a finality that beckons. That there is a question, a question that presupposes the effacing of the named, entails the possibility of an answer. The answer is, of course, marked by its own inherent difficulties. What would be told and to whom? The proper names given within the poem are themselves signs into which other proper names could be—and would have been—folded. (Whence comes the force of biblical naming.) There is, of course the necessity for a form of reiteration and thus for the continuity of naming. There is, if only initially, a direct link here to the point made by Nancy that,

> the exterminated is he who, before dying, and in order to die as the exterminator's representation would have it, is himself emptied of the possibility to represent—or, finally, of the possibility of meaning (*sens*). (*GI*, 90/45)

Although in no sense questioning the perspicacity of Nancy's argument regarding the complex interconnection between the "super-representation" and the Jew (a positioning in which the Jew is given and to that extent takes on the role of the potential destroyer of the Aryan's mythic presence), there is an element that needs to be added. The emptying of meaning is not absolute. The exterminated died *as* Jews. An element of "*sens*" still figured. Something remained. However, that death was not a death as such. It was not dying. Nancy quotes Jean Améry: "No bridge led from death in Auschwitz to *Death in Venice* . . . Dying was omnipresent, but the figure of Death had disappeared" (*GI*, 88–89/44; trans. modified). If "the figure of Death" no longer pertained, no longer figured, but dying in the strict sense used above, the dying of Jews had a harrowing ubiquity, then what endures, takes on the form of a disaster.

What Nancy identifies as "super-representation" works with its own structuring force. On one side there is the image's completion—completion as a form of enactment—whereas on the other there is stripping of meaning from that which stands counter to this conception of the image. A stripping away however necessitating that the Jew endures. What it indicates is that disaster may be an immanent possibility within the structure of representation. Any evocation of the term "disaster" is, of course, already an acknowledgment of the powerful presence of Blanchot's own meditation on this term. For Blanchot, "disaster" is from the start distanced from that which is understood by death. Death, against which disaster is positioned, is not death as finality or completion. It is what could be described as the work of death. Blanchot writes:

> In the Hegelian system (that is, in all systems), death is constantly at work, and nothing dies, nothing can die. What remains after the system—remainder without rest [*reliquat sans reste*]—is the push of dying in its repetitive novelty.[15]

This complex formulation locates death within systems—a location that is always productive and as such can be described as "workful" (*à l'œuvre*)—while indicating, at the same time, that the system can never stem the work of death. The system does not exhaust death; death lives on. Disaster can be understood as the undoing of death, that is, as the undoing of death as that which is "constantly at work" ("*constamment à l'œuvre*"). What is of value for these present concerns is that the distinction between death and the disaster may be fundamental to understanding why it is that continuity is an exacting issue. Continuity may emerge from the position in which to acknowledge the disaster, acknowledging it as the disaster, is to allow for death.

The evocation of the Shoah within Blanchot's *Writing of the Disaster* is of an "event" where, as he writes, "all history took fire, where the movement of Meaning was swallowed up [*s'est abimé*]."[16] And yet, it is also the case that it can be dated historically. This complex co-presence means that although the Shoah is a historical occurrence, thereby enjoining if not necessitating its continual presence as a site of historical investigation, it is equally the case that the site in question has rendered the conventions of history impossible. (Again, the continuity of history, its possibility, is constrained within such a setting.) The Shoah understood therefore as the "disaster" and thus as the site of death's denial—a denial not of dying but of death as Améry notes—opens a form of continuity. The continuity in question would be allowed by what death enables: continuing as allowing to die. This would be a process in which the "allowing to die"—a possibility that the Shoah refused, almost by definition—becomes a form of living on. Here we can mark a conception of memory structured by the concerns of the present: memory as present remembrance.

Completion and finality, the "super-representation's" mythic possibility, through its demand for the realization of final form, necessitated the Jew's destruction. This was a destruction in which anonymity did not pertain to the presence of the annihilated as Jews; they were irrevocably Jews Rather anonymity was the refusal of death.[17] Death as the site of ritual and memory, thus death's creative force, thus death's relation to life, is that which was ruined. That ruination—a ruination without preservation—opens itself up to be thought in terms of the disaster. Pagis' poem, its end, the silence after the "I," acknowledges that the "I" did not continue. That the "I" named Eve died is the staging of an allowing to die. This "allowing" is one that has to be understood as a continuing conditioned by the disaster. Nancy's work takes place within the disaster's insistence. Responding to that insisting—to its detail and its call on thought—is to continue.

NOTES

1. The translation provided by the English translators is as follows: "The eclosure of the world must be thought in its radicalness: no longer an eclosure against the background of a given world, or even against that of a given creator, but the eclosure of eclosure itself and the spacing of space itself." *Dis-Enclosure: The Deconstruction of Christianity*, trans. Bettina Bergo, Gabriel Malenfant and Michael B. Smith (New York: Fordham University Press, 2008), p. 160. Henceforth cited as *D*.

2. Dan Pagis, *The Penguin Book of Jewish Verse*, ed. and trans. by T. Carmi (Penguin Books: Harmondsworth, 1981), p. 575.

3. The reference here is, of course, to Adorno. His argument concerning the problematic undertaking of continuity, be it philosophical or poetic, will be taken up later.

4. In Jean-Luc Nancy, *Au fond des images* (Paris: Galilée, 2003), pp. 57–99. English translation in *The Ground of the Image*, trans. Jeff Fort (New York: Fordham University Press, 2005), pp. 27–51. Henceforth cited as *GI* with the French pagination preceding the English.

5. The presence of the Shoah as both an event for philosophy and an event in which philosophy is already implicated is an enduring concern. That there is no one way of noting that presence and its consequence is significant. What is important about Nancy's undertaking is the interconnection it charts between what he refers to as the "super-representation" and the need to sustain it. There is an important affinity here with a number of positions. One of the most significant is Arendt's argument concerning she calls "totalitarian domination," which is concerned with maintaining a fabricated and therefore mythic entity. See her *The Origins of Totalitarianism* (Harcourt Brace: New York, 1983), p. 438, passim.

6. For a counter instance, there is the argument presented by Elizabeth Costello in J. M. Coetzee's *Elizabeth Costello* (Viking: New York, 2003). Her position is that "[t]o save our humanity, certain things we may want to see (*may want to see because we are human!*) must remain off-stage" (pp. 168–169). The "obscene" should be hidden from view. Here, there is a moral imposition on literature that comes from outside. The position is not Coetzee's since, after all, he presents the very passages that prompt her reflection. What is significant here is the failure by the character Elizabeth Costello to note that the already present implication of language in the problem of presentation cannot be dealt with adequately with modes of censorship, even if they are self-censorship. Censorship would be a form of disavowal.

7. For a detailed discussion of Nancy's work in relation to the question of presentation, see Alison Ross, *The Aesthetic Paths of Philosophy: Presentation in Kant, Heidegger, Lacoue-Labarthe and Nancy* (Stanford: Stanford University Press, 2007), pp. 134–163.

8. The translation of "*le partage de la representation-exposition*" offered here results from the fact that the verb *partager* is itself divided between a "taking part" and a "taking a part." This distinction is usefully offered by Jeff Fort in his translation. Nonetheless, what is fundamental to what will be called the "logic of *partage*" is the idea that it there is both a conception of unity and completion on the one hand and its undoing on the other. The latter is the affirmation of a form of incompletion. What is significant is that both are at work in the construction of representation.

9. Nancy first develops the notion of *partage* in his book *Le partage des voix* (Paris: Galilée, 1982). Although that book ends with the argument that *partage* may provide another way of understanding human commonality, what he refers to as "our being-together" [*notre être-ensemble*], there are no direct intimations of the problems posed by the attempted realization of full presence that is part of such a setup.

10. Nancy identifies this position in the following terms: "The 'Jew' is the representative *par excellence* of the destruction of the representation that we [Nancy] are calling 'super-representation'" (*GI*, 81/40).

11. Nancy's earlier attempt, undertaken with Philippe Lacoue-Labarthe, to engage with the presence of Nazism in terms of its mythic presence is *Le mythe nazi*, available in English in Jean-Luc Nancy and Philippe Lacoue-Labarthe, "The Nazi Myth," trans. Brian Holmes, *Critical Inquiry* 16:2 (Winter 1990), pp. 291–312.

12. T. W. Adorno, "Cultural Criticism and Society," *Prisms*, trans. Samuel and Shierry Weber (Cambridge, MA: The MIT Press, 1982), p. 34. It should be added immediately that Adorno's approach to this question became more nuanced. See, in this regard, "Working through the Past" in his *Can One Live after Auschwitz? A Philosophical Reader*, trans. Rodney Livingstone (Stanford University Press: Stanford, 2003).

13. I have addressed this question in my *Present Hope. Architecture, Philosophy, Judaism* (London: Routledge, 1993). In regards to the continuity of poetry, see the detailed discussion of Edmond Jabès and Paul Celan in Chapter 4.

14. Walter Benjamin, "On the Concept of History" in *Walter Benjamin. Selected Writings Volume 4* (Cambridge, MA: Harvard University Press, 2003), p. 392.

15. Maurice Blanchot, *The Writing of the Disaster*, new edition, trans. Ann Smock (Lincoln: University of Nebraska Press, 1995), p. 45; trans. modified. The project here is to take up the "disaster" as inextricably bound up with the possibility of literature and philosophy after the Shoah. It is not that the Shoah was the disaster. Rather, a thinking of the disaster is the project demanded by the Shoah's actuality, that is, its presence as that which can be, as Blanchot writes, "*a date in history*" (ibid., p. 47). These tentative comments on Blanchot are deeply indebted to a recent conversation with Leslie Hill. His own work on Blanchot remains one of the indispensable touchstones for Blanchot studies. See Leslie Hill, *Blanchot. Extreme Contemporary* (London: Routledge, 1997). See also his *Bataille, Klossowski, Blanchot. Writing at the Limit* (Oxford: Oxford University Press, 2001).

16. *Writing of the Disaster*, p. 47.

17. The reduction of the Jew to the purely anonymous is the risk with Agamben's analysis of the Shoah. Within it, the Jew is positioned as the "homo sacer." What endures as fundamentally problematic within that project is its impossibility

of thinking philosophically the particularity of the Shoah's "victims." I have argued this point in great detail in "Spacing as the Shared. Heraclitus, Pindar, Agamben," in *Work and Death. Essays on "Home Sacer,"* ed. Andrew Norris (Durham: Duke University Press, 2005) and "Particularity and Exceptions: On Jews and Animals," *South Atlantic Quarterly* 107:1 (Winter 2008), pp. 71–87.

PART FIVE

INTERVIEW WITH JEAN-LUC NANCY

FOURTEEN

THE COMMERCE OF PLURAL THINKING

M.-E. M. & P. G.: Our first question concerns what you have written regarding *mondialisation* or "world-forming" and the "auto-deconstruction" of Christianity as a making sense (*faire-sens*) of the world. Our worry is the following: Couldn't this auto-deconstruction, however critical (in the double meaning of the word), amount in the end to the continuation of the Western adventure in its auto-contestation? Isn't there also a contestation of the West that arrives from the outside, and doesn't this form a counter-movement to certain forms of Western hegemony in as much as they take into account a space outside the Western adventure, while not doing so as a remainder, that is to say, merely as non-Western?

J.-L. N.: First, I must answer that the "auto-deconstruction" that you bring up, while "auto," is also deconstructive of the "auto" itself. It should not be confused with autocritique or autogeneration. In effect, it does come from the "self," but it's Christianity that self-deconstructs. This movement, however, neither preserves nor retains more or less secretly the identity of this "self." It affects it (*atteint*), it cuts into it (*entame*), and anyway, for this reason, I think that I would propose in the future not to use the phrase "deconstruction of Christianity," and indicate by other means—I don't know which yet—that "Christianity" does not persist beyond the completion, if there is any, of this movement. Of course, there is a kind of Christian donation (*donnée*), donated (*donnée*) along with Christianity, which engages in a exit move from itself, through a challenge of its own effects, determinations, and so on. Thus, the breaking down of the Church, demythologization, and the like. But in the end, what is engaged is an unlimited putting into play (*mise en jeu*) of any kind of Christian donation. Can we still use the name of God, all things considered? And what about the names of the theological virtues: faith, hope, and charity, even if these names keep in reserve a surplus, an excess that belongs to Christianity—but as not belonging to it either?

Second, I must emphasize that it is precisely not a question of "auto-contestation," as you put it. It does not concern a dispute; it's about wondering—or rather perhaps becoming sensible to—what, from the inmost interiority of Christianity and/or the West itself, is originally, constitutively foreign (meaning as well here, beyond any constitution). What other is buried under the so-called "Western" identity? And if the most salient name of this Western culture is Christianity, what else besides Christianity is buried underneath? Precisely *under* it, not *within* it: not in a secret intimacy that would therefore be preserved across the whole of deconstruction, but somewhere else, more remote or deeper, in a non-intimacy, perhaps...

Third, such a movement cannot bring to the fore a non-Western "remainder," since it's the West itself that is deconstructed. Not simply its assurance, its hegemony, etc., but the very possibility of speaking of the "West"—and thus also of speaking of the "Orient."

I have used the word "dis-enclosure" (*déclosion*), which should be understood not only in the senses I have indicated elsewhere, as the effacement of the limits between faith and reason—an effacement that presumes a recasting of both concepts as well as what they share. It should also be understood as the dis-enclosure of the divisions, the distinctions, the polarities, and the distributions of the world. We can still make use of the very old names of the parts of the world—Europe, Asia, America, and so on. Meanwhile, the real "parts" displace and deform, de- and re-configure themselves. Something is expanding everywhere, surely, and this is what still gets called "Westernization." But this expansion itself, which is a dis-enclosure, ends up negating itself as "Westernization." For McDonald's or fiber optics are already no longer "Western": They are worldwide (*mondial*) in a sense that we still don't not know how to describe better than as "something dis-enclosed" (*du déclos*).

At the same time, all sorts of scattered traits, marks, tastes, and tones continue or rebegin otherwise in shading this "dis-enclosed cloud": certainly languages, dietary or aesthetic tastes, conceptions of work or parenting, as well as old or recent narratives. Just as one day in the Iberian peninsula and in the collection of "Latin" countries, the Visigoth culture was no longer recognizable as such, as distinctive, likewise—at another scale, involving other difficulties—Western culture will no longer be identifiable one day. It will be taken in by another culture by way of a worldwide recasting of culture and cultures. Moreover, *mondialisation* or world-forming is a recasting, a refashioning of the world, a redistribution of all that is shared (*tous les partages*).

Just consider what undoubtedly gave rise to the terms for the "Occident" (or the Arabic *Maghreb*, which has the same sense)—that is to say, "the setting sun"—and the "Orient" (Land of the Rising Sun). Didn't these terms crop up because from both the side of the "setting" and the "rising" sun, Europeans and Japanese found the ocean immense, infinite, or in any case without imaginable horizon? For some the sun set and for others it rose in a region that appeared to present the last outpost of the world, perhaps even its secret. But now we don't see the oceans in the same way: we fly over them, we communicate over them through satellites... Even the semantics of the words "East/West" has weakened.

The "Western" privilege would be its place as that which purposely gets carried away with and outside of itself. It's a place of destabilization, exploration, discovery, and a certain restlessness intimately woven together. Christianity would be the spiritual characterization of this getting carried away with itself (*emportement*). Humanity opens itself through Christianity onto the infinite and begins to worry about its salvation (*salut*)—which, of course, gives rise to a great ambiguity or ambivalence. (In this way, Islam at once represents an intensifying relation of the infinite, if we can say that—marking an infinite remoteness of God, an absolutely irreconcilable transcendence—as well as an opposite movement of assurance through the observation of rules and an allaying of the anxiety concerning abandonment or sin. Now, the movement of the West has been Christian. By this I'm not signaling a "superiority," but only the fact that Islam's assurance has not allayed the unrest in Christianity.)

The dis-enclosure of the West amounts to the proliferation of this getting carried away with and outside of itself—toward the infinite: toward the good or bad infinite, and perhaps the entire question is here.

M.-E. M. & P. G.: You also discuss how the West defines itself over and against myth, how the West's (or philosophy's) founding moment is the exclusion of what it calls, from within, myth. Thus, it seems to have a desire for the affirmation of the "auto," for the establishment of the "auto" against an "other" that is named, identified, and excluded. In this way, are you talking about a different relation to the other (i.e., the foreign element buried under the West)?

J.-L. N.: I think I can answer "yes and no." Yes, it's another relation to the other to the extent that the Occident, first and foremost, dwelled in myths, and that what it excluded while profoundly modifying the word's sense (passing from "spoken stories" to "deceptive fiction") still belongs to it. Just like the later Judeo-Christian and Islamic mythologies (whose enormous differences I leave aside), the whole of Greco-Roman mythology has for a very long time continued to haunt not just our imagination, but also our symbolic system. Oedipus, Moses, and Venus are not unfamiliar in our culture, and they are not simply "figures" in the most external meaning of the term. They are the origins (*foyers*) of signification, such that it's not possible simply to replace them with concepts. In some way, there is in fact an internal alterity, an internal allonomy to any claimed autonomy. Whether collected or invented by Plato, it remains an often repeated question as to how to understand his mythic stories. And not only the so-called "allegory" of the cave or the "myth of Er," but more importantly, all that ties itself to the figure of Eros, as well as to Diotima, to whom she is attached. From there, of course, we can't help but interrogate the very figure of Socrates. Plato constructs this mythic figure prominently and in this way provides philosophy with its own mythology.

Is this alterity fundamentally distinct from the other, from "the foreign buried under the West," as you put it? I am not sure of that, and this is why I also answer "no" to your question. Mythology's other is also as much the Egyptian, African, Mongol, or Celtic foreigner, as the Greek who is a disciple of the Orphic mystery-rites or the heir of Shaman masters. Through many different means and from internal as well as external points of view, an irreducible alterity affirms itself at the heart of the claims for identity. Identity's suture is impossible, and the Occident must learn that an identity occurs only through a displacement of one or several alterities, not through an absorption of others.

This is why contemporary Western thought has registered such an uneasiness over alterity—an uneasiness introduced, in fact, by Hegel, and made worse ever since. But out of this is produced a sort of hypostasis of the "Other" (witness Lacan and Levinas—such a remark is not a covert criticism), whose weakness would be that it always ends up coming back to the Same: The Self needs the other, it must recognize it, it must turn itself toward it, and so forth. By doing so, the self assures its Sameness. I wonder if it would not be better to forget this motif of alterity and to consider, rather, a register of remoteness (*l'éloignement*). I mean something like, "I am at a remove from myself," and "the distance is not to be filled in, it's always farther along." It's in the relation to this distance—surging, gathering momentum, leaping, looking out, etc.—that "I" am, that I "ex-ist." Neither the self nor the Other is distant… only distance.

Myth thus can appear not as providing access to alterity, let alone the alterity of the fictitious with regard to the real, but as that which speaks from afar and which speaks of the remote. The great immemorial Past or the unapproachable Future, the "interiority more internal than intimacy," and finally the "man who infinitely transcends man" ("*homme qui passe infiniment l'homme*") discussed by Pascal. Perhaps we can understand that there is a manner of talking (of story-telling? of signing? I don't know) that essentially converses from a certain remove, and speaks to us of the remote, as opposed to philosophy, which, like the characters in a Platonic dialogue, always wants to discuss that which is most near.

M.-E. M. & P. G.: Next, concerning the problem of the good or bad infinite, couldn't we say that capitalism defines this Western getting carried away with and out of oneself that, in particular, you talked about as the bad infinite? Can the West have the good infinite beyond capitalism? What is the connection between the dis-enclosure of the West and capitalism?

J.-L. N.: Absolutely! I could and should have mentioned it earlier. Capitalism is perhaps better defined as the "bad infinite," or the potentially infinite. The recent developments in financial capitalism, the accumulation of financial abstractions estranged from the real economy that we can't stop denouncing today including from within the most established capitalist institutions, demonstrate this time and again. This means money—money specifically understood as the general equivalence and the harnessing of production by this equivalence in order to augment and accumulate ever more of this equivalent value—is diverted entirely from any relation to worth itself. This incomparable value is neither labor, nor its force, nor its time, but is "man." "Man" as infinite value is not the man of humanism, the man who believes that he knows and can define himself (the man of the rights of man, of a well-tempered rationality, etc.). Again, it's man as that which "infinitely transcends man." But this "surpassing" (*dépassement*) is not potential, it is actual. Here and now, one man is incommensurable and inequivalent to any other, except of course insofar as one is forced to exist only according to this general equivalence…

Dis-enclosing the West means, thus, dismantling the chain of equivalence, opening possibilities of striking (*faire surgir*) the infinite in act. Art, love, and thought are three means—disjointed, they do not form a Whole and in fact prevent any accomplishment of a Whole—of the striking (*surgissement*) of the infinite. And of striking the infinite right at (*à même*) finitude.

M.-E. M. & P. G.: That brings us, it seems, to the question of praxis. How can we articulate or think a praxis of being singular plural that would open rather than close these striking possibilities? Can this be done without repeating the Sartrean gesture by which the thinker (or let's say the intellectual) would be the one who determines or guides praxis? What is thought qua praxis of the dis-enclosure? Is it even possible to say upfront what it can or ought to be (or do)?

J.-L. N.: Exactly. As you suggest at the end of your question, this praxis neither can nor should be programmed. Besides no praxis could come of it. For if "praxis" designates an action that produces the proper subject of action, not an object (like "*poiēsis*"), then this subject in permanent transformation modifies praxis, reinventing it to the extent that it "acts" (*pratique*). (This does not mean, I note in passing, that "*poiēsis*" is necessarily exempt from praxis. But that's another point.)

At the same time, this means that this praxis is not measured by a given, predetermined Idea. Yet, it is not measured against nothing. Let's try saying that it measures itself based on the Idea of what will be unable to saturate the Idea itself. An artist does not measure herself based upon a representation of "perfection," even if he or she has a sort of fantasy of it. The artist measures herself against the undefined or the infinite. And what's more, she doesn't "measure herself" (*se règle*). The lover does not aim for a predestined "love." Nor does the thinker for a predestined thought. However, nothing is without an "aim," nothing is without a predetermination—which can open or contrariwise close down the possibilities. I don't see better examples than invention, a stroke of inspiration, or artistic discovery. Let come the opportunity, the chance, and yet not just anything.

What can I recognizes as the infinite? As having the flavor, the taste, the tone of the infinite? At each possible point of recognition, a mistake is not out of the question… To accept the risk is also part of the chance. Those, curiously, that take the risk of being mistaken leave open the greatest chance for the real chance.

How this inscribes itself in the real, in the most quotidian and modest reality as well as in political choices and strategies… this is not programmable. But it's certain that what is, on the contrary, programmed, has every chance of paralyzing itself. Nevertheless, this is not to affirm just a negative praxology. I think there is, at a minimum, pressure, through a sort of programming or of critical and retentional project, put upon the "intellectual," who would be assumed to provide goals or draw up objectives. She should abstain from providing goals unless placing herself into the action. This would not necessarily be political action (although this could also be the case), but could be the action itself of her discourse: her language, words, rhetoric, or style. Integrity of language, a wariness toward the concept that wants to shine forth as pure Idea, experience of what makes a "style"—or experience of the plastic or sonorous element—collaboration with artists… what do I know? For me today, it's important to share a certain savoir-faire, as occurred recently when putting together a real exposition (of drawings in this particular case), including even relations with the public, which burgeons into many tasks and ideas. Or speaking to children, high school students, or "social workers."

Before coming back to this question of sharing know-how, I would like to ask a question about the relation between ontology and its articulation in everyday life. Heidegger develops his fundamental ontology beginning with Dasein's everydayness, with all the problems this implies for the relation between the authentic and inauthentic. How should one think the relation between, on the one hand, the original plurality of existence (as you develop it in *Being Singular Plural,* for example) and the "fallenness" of the unworld (*immonde*), which you discuss in *The Creation of the World,* if this is not according to the Heideggerian paradigm of the fallenness (*Verfallen*) of the everyday? What explains that the original exposition is able to lead to its opposite, that the "world" can become the "unworld"?

Heidegger himself writes that the "*eigentlich*" is only a modified seizing of the "*uneigentlich,*" as I analyzed it in an already old text, "The Decision of Existence,"[1] that I think is always relevant in this regard: one must not oppose the world and the unworld, although the unworld (*immonde*) can also be the worst (I play on the two possible resources of "*im-monde*": as non-world and as repugnant), the destruction of the world or worse, its sick decomposition, which is disgusting and revolting. It's possible that today we are before a very concrete, very close possibility (even if this means a century or more) of the destruction, the devastation of the world, and the passing to an uninhabitable, unlivable world, as much ethically as physically. Humanity, too, is driven by a death drive.

On the other hand, if it's possible to recreate a "world"—a space of meaning—this can't be determined by a call to some transcendence, whether a god, a value, heroes, or glorious humanity, but only by giving sense to our nonsensical (*insensée*) existence. But this giving sense to the nonsensical must be understood such that non-sense is itself or makes itself "sense." This means that we have to work through and twist the idea of "sense": We have to take leave of horizons, objectives, and aims—all while truly wanting "some sense." What does this mean? In fact, this is what literature does, what art, and what love do. In each form, these three modes of creative ethos make sense beyond sense. And this can invigorate the life of everyone because they circulate across common life, conditioned by how much the public space permits it. As such, this circulation is conditioned on the extent to which politics takes itself to be designed to enable the appearance of these modes of significance, and not to assume for itself the truth of existence. Thus, we must rethink completely the idea of the political itself.

M.-E. M. & P. G.: This brings two things to mind: first, the idea of "literary communism" as you have used it previously in order to name

the relation between the community and writing (as what resists the accomplishment of a community), or in order to otherwise name the political exigency of writing. Finally, there is also the idea of writing that one finds in *Corpus* as that which is "between" the body and sense (as the touching of a body "with the incorporeality of sense"). Is it necessary here to look for the connection between art or the creative ethos that you discussed and politics, that is to say, between the body and sense? And moreover without falling into an aestheticization of politics, as Philippe Lacoue-Labarthe has analyzed it?[2]

J.-L. N.: I'll pick up where you left off with this part of your phrase, "the connection between art… and politics, that is to say, between the body and sense." I can tell you that what necessarily came up at the end of my preceding response—namely, about rethinking the very idea of "politics"—goes directly against the parallel you pose here. In effect, you assimilated "art" to the "body" and "politics" to "sense." Now, specifically I think that we must stop seeing politics as the assumption of sense. It's one of the greatest dangers today for all who take themselves to be "on the left": to continue to take the "political" as the name—in an ultimately vague enough sense—of that place, dimension, ethos, or pathos where/whence "sense" should be achieved, in particular, the sense of being-in-common itself, understood as the condition of sense for each and everyone. Now, if it's true that there is no sense that's not in common (*Il n'y a de sens qu'en commun*), that is not communicated, and that is not communicating, it is no less true that this sense—which *is not signification*, an exchange of signs and signals, gestures, voices, and looks—is, therefore, not or is no longer "political." Perhaps, it had been so for cultivated men of the ancient cities. It had been so perhaps for the aristocracy and then the men of the "robe" and the industrial bourgeoisie, but it has never been the case for the people except in some revolutionary flashes. But these flashes have borne a certain ambivalence while also casting light on a word—*democracy*—as the name for a reassumed sense in politics. But let's not forget that democracy is only political by default: By definition it should renounce producing itself as sense. It can only organize the *possibility* that a sense or a plurality of senses might commence in several ways (in art, in life, in and as bodies). Of course, it can only do so while being open to this sphere of sense—and yet, it can't nor mustn't take it over: This is the whole difference between democracy and any other politics. Thus democracy is at once political and more than political, or better ultra-political (*outre-politique*). (But I am in the midst of telling you what is found in a small book, *Vérité de la démocratie*).[3]

To come back to your question, "literary communism" is not political. It designates what, concerning literature, makes a connection and produces a common (*commun*). For example, it designates how right-wing writers—Flaubert, Baudelaire, among many others—let circulate through language, that is to say, through the subjects of/in this language, some new "sense," some unheard-of sensation or sentiment…

M.-E. M. & P. G.: Returning to the sharing (*partage*) of know-how that you discussed above, I would like you to situate your philosophical style in relation to someone like Badiou. In his *Manifesto for Philosophy*,[4] Badiou speaks of the necessity of de-suturing philosophy from poetry in particular (or art in general) in order to renew or make it possible once more. How do you situate yourself in relation to this project? In what way does your philosophical style and your "engagement" in artistic projects constitute or does not constitute such a suturing that Badiou talks about?

J.-L. N.: Badiou insists on affirming a specificity and a continuity of philosophical style in opposition to what he understands in the Heideggerian expression "end of philosophy." But this expression, which I have happened to take up without supporting more than that, is followed in Heidegger by these words, "and the task of thought." "Philosophy" is opposed to "thought," just as "ontology" was opposed to the "thinking of being" or "the hearing of being." We can argue a long time over these choices of words, but one thing is clear: the "end" in question corresponds to the closure of a world, of "our" world, of the sense of sense, and of the Greco-Judeo-Christian-Islamic world. *Mondialisation* or world-forming means we are moving out of an era, we are changing from a culture, from a world, from a sense of sense, if I can put it this way. Where "philosophy" designates the science of the principle of ends or of being as such, is where even these very concepts of the principle, end, being, as well as those of the subject, knowledge, history, and the like, are carried away in a general mutation of significations. Doesn't Badiou himself continually elaborates categories and a nomenclature? Isn't the Platonic lineage, to which he lays claim, accompanied by serious displacements in relation to Plato?

So that's that for the first term. Next, "poetry." Here again, Heidegger is not far off (as well as Nietzsche, and also Bataille, Derrida, even Deleuze and… Badiou also!). Certainly, Heidegger has given the impression of calling philosophy to disappear gradually into the sublime manifestations of poetry. But if one puts aside for a moment his sometimes unsupportable pathos, what does he want to designate (*désigner*)? Simply, perhaps that it's no longer a matter of signifying (*signifier*) and designating things like we've been doing, but of making a sign (*faire signe*) in another sense: to signal and to indicate, *winken* in German (making a quick signal of complicity, recognition, or affection, without determinate signification). Or let's put it another way: What does the "poem" do? Or literature? They are responsible for the insignificance or ultra-significance (*outre-signifiance*) of language, that is to the say, the infinite distancing of sense and the infinite absenting of truth—an absenting that makes the very revelation of that which is true?

I am not saying that we must poetize—not at all! I am saying that philosophy declares that there is the unnameable, whereas poetry is capable of naming the unnameable—and of rendering it unnameable again while it is naming it. Philosophy is thus always in danger of substituting its unlimited declarations for the unnameability of the unnameable, whereas poetry, on the contrary, names while restoring the unnameable, while making it spring forth right at (*à même*) the name, as the very name itself. But this isn't simple… There is a lot of spurious poetry. "Poetry" is the most ambiguous, twisting, slippery term that there is. It is capable of dazzling, seducing, and enchanting instead of proceeding to the de-nomination that I am trying to indicate here. And yet, it is on this side that "true" poetry resides: on the side of singing and/or story-telling moreover—not on the side of discourse. Discourse attributes, predicates, qualifies, and modalizes (*modalise*); it does not *un-name* (*dé-nomme*).

M.-E. M. & P. G.: To be more precise, for example (although this is not an example relying on art, but one that intrigues me): What does the philosopher provide to "social workers," and what can he or she learn from them? What are the presuppositions and goals of the exchange?

J.-L. N.: In fact, you've changed the subject! You said yourself that you are moving away from art, and in fact, you moved on to a whole other discussion: the relation of philosophy with those who are at work in action or "practice"—you say "social workers" and one can expand that to doctors, psychologists, judges, politicians… Each time that I have had to intervene in this area, I am stricken by the importance that my interlocutors attach to certain motifs—ideas, notions, what have you—which at first appear abstract. If I say that the "being-in-common" does not have a common substance and makes common a nonsubstance, a "nothing," the "between" of "between us" (*entre nous*) (in order to take some prominent examples), I see social workers, to take your category, who find there a resource: They feel relieved from the possible weight of the idea of community; they feel capable of going farther than the ethical denunciation of collective identities. For example, instead of repeating that "race" is a dubious concept, they have something much more consistent: It's the "common being" that is dubious, and "being *in* common" becomes the carrier of sense, of capacities for action. Or again, if I am in front of people—therapists, psychologists—who are questioning themselves, because they are close to the so-called religious disturbances, on the meaning of the "spiritual," I try to say to them that the "spirit" has nothing ethereal, graceful, exalted, or spiritistic, but designates the relation to the incommensurable. This attempt at a designation to them is something, at least, to help their wheels stop spinning in terms of their initial question. At the same time, philosophy does not provide tools; it remains incapable of acting in the proper sense, but it acts upon the agents of action, it provides the momentum, the push...

NOTES

1. Published in English in *The Birth to Presence*.

2. See, for example, Philippe Lacoue-Labarthe, *Typography: Mimesis, Philosophy, Politics*, trans. Christopher Fynsk (Stanford: Stanford University Press, 1998).

3. Jean-Luc Nancy, *The Truth of Democracy*, trans. Pascale-Anne Brault and Michael Naas (New York: Fordham University Press, 2010).

4. Alain Badiou, *Manifesto for Philosophy: Followed by Two Essays* (Albany, NY: SUNY Press, 1999), pp. 61–69.

BIBLIOGRAPHY OF JEAN-LUC NANCY'S WORKS IN ENGLISH

BOOKS

Being Singular Plural. Trans. Robert D. Richardson and Anne E. O'Byrne. Stanford: Stanford University Press, 2000.

The Birth to Presence. Trans. Brian Holmes et al. Stanford: Stanford University Press, 1993.

Corpus. Trans. Richard A. Rand. New York: Fordham University Press, 2008.

The Creation of the World or *Globalization*. Trans. François Raffoul and David Pettigrew. Albany: SUNY Press, 2007.

The Discourse of the Syncope: Logodaedalus. Trans. Saul Anton. Stanford: Stanford University Press, 2007.

Dis-Enclosure: The Deconstruction of Christianity. Trans. Bettina Bergo, Gabriel Malenfant, and Michael B. Smith. New York: Fordham University Press, 2008.

The Experience of Freedom. Trans. Bridget McDonald. Stanford: Stanford University Press, 1993.

The Fall of Sleep. Trans. Charlotte Mandell. New York: Fordham University Press, 2009.

A Finite Thinking. Ed. Simon Sparks. Stanford: Stanford University Press, 2003.

God, Justice, Love, Beauty: Four Little Dialogues. Trans. Sarah Clift. New York: Fordham University Press, 2011.

The Gravity of Thought. Trans. François Raffoul and Gregory Recco. New York: Humanities Press, 1997.

The Ground of the Image. Trans. Jeff Fort. New York: Fordham University Press, 2005.

Hegel: The Restlessness of the Negative. Trans. Jason Smith and Steven Miller. Minneapolis: Minnesota University Press, 2002.

The Inoperative Community. Ed. Peter Connor. Minneapolis: University of Minnesota Press, 1991.

Listening. Trans. Charlotte Mandell. New York: Fordham University Press, 2007.

The Literary Absolute: The Theory of Literature in German Romanticism. With Philippe Lacoue-Labarthe. Trans. Philip Barnard and Cheryl Lester. Albany: SUNY Press, 1988.

Multiple Arts: The Muses II. Ed. Simon Sparks. Stanford: Stanford University Press, 2006.

The Muses. Trans. Peggy Kamuf. Stanford: Stanford University Press, 1997.

Noli Me Tangere: On the Raising of the Body. Trans. Sarah Clift, Pascale-Anne Brault, and Michael Naas. New York: Fordham University Press, 2008.

On the Commerce of Thinking: Of Books and Bookstores. Trans. David Wills. New York: Fordham University Press, 2009.

Philosophical Chronicles. Trans. Franson Manjali. Stanford: Stanford University Press, 2008.

Retreating the Political. With Philippe Lacoue-Labarthe. Ed. Simon Sparks. New York: Routledge, 1997.

The Sense of the World. Trans. Jeffrey S. Librett. Minneapolis: University of Minnesota Press, 1997.

The Speculative Remark (One of Hegel's Bons Mots). Trans. Céline Surprenant. Stanford: Stanford University Press, 2001.

The Title of the Letter: A Reading of Lacan. With Philippe Lacoue-Labarthe. Trans. François Raffoul and David Pettigrew. Albany: SUNY Press, 1992.

The Truth of Democracy. Trans. Pascale-Anne Brault and Michael Naas. New York: Fordham University Press, 2010.

ARTICLES, BOOK CHAPTERS, AND INTERVIEWS

"Atheism and Monotheism." In *Weakening Philosophy: Essays in Honour of Gianni Vattimo*, ed. Santiago Zabala. Montreal: McGill-Queen's University Press, 2007.

"The Being-With of the Being-There." In *Rethinking Facticity*, ed. François Raffoul and Eric Sean Nelson. Albany: SUNY Press, 2008.

"Between Story and Truth." Trans. Franson Manjali. *The Little Magazine* 2.4 "The Wall" (July/Aug. 2001). <http://www.littlemag.com/jul-aug01/nancy.html>.

"The Birth of Breasts." In *The Eight Technologies of Otherness*, ed. Sue Golding. London & New York: Routledge, 1997.

"The Calculation of the Poet." In *The Solid Letter: Readings of Friedrich Hölderlin*, ed. Aris Fioretos. Stanford: Stanford University Press, 2000.

"Chromatic Atheology." *Journal of Visual Culture* 4.1 (April 2005): 116–128.

"Church, State, Resistance." *Journal of Law and Society* 34.1 (March 2007): 3–13. Reprinted in *Political Theologies: Public Religions in a Post-Secular World*, ed. Hent de Vries and Lawrence E. Sullivan. New York: Fordham University Press, 2006.

"*La Comparution*/The Compearance: From the Existence of Communism to the Community of Existence." Trans. Tracy B. Strong. *Political Theory* 20.3 (1992): 371–398.

"The Confronted Community." Trans. Amanda McDonald. *Post-Colonial Studies* 6.1 (2003): 23–36.

"Consecration and Massacre." Trans. Amanda McDonald. *Post-Colonial Studies* 6.1 (2003): 47–50.

"Corpus." Trans. Claudette Sartiliot. In *Thinking Bodies*, ed. Juliet F. MacCannell and Laura Zakarin. Stanford: Stanford University Press, 1994.

"Cut Throat Sun." In *An Other Tongue: Nation and Ethnicity in the Linguistic Borderlands*, ed. Alfred Arteaga. Durham: Duke University, 1994.

"*Das unendliche Ende der Psychoanalyse*." *Journal of European Psychoanalysis: Humanities, Philosophy, Psychotherapies* 12–13 (2001). <http://www.psychomedia.it/jep>.

"*Dei Paralysis Progressiva*." In *Nietzsche: Critical Assessments*, ed. by Daniel W. Conway and Peter S. Groff, vol. IV, *The Last Man and the Overman*. London & New York: Routledge, 1998.

"Deconstruction of Monotheism." Trans. Amanda McDonald. *Post-Colonial Studies* 6.1 (2003): 37–46.

"The Deleuzian Fold of Thought." In *Deleuze: A Critical Reader*, ed. Paul Patton. Oxford: Blackwell, 1996.

"Elliptical Sense." *Research in Phenomenology* 18 (1988): 175–191. Reprinted in *Derrida: A Critical Reader*, ed. David Wood. Oxford: Blackwell, 1991.

"Far Away, Los Angeles." ANY 12: The Dimensions of Play: Ways of Thinking Architecture and the City (Nov./Dec. 1995).

"Freud, so to Speak." *Lacanian Ink* 31 (2008).

"Heidegger's 'Originary Ethics.'" In *Heidegger and Practical Philosophy*, ed. François Raffoul and David Pettigrew. Albany: SUNY Press, 2002.

"Icon of Fury: Claire Denis's *Trouble Every Day*." Film-Philosophy 12.1 (2008): 1–9. <http://www.film-philosophy.com/2008v12n1/nancy.pdf>.

"The Insufficiency of 'Values' and the Necessity of 'Sense.'" *Journal for Cultural Research* 9.4 (2005): 437–441.

"Introduction." *Topoi* 7.2 (1988): 87–92.

"An Interview with Jean-Luc Nancy." In Michel Gaillot, *Multiple Meaning: Techno, An Artistic and Political Laboratory of the Present*. Paris: Editions Dis Voir, 1998.

"Interview with Jean-Luc Nancy." *Topoi* 7.2 (1988): 113–121.

"Is Everything Political? (A brief remark)." Trans. Philosophy M. Adamek. *At the Heart: of Jean-Luc Nancy*. A Special Issue of *The New Centennial Review* 2.3 (Fall 2002): 15–22.

"*Lapsus judicii*." *Pli: The Warwick Journal of Philosophy* 3.2 (1991): 16–40.

"Limits, Borders, and Shores of Singularity." In *Encounters with Alphonso Lingis*, ed. Alexander E Hooke and Wolfgang W Fuchs. Lanham, MD: Lexington Books, 2003.

"Literally." *Angelaki: Journal of the Theoretical Humanities* 7.2 (Aug. 2002): 91–92.

"The Jurisdiction of the Hegelian Monarch." *Social Research* 49.2 (Summer 1982): 481–517.

"*Larvatus pro Deo*." *Glyph* 2 (1977): 14–36.

"*L'Intrus*." Trans. Susan Hanson. *At The Heart: of Jean-Luc Nancy*. A Special Issue of *The New Centennial Review* 2.3 (Fall 2002): 1–14.

"Menstruum universale." *SubStance* 6.21 (1978–1979): 21–35.

"Mundus est fabula." *Modern Language Notes* 93:4 (1978): 635–653.

"The Nazi Myth." With Philippe Lacoue-Labarthe. Trans. Brian Holmes. *Critical Inquiry* 16.2 (1990): 291–312.

"Nietzsche's Thesis on Teleology." In *Looking After Nietzsche*, ed. Laurence A. Rickels. Albany: SUNY Press, 1990.

"Nothing but the World: An Interview with *Vacarme*." *Rethinking Marxism* 19.4 (2007): 521–535.

"Of Being in Common." In *Community at Loose Ends*, ed. The Miami Theory Collective. Minneapolis: University of Minnesota Press, 1991.

"Of Divine Places." *Paragraph* 7 (1986) 1–52.

"On Derrida." A conversation with Sergio Benvenuto. *Journal of European Psychoanalysis* 19.2 (2004). <http://www.psychomedia.it/jep>.

"On the Meanings of Democracy." *Theoria: A Journal of Social and Political Theory* 53.111 (2006): 1–5.

"On the Threshold." *Paragraph* 13.2 "On the Work of Jean-Luc Nancy" (July 1993): 111–121. Reprinted in *The Muses*. Trans. Peggy Kamuf. Stanford: Stanford University Press, 1997.

"Our History." *Diacritics* 20.3 (1990): 97–115.

"Our World: An Interview." *Angelaki: Journal of the Theoretical Humanities* 8.2 (2003): 43–54.

"Philosophy without Conditions." In *Alain Badiou and the Future of Philosophy*, ed. Peter Hallward. London: Continuum, 2004.

"Philosophy as Chance: An Interview with Jean-Luc Nancy." With Lorenzo Fabbri. Trans. Pascale-Anne Brault and Michael Naas. *Critical Inquiry* 33.2 (2007): 427–440.

"*Praesens*." In *Il Dono/The Gift: Generous Offerings Threatening Hospitality/Offerta Ospitalita Insidia*, ed. Antonio Somaini, Gianfranco Maraniello, and Sergio Risaliti. New York: Charta, 2002.

"Question of the common and responsibility of the universal." A dialogue with Artem Magun and Oxana Timofeeva. *What is to be done? A Newspaper for Engaged Creativity* 9 (2005). <http://www.chtodelat.org>.

"The real outside is 'at the heart' of the inside." An Interview with Jean-Luc Nancy. *ATOPIA* 9 (2006). <http://www.atopia.tk>

"Responding for Existence." Trans. Michael Collins. *Studies in Practical Philosophy: A Journal of Ethical and Political Philosophy* 1.1 (1999): 1–11.

"Scene." With Philippe Lacoue-Labarthe. Trans. Meiko Behr. In *Beyond Representation: Philosophy and Poetic Imagination*, ed. Richard Eldridge. Cambridge: Cambridge University Press, 1996.

"Self from Absence to Self." *Lacanian Ink* 33 (2009).

"Sharing Voices." In *Transforming the Hermeneutic Context: From Nietzsche to Nancy*, ed. Gayle L. Ormiston and Alan D. Schrift. Albany: SUNY Press, 1990.

"The So-Called/Self-Saying People." In *Translation, Biopolitics, Colonial Difference*, ed. Naoki Sakai and Jon Solomon. Hong Kong: Hong Kong University Press, 2006.

"Speaking about Art." In *Post-structuralism and Cultural Theory*. New Delhi: Allied Publishers Pvt., 2006.

"Strange Foreign Bodies." With Philipp Warnell. *Lacanian Ink* 32 (2008).

"The Surprise of the Event." In *Hegel after Derrida*, ed. Stuart Barnett. New York: Routledge, 1998.

"The Technique of the Present." In *On Kawara—Paintings of 40 Years*. New York: David Zwirner, 2004.

"Thinking Better of Capital (An Interview)." *Studies in Practical Philosophy* 1.2 (1999): 214–232.

"To the exhausting Nude." *Lacanian Ink* 30 (2007).

"The Two Secrets of the Fetish." With Thomas C. Platt. *Diacritics* 31.2 (2001): 3–8.

"The Unsacrificeable." *Yale French Studies* 79 (1991): 20–38.
"The War of Monotheism." Trans. Amanda McDonald. *Post-Colonial Studies* 6.1 (2003): 37–46.
"Thinking Better of Capital, An Interview." *Studies in Practical Philosophy*, 1.2 (1999): 214–232.
"The Two Secrets of the Fetish." *Diacritics* 31.2 (2001): 3–8.
"War, Law, Sovereignty—Techné." Trans. Jeffrey S. Librett. In *Rethinking Technologies*, ed. by Verena Andermatt Conley. Minneapolis: University of Minnesota Press, 1993.
"Wild Laughter in the Throat of Death." *Modern Language Notes* 102.4 (1987): 719–736.
"Within my breast, alas, two souls . . ." *Topoi* 25.1 (2006): 69–73.
"You ask me what it means today . . ." *Paragraph* 13.2 "On the Work of Jean-Luc Nancy" (1993): 108–110.

CONTRIBUTORS

Stephen Barker is associate dean and head of doctoral studies in the Claire Trevor School of the Arts at the University of California at Irvine. Working centrally in critical, aesthetic, and performance theory, he has written books and articles on Nietzsche, Derrida, Beckett, Blanchot, and Artaud, among others. His most recent book, *Thresholds: Limit-Play In and After Derrida*, is forthcoming. He is among the founders of the journal *Derrida Today* and is on the faculty of the London Graduate School. Barker has translated a number of recent volumes by French philosophers Bernard Stiegler and François-David Sebbah for Stanford University Press.

Andrew Benjamin is professor critical theory and philosophical aesthetics at Monash University. He recently published *Of Jews and Animals* (Edinburgh University Press, 2010) and *Place Commonality and Judgement: Continental Philosophy and the Ancient Greeks* (Continuum, 2010).

Alfonso Cariolato received his PhD in philosophy from the Universities of Strasbourg and Padua under the supervision of Jean-Luc Nancy and Franco Volpi. He is now research fellow at the University of Padua. He has published many essays, as well as five books: *Il luogo del finito* (2003), *I sensi del pensiero* (2004), *L'Existence nue. Essai sur Kant* (2009, with an introduction by Jean-Luc Nancy), *Dare una voce. La filosofia e il brusio del mondo* (2009), and *Le geste de Dieu. Sur un lieu de l'Éthique de Spinoza* (2011, with marginalia by Jean-Luc Nancy).

Peter Gratton is assistant professor of philosophy at the Memorial University of Newfoundland in Canada. He is author of *The State of Sovereignty: Lessons from the Political Fictions of Modernity* (SUNY Press, 2011) and co-editor (with John Panteleimon Manoussakis) of *Traversing the Imaginary: Richard Kearney and the Postmodern Challenge* (Northwestern University Press, 2007).

Graham Harman is associate provost for research administration and a member of the philosophy faculty at the American University in Cairo. He is author of the following books: *Tool-Being* (2002), *Guerrilla Metaphysics* (2005), *Heidegger Explained* (2007), *Prince of Networks* (2009), *Towards Speculative Realism* (2010), *Circus Philosophicus* (2010), *L'Objet quadruple* (2010),

The Prince and the Wolf (with Bruno Latour and Peter Erdélyi, 2011), and *Quentin Meillassoux: Philosophy in the Making* (2011).

Ben Hutchens has an Oxford DPhil and has been a Fulbright Scholar. He is author of *Jean-Luc Nancy's Exposition of Freedom: The Critique of Kant* (SUNY Press, forthcoming) and editor of *Jean-Luc Nancy: Justice, Legality, World* (Continuum Press, 2012). He is also author of *Jean-Luc Nancy and the Future of Philosophy* (McGill-Queens/Acumen, 2005) and *Levinas* (Continuum, 2004).

Martin McQuillan is professor of literary theory and cultural analysis, dean of the Faculty of Arts and Social Sciences, as well as co-director of the London Graduate School at Kingston University in London. His recent publications include *Deconstruction After 9/11* (Routledge, 2008) and *Roland Barthes, or, The Profession of Cultural Studies* (Palgrave Macmillan, 2010). He is editor of *The Politics of Deconstruction: Jacques Derrida and the Other of Philosophy* (Pluto Press, 2007), *Deconstruction Reading Politics* (Palgrave Macmillan, 2008) and *The Origins of Deconstruction* (Palgrave Macmillan, 2010), and is also series editor for "The Frontiers of Theory" list published by Edinburgh University Press.

Marie-Eve Morin is assistant professor of philosophy at the University of Alberta in Canada. She is author of *Jenseits der brüderlichen Gemeinschaft. Das Gespräch zwischen Jacques Derrida und Jean-Luc Nancy* (Ergon, 2006) and is now preparing a book on Jean-Luc Nancy for Polity Press' Key Contemporary Thinkers series. She has published several articles on Jean-Luc Nancy's work including "Towards a Divine Atheism: Jean-Luc Nancy's Deconstruction of Monotheism and the Passage of the Last God" in *Symposium* (2011) and "Thinking Things: Heidegger, Sartre, Nancy" in *Sartre Studies International* (2009).

Jean-Luc Nancy is emeritus professor of philosophy at the University of Strasbourg and professor of political philosophy and media aesthetics at the European Graduate School in Switzerland. He is the author of many books including *The Creation of the World* or *Globalization* and co-author (with Philippe Lacoue-Labarthe) of *The Title of the Letter: A Reading of Lacan* and *The Literary Absolute: The Theory of Literature in German Romanticism*, all published in English translation by SUNY Press.

Andrew Norris is associate professor of political science and affiliated professor of philosophy at the University of California, Santa Barbara. He is editor of *Politics, Metaphysics, and Death: Essays on Giorgio Agamben's* Homo

Sacer (Duke University Press, 2005) and *The Claim to Community: Essays on Stanley Cavell and Political Philosophy* (Stanford University Press, 2006) and co-editor of *Truth and Politics* (University of Pennsylvania Press, forthcoming). He is currently completing a book titled *Publicity and Partiality: Political Reflection in the Work of Stanley Cavell.*

Anne O'Byrne is associate professor of philosophy at Stony Brook University. Her work occurs at the intersection of ontology and political philosophy, engaging a range of thinkers that includes Heidegger, Arendt, Dilthey, Derrida, and Nancy and a range of issues including identity, natality, embodiment, education, history, gender, and genocide. She is author of *Natality and Finitude* (Indiana, 2010), co-translator (with Robert Richardson) of Nancy's *Being Singular Plural* (Stanford, 1996) and translator of his *Corpus II* (Fordham, forthcoming 2012).

David Pettigrew is professor of philosophy at Southern Connecticut State University. He is co-translator of Jean-Luc Nancy's *The Title of the Letter: a Reading of Lacan* (with Philippe Lacoue-Labarthe, SUNY Press, 1992) and *The Creation of the World* or *Globalization* (SUNY Press, 2007), co-editor of *French Interpretations of Heidegger* (SUNY Press, 2008), and co-translator of Juan-David Nasio's *Oedipus* (SUNY Press, 2010) (all with François Raffoul). He is also co-editor of the book series *Contemporary French Thought* at SUNY Press. His current work bears on ethical responses to genocide, specifically seeking pathways to justice in the aftermath of the genocide in Bosnia (1992–1995). He has co-produced a documentary film about the genocide in Bosnia titled, *The Geography of Genocide in Bosnia: Redeeming the Earth* (US, 2009, 50 min.).

François Raffoul is professor of philosophy at Louisiana State University. He is author of *Heidegger and the Subject* (Prometheus Books, 1999), *À chaque fois Mien* (Galilée, 2004), and *The Origins of Responsibility* (Indiana University Press, 2010). He has co-edited several volumes, *Disseminating Lacan* (SUNY Press, 1996), *Heidegger and Practical Philosophy* (SUNY Press, 2002), *Rethinking Facticity* (SUNY Press, 2008), *and French Interpretations of Heidegger* (SUNY Press, 2008). He is co-translator of several books by Jean-Luc Nancy, including *The Title of the Letter: a Reading of Lacan* (with Philippe Lacoue-Labarthe, SUNY Press, 1992), *The Gravity of Thought* (Prometheus Books, 1998), and *The Creation of the World* or *Globalization* (SUNY Press, 2007). He is co-editor of the book series *Contemporary French Thought* at SUNY Press.

Christina Smerick is Shapiro chair of Jewish-Christian Studies and associate professor of philosophy at Greenville College in Greenville, Illinois. She received her PhD in philosophy from DePaul University. Her most recent publications include "Taking Thomas To Temple: Introducing Evangelicals to the Jewish Jesus," in *The Jewish Jesus* (Purdue University Press, 2011); "The Failure of Hate: Love, Hate and Hope in Jean-Paul Sartre," in *Philosophy Today*; and "'And G-d Said': Language, Translation and Scripture in Two Works by Walter Benjamin," in *Shofar: An Interdisciplinary Journal of Jewish Studies*.

William Watkin is professor of contemporary literature and philosophy at Brunel University in West London. He is author of *In the Process of Poetry: The New York School and the Avant-Garde* (Bucknell, 2001), *On Mourning: Theories of Loss in Modern Literature* (Edinburgh, 2004) and *The Literary Agamben: Adventures on Logopoiesis* (Continuum, 2010). He has just completed his fourth monograph provisionally titled *Agamben and Indifference*. He has also published various articles on modern and contemporary poetry and the work of Agamben, Derrida and Nancy. He is currently working on a full-length study of the philosophy of indifference.

INDEX